"Ronnie Campbell and David Baggett's *A Personal God and a Good World* effectively and succinctly presents the case for theistic personalism over against the classical theistic model of God. In their examination of the divine attributes, Campbell and Baggett address misperceptions and misrepresentations of theistic personalism while fair-mindedly describing and critiquing the classical theistic model—as well as other theological approaches such as open theism, panentheism, and more. This book is a clear, readable, effective, and inspiring exploration of the attributes of God and their coherence."

—**Paul Copan**, Pledger Family Chair of Philosophy and Ethics, Palm Beach Atlantic University

"*A Personal God and a Good World* is a sophisticated but extremely clear investigation into the nature of God. The authors defend a version of theistic personalism in which God is temporal but also immutable and impassible. In addition, they explore distinctively Christian doctrines such as the Trinity, salvation, heaven, and hell. Their work is evenhanded, charitable, well-documented, and interesting."

—**Gregory E. Ganssle**, chair, department of philosophy, Talbot School of Theology

"In *A Personal God and a Good World*, Ronnie Campbell and David Baggett go to great lengths to show how our concept of God is intimately connected to our concept of goodness, and this all impacts not only how we think about God and morality but how we think about the moral status of God's solution to the problem of evil in the world. After making the case that the biblical concept of God is best resembled by the model of God known as theistic personalism, Campbell and Baggett show how this concept of God best explains not only that our world is governed by an objective morality but also how this particular model of God makes the best sense of the Christian moral story."

—**Andrew Hollingsworth**, assistant professor of theology and Christian Philosophy, Brewton-Parker College

"Francis Schaeffer often described the relationship between general revelation and special revelation as finding two halves of a book in an old house: one half in the attic and the other half in the basement. If you only found one half you could know a few things that were probably true of the other half, but you couldn't re-create the half you were missing from the half you found. But when we bring these two revelations together and realize how well they fit together, our confidence that the Bible is true soars because it matches so well with what we see and experience in the world around us. In this book, Baggett and Campbell do an excellent job showing us this is exactly what we discover when it comes to the moral realm."

—**Adam Lloyd Johnson**, president, Convincing Proof Ministries

"*A Personal God and a Good World* offers an illuminating and nuanced exploration of who God is and why it matters by adeptly addressing the central issues of the Christian faith. With a clear and approachable style, the authors present an insightful and compelling case that God is personal and engaged in genuine back-and-forth relationship with creatures for God's love as the metaphysical ground for Christian ethics. Highly recommended for those seeking a profound yet accessible exploration of God's nature, the ground of morality, and the intersection between them."

—**John C. Peckham**, research professor of theology
and Christian philosophy, Andrews University

A
PERSONAL GOD
and a
GOOD WORLD

A
PERSONAL GOD
and a
GOOD WORLD

The Coherence of the Christian Moral Vision

RONNIE P. CAMPBELL JR.

and

DAVID BAGGETT

ACADEMIC®
BRENTWOOD, TENNESSEE

From Ronnie P. Campbell, Jr.

To Debbie

A constant source of friendship, patience, and love.

* * *

From David Baggett

To Marybeth

Ditto

CONTENTS

ACKNOWLEDGMENTS

With the making of any book, there are too many people to thank. We would like to highlight a few. We would first like to thank the folks at B&H Academic for their kind support and encouragement throughout this whole process. Michael McEwen, our content editor, has been an absolute joy and delight to work with. His comments, along with the comments of an anonymous reviewer, were helpful in crafting our final product. We would also like to thank Madison Trammel for his interest in this project and his constant encouragement throughout the process.

We would also like to thank Matthew Hamilton for his assistance with footnotes and the bibliography. Matthew went above and beyond his normal graduate assistant duties to aid us in this work. A big thank you goes out to him!

Finally, we would like to thank our families. Ronnie would like to thank his wife, Debbie, and four children, Abbey, Caedmon, Caleb, and Zeke for their continual encouragement and love. You all bring me deep joy and make life more interesting! David would also like to thank Ronnie Campbell, a kindred spirit, dear friend, and brother in Christ, for the invitation to join this venture. It was an unmitigated privilege and great joy.

INTRODUCTION

How people understand God has significant implications for their worldview, affecting nearly everything—contrary to claims that God's existence or nature is largely irrelevant, affecting little or nothing. That and who God is makes a tremendous difference. We don't mean only in the sense of whether one is a Christian, Muslim, Hindu, atheist, or Buddhist—though that's hugely significant! But we mean even for those who share the same general worldview. Not all Christians believe the same thing about God, and recognizing these differences is important, especially as we consider the moral landscape of our world. Who God is remains a question of great practical and existential import.

In this short book, we wish to explore the connection between the Christian view of God, as we understand it, and (among other things) morality. We do not aim to provide anything like an abductive moral case for God's existence—the notion that God is the best explanation of (say) moral values or moral duties. Our goal is more modest than that. Instead, we argue that God as we understand him makes good sense of a range of important realities, moral ones among them. The abductive case can be made but is for other occasions; here we see our book as simply one step toward such a goal, one piece of a much bigger puzzle.

In this book we argue for a view known as theistic personalism. More specifically, our view is a form of modified classical theism (also known as neo-classical theism). Christians believe that God is deeply personal—tripersonal to be exact. Our understanding of a personal God shapes how we view the moral landscape of our world. Our approach is largely Anselmian in nature. We aim to present a view that is both coherent internally and consonant with scriptural teaching on God and moral reality.

This book features philosophical theology, though not merely that. It has the advantage of being written by a philosopher (Dave) and a theologian (Ronnie). We unapologetically engage in a variety of cross-disciplinary studies, examining biblical, theological, and philosophical dimensions of our overall thesis.

The book is structured in three basic parts. Part 1 (chapters 1–2) gives a general defense of Anselmian theism and broadly lays out a case for how moral truths provide a powerful evidential consideration in favor of God's reality. We then focus our efforts on theological method as it pertains to the doctrine of God, rounding it out by comparing models of God. Part 2 (chapters 3–5) takes aim at defending modified classical theism. Part 3 (chapters 6–9) argues how the triune God of Christian theism makes good moral sense of our universe by examining a variety of Christian doctrines.

Our ultimate aim in this book is to help the reader understand that our thoughts on God matter and have significant moral implications. They shape not only how we view the God/world relationship, but others such as our understanding of divine providence, miracles, human dignity and worth, the problem of evil, salvation, and the afterlife.

PART 1

1

Anselmian Theism and
Moral Reasons for God

The insights and categories of philosophy can help elucidate many branches of theology, including systematic theology, biblical theology, and natural theology. Natural theology, at least in part, is the effort to use the light of reason to describe the relationship between faith and reason and examine the epistemic status of belief in God; so it provides an appropriate launching point for our investigation. To speak of "God," of course, raises an important preliminary question about intended referent, so this will be the first question to explore.

Often in colloquial usage, "God" or "gods" is meant to refer not to a person or persons necessarily but simply to something that is most esteemed or perhaps even worshipped. "Golf is my god," for example, would mean something like "Golf is what I love the most" or "Golf is a higher priority of mine than anything else." Using language this way resides somewhere in between idiosyncratic usage and standard usage. It is unlikely to be taken seriously as a substantive theistic claim, and yet it captures an important aspect of any legitimate concept of God—God is worthy of worship and love.

By definition, even a little conversational cooperation would suggest that God deserves to be worshipped. Perhaps we could say that this is just part of the conceptual meaning or analytic import of "God." Although this by no means establishes that God actually exists, it nevertheless suggests that *worship-worthiness* must be an attribute of anything or anyone that legitimately inhabits the office of deity. The question of God's existence is important, but existence claims need first to be clear about what is affirmed or denied. So there is prudence in holding the matter of God's existence in abeyance for a bit longer until we can first explore the concept of God.

One powerful way to identify what God must be like if he is worthy of worship is to think about those traits that are great-making properties and then to ascribe their maximal expressions to God. Although some might wonder how practicable this is, a wide swath of shared value intuitions has shown it to be a fruitful approach. For example, having power is a great-making trait, as is having knowledge, as is being good, morally or otherwise. And to have such traits to the maximal degree is greater than having them only in some measure or to some limited extent. Moreover, having all these traits together is greater than having only one or two of them. So a worship-worthy God, by this methodology, instantiates all the great-making properties to the maximally compossible degree.

Such a conception of God is sometimes called an Anselmian picture of God, so named because of the great medieval thinker St. Anselm, who thought of God in such terms. He was also known for the ontological argument for God's existence, but an Anselmian God need not be predicated on the ontological argument. Recall that here we are still just sketching what the conception of God involves, not yet establishing God's existence. As will become obvious, however, such a depiction of God's nature will prove itself relevant to the epistemic question of God's existence and the rationality of religious belief.

Two Challenges to Anselmianism

A Conceptual Challenge

Before pursuing the question of whether God is real, let's first consider two challenges to this sort of Anselmian picture of God. Others have taken up challenges against a "greatest being" methodology, but here we will limit ourselves to these.[1] First, suppose someone were to suggest that, contra Anselmianism, one of the great-making properties, omnibenevolence (being all-good) for example, is not essential to who God is after all. Here is how.

Imagine a creature who is omnipotent, omniscient, and the like, but who lacks the property of being omnibenevolent. This being, we are to suppose, may well be a decent enough chap but is not wholly good or, as some might say, impeccable. We can imagine that such a being neverthe-less created us, upholds the universe by his power, is all-powerful, and is all-knowing but just less than perfectly good and loving. Intuitively, so the argument goes, we would still call such a being God, which goes to show that God's omnibenevolence is not an essential property of his, a property without which a being could not qualify to be called God. The argument amounts to a rejection of the notion that it is a conceptual or nonnegotiable truth that God is morally good.

It seems that such an argument exploits the fact that there are tradition-ally two different ways of thinking about God: specifically, what we call *per-fect being theology* and what we often call *creation theology*. According to such a bifurcation, there is the Anselmian God of the philosophers, like the maxi-mally greatest being, on the one hand. On the other, there is the God who has actively created and entered into the world, the God of experience—like the God of the Bible. It is easy to start with creation theology or experiential theology and argue that some aspect of Anselmianism is not necessary for

---

[1] Thomas V. Morris takes up a number of such challenges in *Anselmian Explorations: Essays in Philosophical Theology* (Notre Dame, IN: University of Notre Dame Press, 1987).

thinking about God, simply because it was not hard-baked into the concept from the start in that tradition. Then we find ourselves at the crossroads of different traditions and are left wondering how consistent they are.

Thomas V. Morris takes on another version of this sort of challenge in *Anselmian Explorations* in the chapter entitled "The God of Abraham, Isaac, and Anselm."[2] He asks readers to imagine the Anselmian God without moral qualities at all since, say, they do not exist.[3] But this being has aseity (absolute ontological independence), omnipotence (being all powerful), and existence in every possible world. Now, in one world, there is a creator ("c") without maximal perfection, and we are tempted to call him God. Yet in that same world there would be an Anselmian being in the background responsible for c's existence and power. So who is God now? Surely not c.

It is true that moral goodness is not ascribed to every conception of God or the gods. The Greek pantheon of deficient and fallible deities comes to mind about which Socrates and Euthyphro had a dustup. But the argument under consideration aims to use "God" in a more standard sense to encapsulate something like the God of classical theism or theistic personalism. Again, some uses of "God" don't have the notion of perfect goodness built into it, but arguably in the Western tradition, with its exalted, typically Anselmian conception, something like perfect goodness does tend to be presupposed.

So what concerns us here is a potential equivocation. If, as is not uncommon, we were to affirm one reading of "God is morally good," that would mean we think no entity could inhabit the office of deity without being morally good. (This can be called a *de dicto* reading.) That's at least in close proximity to affirming the conceptual truth that God is morally good. Another reading (called the *de re* reading) is even more explicit: the being

---

[2] Morris, *Anselmian Explorations*, 10.

[3] So-called "error theorists," to adduce one example, argue that objective moral properties do not exist. In J. L. Mackie's case, he argued this because of what he considered the metaphysically odd features such properties would need to feature—like overriding authority that trumps one's personal predilections. Those of a naturalistic persuasion, for understandable reasons, might be inclined to adopt such a position.

who is God himself has the necessary or essential property of being good. This seems very much like building the quality of moral goodness into one's theology of God after all.

The argument under consideration assumes that it would be a justified and intuitive step to call a less-than-wholly-good being God. Accordingly, it would not be the case that God does not exist but rather that God would turn out to be different from what we had envisioned. Suppose, however, we were to alter the thought experiment and suggest that the being in question is not just lacking in perfect moral goodness by a negligible margin but has an irremediable and vicious mean streak that manifests fairly frequently. Let's call such a being "Biff." Would we still call Biff God? More to the point, *Should* we?

Again, on a *de dicto* analysis of "God is good," we should *not*, because Biff would be disqualified from holding the office of deity. Likewise, we certainly should not say Biff is God if God is understood to be good necessarily, since not only is Biff not perfectly good, he is not morally good at all.

The argument under critique also arguably would show too much, for by parity of reasoning, we could run a similar thought experiment with respect to each of God's putative great-making properties. If such reasoning works, it would show that God possesses for an essential property none of the great-making properties.

For example, suppose the being who created the world has all the Anselmian attributes except being fully omniscient. He knows nearly everything but not everything. There you have it: it would still be appropriate to call such a being God, the argument suggests, so omniscience is not an ineliminable part of our concept of God. Likewise with omnipresence. What starts with a seemingly small concession ends up entirely vitiating the picture of God as traditionally conceived.

We harbor the suspicion that much of the purchase of the thought experiment comes from the hypothesized being in question residing so conceptually close to God as traditionally conceived. So let's alter the thought experiment a bit. Imagine that the being were really morally vicious and cruel but had the other great-making properties. It seems to us that we would be within our epistemic rights to say, in that case, that whereas God does not exist, something more like the devil does. Of course others might demur and insist that God exists but is just cruel. This owes a great deal to equivocation on "God," but for now our point is that a being like the devil is far from worship-worthy.

Can we in some loose sense conceive of God as without the quality of moral goodness? Perhaps, but it is not at all clear that anything of substance follows from that. Suppose we conceive of some mathematical theorem as false. Still, if it is true then it is necessarily true. It may be conceivably false in some fuzzy way, but a necessary truth would not be thereby vitiated. Likewise with the necessity of God's goodness, mere imaginability is a nearly feckless notion compared to the convictions of deep ingression concerning the insoluble link between God and goodness in the minds of traditional theists. Mere epistemic possibility does not entail anything like genuine metaphysical possibility. Some people admittedly have a modest conception of "worthiness of worship," but we opt for a richer conception entailing moral perfection, including perfect moral goodness. In part we make that decision because we want to engage the God of Jesus (and parts of traditional monotheism).

An Old Testament Challenge

Yoram Hazony, author of *The Philosophy of Hebrew Scripture*, expresses skepticism toward the idea of a perfect God. He suggests that there are two compelling reasons why the God of classical theism (or theistic personalism) should be rejected: first, reconciling the existence of evil with God's omniscience, omnipotence, omnibenevolence is too great a challenge. Second, he says, such a picture fails to match the Old Testament portrayal of God. The problem of evil will be taken up in a later chapter; here we will say just a few words about that challenge but then respond at slightly greater length to the challenge to Anselmianism that Hazony thinks the Old Testament poses.

Hazony insists that the problem of evil shows that God cannot be both all-good and all-powerful, for if he were, then there would not be injustices in the world. He chalks up affirmation of such perfections more to the influence of Greek philosophy than to biblical thought. Regarding the God of the Old Testament, he writes that the God of Hebrew Scripture is not depicted as immutable but rather is one who changes his mind about things (for example, he regrets having made man). He is not all-knowing, since he is repeatedly surprised by things (like the Israelites abandoning him for a statue of a cow). He is not perfectly powerful, either, in that he famously cannot control Israel and get its people to do what he wants. Hazony says forthrightly that the problem of evil renders reconciliation of such standard perfections as omnipotence and omnibenevolence either highly unlikely or flatly impossible.[4]

Hazony's claims, however, are predicated on an unrefined conception of omnipotence and the other great-making properties. Talk of perfection only makes sense in terms of achieving the right balance of properties, not by maximizing a thing's constituent principles simultaneously. To speak of a "perfect bottle," for example, is colloquial at best, confused at worst. The question of how many drops of liquid are contained in the "perfect bottle" admits of no objective answer. In contrast, God's perfections do admit of "intrinsic maxima." God has as much power, knowledge, and goodness as are mutually compatible and compossible.

If God sovereignly chooses to confer on human beings meaningful agency and libertarian freedom, that does not show that God is not omnipotent.

---

[4] For a succinct formulation of Hazony's view, see Yoram Hazony, "An Imperfect God," *New York Times*, November 25, 2012, https://www.nytimes.com/2003/12/14/books/chapters/an-imperfect-god.html and "A Perfect God," by Tom Morris and David Baggett, *First Things*, January 28, 2013, https://www.firstthings.com/web-exclusives/2013/01/a-perfect-god. For a slightly longer treatment of some of the same themes, see Yoram Hazony and Dru Johnson, eds., *The Question of God's Perfection: Jewish and Christian Essays on the God of the Bible and Talmud* (Boston: Brill, 2019), esp. ch. 1. The whole volume is well worth reading, containing marvelous chapters by Stump, Leftow, Goodman, and others.

Omnipotence need not entail meticulous providence in every detail. Hazony also errs in taking the great "I am" declaration of God to be an indication of God's incompleteness and changeability, rather than, as seems the more straightforward meaning, God's uncreatedness and ontological independence.

One reason Hazony makes these claims is that he wishes to emphasize the need for tentativeness and provisionality in theology and to remind us that our knowledge of God remains fragmentary and partial. In Hazony's view, "The belief that any human mind can grasp enough of God to begin recognizing perfections in him would have struck the biblical authors as a pagan conceit." According to the Hebrew Bible, Hazony insists, God represents the embodiment of life's experiences and vicissitudes, from hardship to joy. Although God is ultimately faithful and just, these are not perfections or qualities that obtain necessarily. "On the contrary, it is the *hope* that God is faithful and just that is the subject of ancient Israel's faith." He concludes by arguing that his view is one that ought to appeal to people of faith today: "With theism rapidly losing ground across Europe and among Americans as well, we could stand to reconsider this point. Surely a more plausible conception of God couldn't hurt."[5]

By way of reply, is theism really losing ground, or merely certain religious institutions? And what does it even mean to speak of the Hebraic depiction of God as *more realistic* than the idea of God as altogether perfect? It is certainly more *anthropomorphic*, or to put it more precisely, *anthropopathic*: portraying God as if he had human passions. But does that make it more "realistic"? And why does the fact that Scripture may not read like a philosophical text compromise the philosophical work of evincing such a conception, or render the effort artificial or invalid?

The claim that the notion of a perfect God is a Greek convention incorporated into theology is an allegation that overlooks the role of what

---

[5] See Yoram Hazony, *The Philosophy of Hebrew Scriptures* (Cambridge: Cambridge University Press, 2012). References adduced here are from his aforementioned shorter piece from 2012 in the *New York Times*.

theologians refer to as "general revelation." The Greeks had no corner on the market of reason. Plenty of Greeks—Euthyphro, for example—believed in all sorts of rather morally deficient gods. Indeed, we could return the favor and suggest that it is actually Hazony's conception of God that's more influenced by Greek ideas in this regard than by Scripture. The fact remains that in the New Testament we find ample indications of a morally perfect and perfectly loving God. This happy congruence and convergence of the *a priori* deliverances of reason and the *a posteriori* deliverances of Scripture is no surprise if there is deep resonance between the outcomes of general and special revelation, the latter performing an ampliative function for the former.

The Existence Question

Earlier it was suggested that one's conception of God will prove relevant to religious epistemology. To think of God as essentially worship-worthy infuses religious epistemology with moral concerns. Before considering questions of God's existence, there is wisdom in clarifying our salient conception of God. Now, if "God" is a title, requiring its bearer to be worthy of worship, this means that any evidence we find must be fitting to God's character construed in such a way, lending itself to a personal being and a morally perfect agent.

What does being worthy of worship involve? Epistemologist Paul K. Moser argues that though nobody shows this better than Jesus did, most apologists gravitate instead to abstract arguments that risk missing the point. Right or wrong, Moser thinks such efforts tend to result in some bad arguments, but if Moser is on to something, the most relevant evidence to consider should arguably pertain to God's moral character and what that involves for us.

We should ask questions like the following: Who am I as an inquirer about God as I ask for evidence for God's existence? What do we expect the evidence to be, and, importantly, what are we going to do with it? If the whole endeavor simply has for its goal becoming puffed up or accusing others of irrationality, we are arguably not yet ready to receive the evidence, in which case a God worthy of the title may well elude us and not furnish us with the eyes with which to see the evidence. Divine hiding is a theme rampant throughout the Bible, and it is there for a reason.[6] As Moser puts it, we should not expect God to be trivially obvious.[7]

The Role of Conscience

As for where to look for the relevant evidence, perhaps it should be in the deepest center of human moral agency: the moral conscience. Our conscience challenges us to renounce selfishness and become oriented toward others. The place where God self-manifests and gives evidence of divine reality is often in the conscience. The conscience is indicative of fundamental reality because of the way it works so concretely. To be a personal agent is to be an intentional agent, setting goals and the like. The important question about conscience is whether its evidence indicates intentional agency.

Since conscience can lead people who are responsive to it away from selfishness and can deepen concern for others in a way that is purposive, there is reason to think it is deeply personal. We are moved less by abstract principles than by something intentional, something personal, so among the most relevant evidence for God to consider is human moral experience

---

[6] There tend to be two salient sorts of divine hiddenness covered in the relevant literature. One is the sense of God's absence in times of trouble, a motif throughout Scripture, such as in the Psalms. The other, distinctly more modern discussion, pertains to lack of perceived evidence for God's reality. Our focus here will center more on this second matter and will broach the issue of what expectations are appropriate about the nature of the evidence sought.

[7] See Paul K. Moser's *The Elusive God: Reorienting Religious Epistemology* (Cambridge: Cambridge University Press, 2009), *The God Relationship: The Ethics for Inquiry about the Divine* (Cambridge: Cambridge University Press, 2018), *The Evidence for God: Religious Knowledge Reexamined* (Cambridge: Cambridge University Press, 2009), and *The Divine Goodness of Jesus: Impact and Response* (Cambridge: Cambridge University Press, 2021).

where people are morally challenged in a way that is indicative of God's character. Because there is a side of the human condition that resists and does not want to find any such evidence, moral candor and a willingness to comply with the dictates and deliverances of conscience is vital.

Here is where epistemology becomes morally robust. Moser points to a central question of Plato's *Republic*, namely, Is the just life really worthwhile? Can it be sustained? Will there be ultimate justice and a balancing of the scales? These pose a formidable challenge to secular ethics, Bertrand Russell's transparent bravado in "A Free Man's Worship" notwithstanding. On the matter of whether the good life is redolent with lasting meaning, a naturalist view is at a serious disadvantage for lack of requisite resources.

The challenge, Moser argues, is whether we can be candid enough to leave room for such evidence—to give it honest attention, to be morally attentive and responsive. Conscience constantly challenges us to be responsive to moral intrusion. Are we willing to allow ourselves to be radically challenged and to undergo a change of priorities?

John Henry Newman pushed a similar point by accentuating the central importance of the conscience, making possible knowing God himself. Newman didn't think of conscience so much as a rule of right conduct than as a sanction of right conduct—this is its primary and most authoritative dimension. Here is how he wrapped up his appraisal of the phenomenology of conscience:

> Conscience has an intimate bearing on our affections and emotions, leading us to reverence and awe, hope and fear, especially fear. Wrongdoing generates a lively sense of responsibility and guilt. These various perturbations of mind which are characteristic of a bad conscience, and may be very considerable—self-reproach, poignant shame, haunting remorse, chill dismay at the prospect of the future—and their contraries, when the conscience is good, as real though less forcible, self-approval, inward peace, lightness of heart, and the like—these emotions constitute a specific difference between

conscience and our other intellectual senses—common sense, good sense, sense of expedience, taste, sense of honour, and the like.[8]

Newman inferred from the characteristically moving and holistic nature of the conscience that it involves recognition of a living object toward which it is directed, specifically, one to whom we are responsible, before whom we are ashamed, whose claims upon us we fear. In this way, moral experience, for Newman, provides more than a propositional way to know that God exists, but an experiential knowledge of God himself, because a properly functioning conscience is something much like the voice of God himself speaking to us. The intensely personalist nature of moral experience gives morality a distinctively powerful place in natural theology for enabling us to know the reality of God—both his existence and his nature.

Two Kantian Arguments and Lotze's Dictum

Both Moser and Newman expressed doubts about other forms of natural theology, as did Immanuel Kant. We mention this not because we share their skepticism, but because we wish to emphasize that, despite their skepticism, all of them remained eminently open to the evidential significance of morality. One of the reasons we do not tend to share their skepticism about other arguments for God's existence is because they can be helpful to vindicate aspects of our moral experience. In light of debunking objections to moral knowledge, for example, a teleological set of considerations can help the theist retain principled confidence in the reliability of salient moral deliverances.[9] However, here we will retain our narrower focus on the evidence that comes from morality in particular, without implying by

---

[8] John Henry Newman, *An Essay in Aid of a Grammar of Assent* (Notre Dame, IN: University of Notre Dame Press, 1979), 100.

[9] See Logan Paul Gage, "Newman's Argument from Conscience: Why He Needs Paley and Natural Theology After All," *American Catholic Philosophical Quarterly* 94, no. 1 (2020): 141–57.

this delimiting strategy that other forms of natural theology are lacking in persuasive force or evidential significance.

Before Kant, the moral argument tended to manifest in only fragmentary and partial forms; important precursors included John Locke and René Descartes, Blaise Pascal and Joseph Butler, George Berkeley and Thomas Reid. One can argue that the roots of the moral argument can be traced to Plato himself! It was with Kant, however, that the moral argument began to show up in a robust and explicit way, especially in the two variants he offered, namely, an argument from grace and an argument from providence.

His *argument from grace* will be discussed later, but it pertains to whether morality is even possible in light of its uncompromising standards well beyond our capacity to meet on our own. Kant's *argument from providence* appeals to God's loving sovereignty as a robust explanation of an ultimate airtight connection between happiness and virtue, necessary for morality to be fully stable rationally. This argument will prove relevant in a later chapter. Together these arguments provide principled reasons to undergird the two aspects of "moral faith" needed to make full sense of morality—that morality is possible and the virtuous are ultimately joyful and satisfied.

Hermann Lotze put his finger on what is arguably the motivating principle of moral arguments for God's existence. Mark Linville dubs "Lotze's Dictum" the notion that the true beginning of metaphysics lies in ethics.[10] The gist of the Dictum is that ethical ideas about value or worth hold a certain primacy for the interpretation of reality—metaphysics ought to be founded on ethics, objectively construed. This is a departure from the modus operandi of many, which starts with metaphysics and then shoehorns morality into whatever strictures and constraints the prior

---

[10] See Mark Linville, "The Moral Argument," *The Blackwell Companion to Natural Theology*, ed. William Lane Craig and J. P. Moreland (Malden, MA: Blackwell, 2009).

metaphysical construct imposes. Lotze instead saw that morality ought to be allowed a preeminent place at the table in the quest to figure out the nature of reality.

Lotze had an enormous influence on a host of nineteenth- and early twentieth-century British figures, from A. E. Taylor to William Sorley, from Hastings Rashdall to Clement Webb, who spent their careers living with the moral argument and explicating fresh variants of it. More recently, there has been a huge resurgence of interest in the moral argument. When asked which argument from natural theology he thinks is the best, Alvin Plantinga has answered the moral argument.[11] When asked which argument has the largest impact in his debates on college campuses, William Lane Craig says the moral argument. The existentially central questions with which the argument is concerned, its rich and fertile history, and its contemporary formulations at the highest level of philosophical rigor all seem to underscore its abiding importance and remarkable staying power. For just such reasons, moral considerations will figure prominently in this book's distinctive take on philosophical theology.

Bare Natural Theology and Ramified Theology

Whereas the moral evidence to which Kant pointed involved matters of moral performance and rationality, and Moser and Newman would accentuate the conscience, other pieces of moral evidence include binding moral obligations, essential human equality, the dignity and value of people, moral knowledge, moral regrets, moral freedom, and still others. Another important but less frequently discussed part of moral phenomenology is a nagging sense that there will be a moral reckoning of sorts.

---

[11] Interestingly, this was after Plantinga had largely ignored the argument earlier in his career, in his *God and Other Minds*, for example. See Jerry L. Walls and Trent Dougherty, *Two Dozen (or So) Arguments for God* (New York: Oxford University Press, 2018), 447.

A fascinating exercise is to read Acts 17 and the Platonic dialogue of the *Apology* side by side. Both scenes are set in Athens, and Socrates and the apostle Paul make for an engaging comparison and contrast. Both saw themselves as on a divine mission; both questioned prevailing theological assumptions; both insisted on attentiveness to the evidence. As much as Socrates, Paul was skeptical both of the legends and of the Homeric spirit, which privileged an ambitious range of beliefs to cover one's theological bases over a serious examination of where the evidence leads.

Both were also committed to belief in a coming reckoning of some sort, but the most significant contrast between Paul and Socrates pertained to the issue of *ignorance*. Whereas Socrates claimed to be largely ignorant of the answers to the ultimate questions, Paul said that the hour of ignorance was over because of the resurrection (*anastasis*) of Jesus. It seems unlikely that the residents of Athens would have missed the obvious contrast with their most famous native son. Interestingly enough, though, as much as Socrates claimed ignorance, his conviction of a judgment to come escaped unscathed.

On the assumption that a reckoning will come, this piece of general revelation, too, may provide a measure of moral evidence for theism: that there is One to whom we are accountable after all, as Newman put it. This inches toward an example of what Richard Swinburne calls "bare" natural theology (BNT), which gets us to a generic theistic concept of God, one that can be shared among most all theists. This is not just any "god," so to speak, but a God who is omnipotent, omniscient, and perfectly good. "Ramified" natural theology (RNT), on the other hand, is an exercise in or a "natural extension" of BNT, and it takes us from a generic theism to particular religious claims, such as those of Islam or Christianity.[12]

Consistent with the project of RNT, we wish to emphasize the way that moral apologetics, on the foundation of natural theological arguments

---

[12] Richard Swinburne, "Natural Theology, Its 'Dwindling Probabilities' and 'Lack of Rapport,'" *Faith and Philosophy* 21, no. 4 (2004): 533.

for theism per se, can extend the case for God's existence by fleshing out distinctively moral aspects of God's character. In so doing, moral evidence for God's existence and essentially loving character can bolster the case for specifically Christian points of theology. Not only do moral arguments for God, as put forth by RNT, distinguish Christian theism from various other theisms, it also serves to make certain distinctions within Christian theism itself. In a Swinburnian spirit we dub this argumentative strategy doubly ramified natural theology, the explanation of which is forthcoming.[13]

What, then, are some of the biblical intimations of God's perfectly and essentially loving nature? What within Christian theology will point the project of RNT with respect to moral arguments for God in the right direction? This step of the argument can be thought of as an extension of a BNT moral case for God toward the specific theology (via RNT) that best explains and models God's omnibenevolence.

The first distinctively Christian teaching germane to God's omnibenevolence and essentially loving nature is the trinitarian understanding of God. God exists in three Persons, who have always existed in a relationship of perfect love with one another.[14] Nontrinitarian theistic religions cannot say the same and are at a distinct disadvantage in explaining how God's nature could be essentially one of love. C. S. Lewis famously wrote, "All sorts of people are fond of repeating the Christian statement that 'God is love.' But, they seem not to notice that the words 'God is love' have no real meaning unless God contains at least two persons. Love is something that one person has for another person. If God was a single person, then before the world

---

[13] See David Baggett and Ronnie Campbell, "Omnibenevolence, Moral Apologetics, and Doubly Ramified Natural Theology," *Philosophia Christi* 15, no. 2 (2013): 111–26.

[14] In lieu of trying to encapsulate the doctrine of the Trinity in a verse or two, readers are directed to Brandon D. Smith, ed., *The Trinity in the Canon: A Biblical, Historical, and Practical Proposal* (Brentwood, TN: B&H Academic, 2023). I (Dave) wrote the last chapter in the volume, entitled "Apologetics and Worldview," 431–62.

was made, he was not love."[15] If the world were necessary for God's love to be operative, that would also threaten God's aseity.

A trinitarian theist might argue that any kind of monotheism, apart from a dynamic relationship of divine persons, in some sense, collapses into something like panentheism—where God, to some extent or another, depends on the world for his existence—particularly if such nontrinitarian theists want to maintain that "God is love." Perfect love requires relationship with an "other." A trinitarian conception of God can maintain, on the one hand, that "God is love," and, on the other, that God exists *a se* ("from himself"). If a theist wants to claim that God is perfectly loving, then there must be an object of God's love. If the object is a creature, then God needs the creature in order to be perfectly loving. This in turn would call into question whether God is a necessary being. Therefore, it would seem that a trinitarian conception of God makes better sense of God's aseity and freedom, his perfect love, and his transcendence.

Reflection on the Christian doctrine of Trinity, particularly with respect to the doctrine of *perichoresis*, provides a glimpse of what an omnibenevolent and all-loving God would look like. In other words, this is the kind of thing one might expect if God were, at bottom, all-loving and good. If J. P. Moreland and William Lane Craig are correct in describing God as "a triad of persons in eternal, self-giving love relationships," then within the triune God is the deepest loving relationship in all of reality.[16] This relationship—the perichoretic relationship between the Father, Son, and Holy Spirit—forms the heart of Christian theism. The concept of perichoresis is intricately connected to the Christian belief that God is love. "God is love" is not merely a statement about God's character or his actions toward his creatures. It is at root and most fundamentally a claim about the very nature of the inner life of the triune

---

[15] C. S. Lewis, *Mere Christianity* (New York: Macmillan, 1960), 151.

[16] J. P. Moreland and William Lane Craig, *Philosophical Foundations for a Christian Worldview* (Downers Grove: IVP, 2003), 595.

God. God's nature is such that the three persons of the Trinity exist in eternal self-giving love. There is complete indwelling and mutual inter-penetration between the persons of the Trinity, or as Karl Barth describes it, "complete participation."[17]

As Stephen T. Davis suggests, with respect to perichoresis, at "the core of God's inner being is the highest degree of self-giving love. The Persons are fully open to each other, their actions *ad extra* are actions in common, they 'see with each other's eyes', the boundaries between them are transparent to each other, and each ontologically embraces the other."[18] At the core of all of existence is a dynamic "loving relationship among persons."[19] God's loving nature, in turn, works its way out in God's dealings with his creatures. So Christianity has in the Trinity, especially when considering the doctrine of perichoresis, the needed resources for arguing that God is essentially loving, a requirement of omnibenevolence.

Second, human beings are said to be made in God's image, and in fact the command to love each other is rooted in God's loving nature. If God is not essentially loving, it is much harder to understand how his command to love our enemies (Matt 5:43–44) would retain its authority. The issue of human dignity and worth and its connections to Christian theology will be taken up in a later chapter.

This leads to a third central Christian teaching, the death of Christ on the cross. God the Son's work in becoming incarnate and atoning for the sins of the world (John 3:16; 1 John 2:2) is the very kind of thing that one might expect if God were an omnibenevolent being, a claim that fits neither with other theistic religions nor altogether comfortably with certain

---

[17] Karl Barth, *Church Dogmatics*, vol. 1, part I, "The Doctrine of the Word of God," ed. G. W. Bromiley and T. F. Torrance (New York: T&T Clark International, 2004), 370.

[18] Stephen T. Davis, *Christian Philosophical Theology* (New York: Oxford University Press, 2006), 72.

[19] Stephen T. Davis, "God's Action," in *In Defense of Miracles*, ed. R. Douglas Geivett and Gary Habermas (Downers Grove: IVP, 1997), 176.

Augustinian models of Christian theism, but is, nevertheless, an inference derived from the moral argument for God.[20]

Here we part company with those who believe in limited atonement because the Bible says that we know God loves us because Jesus died for us. If Jesus did not die for some, then God has not shown his love for them in any ultimately significant way. No greater love has a man than to lay down his life for his friends (John 15:13). The defense that God loves the nonelect differently does not work; *differently* is fine, *not recognizably at all* is not. It is not that God had an obligation to save anyone. Out of love surely he would, and a moral argument pointing to the God who is goodness itself would do no less. God may well love each person differently, but as C. S. Lewis once wrote, he also loves each one infinitely.

In his book *The Difficult Doctrine of the Love of God*, D. A. Carson struggles with this idea that God loves all.[21] We are in agreement with him that we have to understand the love of God in connection with God's other attributes, including his holiness, his sovereignty, and his wrath. Where we tend to differ is with his privileging the question of what God's love looks like when considered in the light of such other qualities, while he neglects to

---

[20] Matthew J. Hart is an example of such Augustinianism, offering some reasons why God, despite being able to save everyone without violating anyone's free will, might not save some, perhaps many. One of the goods he thinks might justify God's creating many occupants of hell is the deepened sense of gratitude the saved would have in recognizing the "likelihood of the alternative." When the elect see in hell all their friends and associates who were just like they were in so many ways, they will feel all the more keenly how blessed they are to be saved. This provides a reason why God would determine things so the number of the damned would "far outstrip the elect." Indeed, the more such reprobated companions the elect have, "the more appropriate or 'truer' it will be for them to say, 'I could have been damned,' and their gratitude at being in heaven will increase—in proportion to both the number of these companions and the similarity of situation of these companions to themselves." *Calvinism and the Problem of Evil*, ed. David E. Alexander and Daniel M. Johnson (Eugene, OR: Pickwick, 2016), 258.

[21] D. A. Carson, *The Difficult Doctrine of the Love of God* (Wheaton: Crossway, 2000).

ask what those other qualities look like in the light of divine love—which is particularly regrettable given the utter centrality of God's love in his nature. God is not just loving, but love itself. It is true that the contemporary notion of love is too often degraded, watered down, and sentimentalized, but Carson's fairly consistent intimation is that those who do this are those who do not buy into his theological paradigm. Repeatedly smuggling in such a claim does nothing to strengthen the point and potentially conceals the way he fails to come to terms with what genuine love entails.

Carson's claim is that believing in a God of love is easy, whereas believing in a God of wrath and justice is hard. Although an interesting claim, it's demonstrably false. Many people harbor grave doubts about God's love for them, including Christians. And plenty of people believe in something like hell, while similarly entertaining deep doubts they can reconcile such doctrines with anything like recognizable love. Altogether too many, we fear, down deep do not really believe God loves everyone, taking the "hating Esau" with wooden literalness. To say, as Carson does, that God's love for the nonelect is manifested in God's "salvific stance" toward them seems worse than disingenuous.[22] All he in essence is affirming is that God, in dissembling fashion, projects the impression of offering to them a genuine chance at salvation when in point of fact and in actuality he is not and they are without hope. Yet Jesus, he wants to affirm, in some real sense died for them and God genuinely loves them, which seems incoherent. In fact, it is hard to see how the problem of evil does not become simply intractable on a view such as his, replete as it is with a compatibilist understanding of human freedom and impotent salvific stances.[23] Theism, and particularly

---

[22] Carson, 17–19.

[23] A compatibilist view of freedom treats something in the vicinity of doing what one wishes to do as not just necessary but sufficient for free will, even if we have no ultimate volitional control over our desires. On a theological compatibilist view, God could have saved everyone without violating anyone's free will, but chose not to. We instead adopt a view of agency, made possible by God's grace, that is furnished to all and makes alternatives possible.

a Christian concept of God, would certainly suffer for the failure of God's goodness and love toward all being sufficiently recognizable.

The fourth central Christian teaching—God as a loving being is intimately connected to God as a morally perfect being—means that God cannot be morally perfect without being essentially loving and vice versa. Let us suppose we were to look at how God's other attributes fit with a God who is essentially love, as suggested by Carson. It would seem that the various attributes would work in conjunction in such a way that they consistently exemplify God's essential nature. But are all attributes on par with one another? Suppose that God had never created. Would God then be sovereign? Yes, but God's sovereignty over an actualized creation would be quite different from, say, over no creation at all. It would seem, then, that the exercising of God's sovereignty is at least grounded in some other attribute such as his necessity, aseity, or freedom. We might speak of these as grounding attributes. How God exercises his sovereignty is grounded in God's necessity or freedom or aseity, but more on sovereignty and aseity below.

What of love? It would seem that love, too, is a grounding attribute. The book of 1 John emphasizes that "God is love." As noted above, God is a Trinity of persons and not merely one person; moreover, it is God's essential loving nature that grounds the ethical command for humans to love one another. But the author of 1 John also emphasizes that "God is light." Both "God is love" and "God is light" are ontological claims about the nature of God. With respect to the latter, the word "light" is used metaphorically by the author; nevertheless, within context its use captures a variety of concepts, particularly God's moral perfection, truthfulness, and impeccability. God cannot do anything contrary to exemplifying these qualities. This is affirmed when the author asserts that within God there "is no darkness at all" (1 John 1:5 ESV). For the author, God as light and God as love become the theological grounds for ethics for the Christian community; the two are deeply connected.

Walking in the light for the Christian requires not only living a life that is truthful and pure but also to love one's brother or sister, seeking the good and best for the other. The reason why believers are to do this is found in God's demonstration of love toward us by sending his own Son who died for the sins of the world. Further, failure to love is a failure to be in the light as God himself is in the light. The logic for the writer of 1 John is twofold. On the one hand, God cannot do other than what his nature allows, yet, on the other, God does not require of us, with respect to moral goodness and love, what is not true of himself. God's moral goodness grounds God's love, and God's love directs God's moral goodness, just as "walking in the light" requires that one love one's brothers and sisters, seeking out their best. Failure to love means that one is not walking in the light.

With respect to God's perfect freedom, there seems to be, at least, some limitations on that freedom, though of course any such constraints are intrinsic to God's nature and reflections of his perfection.[24] If "God is light" and in him there "is no darkness at all," then what God does out of perfect freedom must be done in love toward his creatures and must be grounded in his perfect goodness. Moreover, to love is to seek what is best for the other, as is exemplified in the heart of the interpenetrating relationship of the divine Trinity. Thus in his aseity and sovereignty, while not depending on or needing anything for his own existence or being, God, out of love, seeks out the best for his creatures. What is best for God's human creatures is for them to be in union (fellowship) with their Creator and with other humans, living a pure and sinless life, while loving God and others. Grace motivated by perfect love does not fail to be grace—amazing grace.

This leads to the last point to emphasize: *doubly ramified natural theology*. The more fine-grained analysis of natural theology made possible by bringing to bear specific theological insights cannot avoid this simple fact:

---

[24] Sometimes any talk of "limitations" on what God can do strain credulity, but bear in mind two points. Any constraints on God's behavior are internal to his nature, and the Bible itself makes clear there are some things God can't do—deny himself, for example. It isn't that God lacks freedom; rather, he's completely free from any moral or metaphysical imperfections.

Christian theology itself is a vexed and ongoing discussion, involving a number of disputes over quite central questions—even if outside the innermost core of beliefs common to all Christians. And this means that a God in whose image we have been made, a trinitarian God who took human form to die for the sins of all, and a God who is omnibenevolent, not only distinguishes Christian convictions from naturalistic ones and non-Christian theological convictions. It also generates further distinctions among professing Christians—distinctions relevant to the confidence with which Christians can claim God loves everyone, what they mean when they say it, and how principled they can be in the grounding of human rights, in their handling of the problem of evil, and in the viability of moral apologetics.

An Expansive Epistemology and Moving Forward

The operative conception of God in this volume is Anselmian, then, in two senses. First, God is thought of as eminently worthy of worship in part because he is the possessor of all the great-making properties to the maximally composible degree. Second, like Anselm himself, we are Christians, and our conception of God is also conditioned by distinctively Christian theology. As this is not a book on apologetics, we have simply gestured toward the sorts of arguments that, to our thinking, warrant our generally theistic and specifically Christian convictions. The particular line of evidence to which we have devoted the most attention is morality, and we did that for several reasons.

First, we consider moral truths to be a powerful evidential consideration in favor of God's reality. Second, starting with the notion of God's worship-worthiness gives us additional reasons to fuse religious epistemology with a robust moral apologetic. Third, biblical faith, contrary to Enlightenment depictions, is less about epistemic disadvantage than principled trust in God's abiding faithfulness. What better reason to trust God's faithfulness than to find good reasons to believe in his perfect goodness and abiding love? Fourth, and finally, we thought it would be a useful and effective strategy in our introductory chapter to give God's perfect goodness and love center stage as an overarching theme, recurring motif, and undergirding structure.

This approach will afford us the opportunity as we proceed to bring to bear the powerful implications of God's perfect, necessary, and recognizable love. What we hope to show by the book's end is some of the vast swath of applications such theology possesses when God's love is grasped rightly and its implications laid out clearly. Receptivity to the deliverances of powerful moral truths also requires something of an *expansive epistemology*—a willingness to follow a wide assortment of evidences to their natural conclusions. Such evidences exceed the parameters of a narrow empiricism or truncated rationality but are wide and eclectic in scope, ranging from the aesthetic to the relational, from the imaginative to the affective, and of course from the ethical to the evaluative. Such a broad approach captures what William Wainwright means by "passional reason," and what C. S. Lewis meant by a "logic of relations."[25]

What close study of the history of the moral arguments for God's existence reveals is that its luminaries were never narrow logic choppers or abstemious empiricists. They were open to the deliverances of literature, poetry, emotions, and beauty. They did not confine their attention to a myopic range of thinkers; rather, they read widely with an open mind and heart and heeded what they read. Students of the human condition, steeped in life's travails, aware of its challenges, acquainted with grief and loss, they took seriously not just the premium of avoiding error but also the needed risks occasionally required to apprehend and appreciate the truth. In the pages to come we aim to emulate their example of deep faith and wide rationality.

---

[25] See William Wainwright, *Reason and the Heart: A Prolegomenon to a Critique of Passional Reason* (Ithaca, NY: Cornell University Press, 2006).

2

The Christian Concept of God

What we're interested in in this book is the Christian idea of God and especially how this God makes moral sense of our world. We believe, at the heart of Christian theism is a loving and personal God, and what we believe about this God has significant implications for a variety of other Christian doctrines. No run-of-the-mill god will do!

As already mentioned, our approach is Anselmian, prioritizing perfect being theology. But there's more to the story. In this chapter we explore method in relation to the doctrine of God, followed by an examination of four live models available for Christian theists—classical theism, modified classical theism, open theism, and essential kenosis theism. We shall also compare two other broad umbrella models: theistic personalism and eternalism. Our work in this chapter, though preliminary, sets the stage for an overall case for theistic personalism, which we shall develop in the next three chapters.

God or Scripture?

Generally, theologians fall into one of two camps. One camp proposes that we begin with our thoughts on God apart from Scripture (*sensus divinitatis*); the other camp suggests that we begin with Scripture allowing it solely to inform our thoughts on God (*sensus literalis*). But as Kevin Vanhoozer has argued, both starting points run up against difficulties.[1]

Beginning our thoughts on God apart from Scripture often leads to idolatry. Because of the effects of sin on our thinking, we are prone to make God into our own image. "[W]hat we say about God on the basis of our own ideas may well reveal more about us, our social location and our sinfulness, than it does about God," suggests Vanhoozer.[2] There is still a further difficulty of beginning with God apart from Scripture: how should we define "perfection"? The temptation is to begin "from below," using human experience and culture to work our way up to an understanding of what God is like. But such an approach doesn't always bode well. He offers a case study in the work of theologian Sallie McFague. In her book *Models of God*, she contends that the Bible doesn't really give us information about God. Rather, we should view it as a model of how one should approach theology, using metaphor and various images to speak about God and God's relationship to the world. Given that our own situation and culture exceedingly differs from that of the biblical writers, we are free then to use different metaphors and images that give us insight into God and the God/world relation that specifically address issues we face today from our own experience. McFague begins from a feminist framework, rejecting metaphors that smack of patriarchalism, such as "Lord" or "King." She prefers understanding God as "the Lover of the world" and looks to the world as God's body, especially in light of the ecological crisis of our times. Thus

[1] Kevin J. Vanhoozer, *First Theology: God, Scripture, and Hermeneutics* (Downers Grove: IVP, 2002), 25–28.
[2] Vanhoozer, 25.

the bottom-up approach tends toward the danger of making God into one's own image with idolatry running amok, especially if there are no controls on defining perfection.

But what of beginning with Scripture, allowing it to inform our thoughts on God? As Vanhoozer warns, this, too, has its dangers. First, there is a strong tendency for some to view the Bible as merely a human book. Such an approach, however, hinders the person from ever finding any hint of divine authority in the Scriptures. Second, some advocate for taking the Bible in its "plain," "ordinary," or "common" sense. Yet, as postmodernists have rightly pointed out, common sense is neither common nor universal, and such a reading of Scripture falls victim to cultural relativism.[3]

Where, then, should we begin? Following David Kelsey's insight that theologians often form their views on God and Scripture together, Vanhoozer proposes a "both/and" approach to theology, which he calls "theological hermeneutics" (*sensus scripturalis*).[4] Kelsey recognized that theologians often appeal to the Bible's authority in a variety of ways, as Vanhoozer explains: "Before using the Bible as authoritative, theologians make a judgment as to *how* the Bible will be brought to bear authoritatively: *as* doctrine, *as* myth, *as* history, *as* story, and so on. To view the Bible *as* such and such is to construe it."[5]

A theologian like B. B. Warfield understands the Bible *as* doctrine, whereby he understands God as a personal agent who reveals truth through the Scriptures. Rudolph Bultmann, on the other hand, views Scripture as myth and merely a human work, but, yet, has the power for human transformation. God is not the personalistic revealer of truth; rather, God is the power behind human existential realization.[6] Kelsey's analysis highlights the important insight that one's view of God affects how one interprets

---

[3] Vanhoozer, 25.
[4] Vanhoozer, 38.
[5] Vanhoozer, 29.
[6] Vanhoozer, 30.

Scripture and vice versa. Vanhoozer encourages theologians to "resist the pernicious either-or and affirm instead a both-and approach" and instead "interpret Scripture as divine communicative action in order to know God; we let our knowledge of God affect our approach to Scripture."[7]

We find wisdom in Vanhoozer's approach. Through prayerful reflection on the Bible, human reasoning, and moral intuition, we can begin to fine-tune a faithful conception of the God of Christian faith. Is this enough? Might we go further in laying out a set of principles that guide our journey in understanding the Christian idea of God? We believe we can.

Via Triplex and Three Regulative Principles

Classical theists have generally used three deductive methods when contemplating the divine nature and attributes. Together these methods are known as the *via triplex*. The first of the three is the *via eminentiae* (the way of eminence). This approach takes the so-called *communicable* attributes, that is, those attributes thought to be shared by God and creatures, and maximizes them with respect to the divine nature. For example, human creatures are said to have power, knowledge, and goodness; most theists take it that God has these to the maximal degree. God is not only powerful, good, and wise, but God is omnipotent (all-powerful), omnibenevolent (all-good), and omniscient (all-wise).

The second is the *via negativa* (the way of negation). Theologians who emphasize this method contrast the transcendent God with transient and fleeting creation, placing emphasis on what God is not. This method has led some to extreme skepticism; however, some view it as a backdoor way of saying something about God, namely, that God is immutable (without change), impassible (without passions and free of suffering), timeless and spaceless (without temporal or spatial location or extension), simple (identical to his nature and existence) and non-composite, immeasurable, and so

---

[7] Vanhoozer, 38.

on. Unlike the communicable attributes, these divine perfections are not shared with creatures and belong solely to God.

The third and final is the *via causalitatis* (the way of causation). Here, theologians draw on God as the First Cause, as found in Thomas Aquinas's Five Ways, as a source for understanding certain divine attributes, especially such attributes as necessary existence, self-existence, and aseity, as well as omnipotence, omniscience, and omnibenevolence, which are also ascertained through the *via eminentiae*.[8]

While longstanding in Christian tradition, overemphasis on the *via triplex* leads to a serious problem—a method that takes scriptural revelation as an afterthought in reflection on the doctrine of God. In his book *The Untamed God*, Jay Wesley Richards lays out the problem well. According to Richards, Thomas Aquinas, along with the early Reformers and Protestant Scholastics (who followed Thomas), began their doctrine of God by laying out the divine attributes and then moving on to such doctrines as the Trinity, incarnation, and so forth.[9] The ordering itself isn't problematic; the problem arises from how the divine attributes are to be understood in relation to what God has revealed about himself through Scripture, especially when taking into consideration such doctrines as the Trinity and incarnation. On this, Richards continues:

> The problem, obviously, is that any Christian doctrine of God has to take into account certain biblical claims about God, especially those surrounding Jesus' life, death and resurrection, which were subsequently codified in the early ecumenical creeds at Nicaea (325) and Chalcedon (451). No doubt Thomas Aquinas and the Protestant Scholastics had every intention of doing this. They frequently cite biblical texts as support for the attributes derived from the *via triplex*, even if the biblical texts do not always bear all the

---

[8] Jay Wesley Richards, *The Untamed God: A Philosophical Exploration of Divine Perfection, Simplicity and Immutability* (Downers Grove: IVP, 2003), 24.

[9] Richards, 26–27.

weight of the attribute defended. Despite good intentions, however, the three ways can take on a deductive, a priori character.
When this occurs, what is ascribed to God seems to result primarily from intuitions about what constitute maximal greatness
or aseity, or what is considered a deficiency in the physical world,
with which God must be contrasted. Such a procedure can create
a conflict in a Christian concept of God, which derives its content
not simply from general metaphysical intuitions but from unique,
contingent things that God has done in history and, in particular,
in Jesus Christ.[10]

One solution to the problem, suggests Richards, is simply to give up the
thing causing the conflict. For example, suppose there is a conflict between
the *via negativa* and one of the teachings of the New Testament (or, perhaps,
a teaching found in one of the ecumenical creeds). A person with the proclivity toward developing their doctrine of God, say, from the Bible alone
may find it an appropriate action simply to jettison the *via negativa*. But
such a solution is too hasty. Richards suggests that the theologian first recognize three "regulative principles," which he takes to be universal in Christian
theology: "normativity of Scripture," the "Principle of Perfection," and the
"Sovereignty-Aseity Conviction."[11]

Protestants have long held to the idea of *sola Scriptura*, but some have
grossly misappropriated it to mean that the theologian should use Scripture
apart from tradition or other sources to develop one's idea about God.
Rather, *sola Scriptura* emphasizes that the Bible should take priority for
our ideas and beliefs about God, or as Richards puts it, "The theologian's
metaphysical and ontological commitments should emerge from, or be
consistent with Scripture," and that "the theologian should use philosophical forms that comply with that commitment."[12] Therefore, when we speak

---

[10] Richards, 30.
[11] Richards, 30–31.
[12] Richards, 30–31.

of biblical normativity, what we mean is a "commitment to the witness of Scripture and divine revelation."[13] Richards takes it that the other two principles, the Principle of Perfection (PP) and Sovereignty-Aseity Conviction (SAC), stand behind or motivate the *via triplex*. PP refers to God's divine perfections or God's maximal greatness—the Anselmian notion that God is "that than which none greater can be conceived." SAC, on the other hand, refers to God's self-existence and utter independence from the world (or anything else for that matter). In other words, God is not dependent on anything outside of himself. Furthermore, God exercises divine control over all things that exist. According to Richards, PP seems to motivate the *via eminentiae*; whereas SAC seems to stand behind the *via negativa* and *via causalitatis*.[14]

According to Richards, these three principles often stand behind many of the disputes related to the doctrine of God. Why then should we hold on to the PP and SAC and not just use Scripture alone? Wouldn't this be a simpler solution? After all, aren't PP and SAC nothing more than philosophical assumptions? Not exactly. Both themes have substantial warrant in Scripture.[15] A proper Christian response, says Richards, requires that the theologian not abandon them opting for *sola Scriptura* alone. Theologians "should avoid hastily contrasting, say, the attributes of classical theism and the proper attributes that should derive from a biblical grounded doctrine of God," yet, "[w]hen conflict results within a doctrine of God, theologians must seek resolution by modifying PP and SAC to conform to biblical normativity."[16]

We find Richards's proposal a good method, one which we will adopt moving forward. While PP and SAC are strong regulative principles, given our commitment to Christian Scripture and divine revelation, these should

---

[13] Richards, 32.
[14] Richards, 33.
[15] Richards, 35–36.
[16] Richards, 42.

be used with caution and nuance. Now that we've put forth a method, let's consider the Christian concept of God.

Essences and Attributes

Christians affirm a form of theism called "monotheism," a view shared with Muslims, Jews, Hindus, and certain African religions. In contrast to polytheists, monotheists affirm that only one God exists, and this God is eternal and the Creator of all things. In contrast to pantheists, monotheists reject the idea that God is identical to the world. Instead, monotheists hold to a form of dualism, whereby God and the world are ontologically distinct. Yet, unlike deists, who affirm a radical transcendence, God does not stand aloof. God, though the transcendent creator of all things, remains immanent and intimately engaged in the world through a variety of means (providence, miracles, etc.). On the other hand, monotheists generally avoid panentheism, the belief that God is in the world or the world is somehow in God.

What largely sets Christian monotheism apart from other monotheistic proposals is the belief that God is tripersonal—Father, Son, and Holy Spirit. Christian monotheism centers on the claim that God became flesh in the Second Person of the Trinity and dwelt among human beings (John 1:14). So, whatever else we say about the divine nature, it is imperative that we keep before us the doctrines of incarnation and Trinity.

Christians have long held to a number of other key doctrines about God, namely, that God is incorporeal, eternal, omnipotent, omniscient, omnibenevolent, omnipresent, necessary, *a se*, and the sovereign creator of all things. Most Christians agree on a list of divine attributes but differ on how to cash them out. Some Christian theists hold to several other attributes, such as atemporality, immutability, impassibility, simplicity, and pure actuality.

What do Christians mean by such terms as "attributes" or "perfections," and in what sense are they distinct from a "nature" or "essence"? Much of how one answers this question rests on one's starting point. To begin with, an "attribute" or "perfection" is a property. Being six feet tall, being horned, or having four legs are all examples of properties that some entity might have. Properties come in two forms: "essential" and "nonessential." Essential properties are the kinds of things that if an individual or entity did not have them, then it would not be what it is. Nonessential properties, on the other hand, are accidental or contingent and the kinds of things that if they were different or changed, the entity would remain what it is. Take, for example, changing one's hair color from blond to brown. Though the color of one's hair has changed, the person remains essentially who she is at the core of her essence. One's hair color is an example of a nonessential or *accidental* property.

How does this translate to our understanding of God? God, too, has certain properties. Each of God's attributes (essential to God's nature) may be classified as properties. We can speak of God as having the property of being "Lord over Israel." But being Lord over Israel is not something that is essential to God's nature (unless, of course, one believes that God is not free or that God creates and acts providentially by divine necessity). When it comes to God, "attributes" and "perfections" are often used interchangeably, since when we speak of God's attributes, we mean that God has them maximally.

Take, for example, something like power. Alligators, mice, and humans each have different levels and means of exercising power, but when we speak of divine power, we mean God's power is in a class all alone (*sui generis*). God's power is not like that of a creature's, which is limited and derivative. Rather God's power is maximally great (though, theologians have differing views on just what maximal greatness looks like with respect to God's power) and something that is essential to the divine nature, what we called in chapter 1, "great-making properties."[17] On Anselm's conception, God is "the greatest possible" or "maximally perfect" being, and as Thomas Morris

---

[17] Thomas V. Morris, *Anselmian Explorations: Essays in Philosophical Theology* (Notre Dame, IN: University of Notre Dame Press, 1987).

suggests, "God is thought of as exemplifying necessarily a maximally perfect set of compossible great-making properties."[18]

How do the divine attributes or perfections relate to the divine "nature" or "essence"? Though these terms have been used in various ways throughout the history of Christian theology, they are often used interchangeably today. When we think of an essence or a nature, we're speaking of the kind of thing something is. For example, a rabbit, dog, or cat has a certain set of features that make it just what it is. Perhaps, the same can be said of God. God has certain properties that make him just what he is. Now, there is much dispute as to what this looks like for God. Christian theists, like Thomas Aquinas, have argued that God doesn't have a nature or properties distinct from himself. To suggest otherwise would compromise divine aseity. It would also mean that God is a composite being, and hence dependent on his component parts. Aquinas's view, however, rests on his controversial doctrine of divine simplicity, which suggests that God just is [identical with] his attributes. Others, like Alvin Plantinga, reject the Thomistic view of divine simplicity, arguing that God does, indeed, have a nature. This doesn't mean that God is somehow cobbled together, but it does mean for Plantinga that God has a nature that stands behind the divine attributes.[19] How one understands the relationship between God's essence/nature and the divine attributes rests largely on how one understands the doctrine of divine simplicity, which we'll explore more in chapter 4.

Models of God within Christian Thought

Having made preliminary delineation between the divine essence and attributes of God, let us now briefly consider four unique models that serve as live options for the Christian concept of God: classical theism, modified

---

[18] Morris, 12.

[19] For an extended discussion, see Alvin Plantinga, *Does God Have a Nature? The Aquinas Lecture, 1980* (Milwaukee: Marquette University Press, 1980).

or neo-classical theism, open theism, and essential kenosis theism. It is not enough that models share common belief that God has certain attributes. After all, a good number of theists, whether Christian or not, share the belief that God is omnipotent, omniscient, eternal, and so on. Each model must say something unique about the divine nature that differs from its rivals.[20]

Classical Theism

Perhaps, the most widely held view in Western Christian thought is classical theism, promoted by such key historical thinkers as Augustine, Boethius, Anselm, Thomas Aquinas, and Protestant Scholastics. According to this view, God is omnipotent, omniscient, omnibenevolent, omnipresent, *a se*, and necessary. Classical theists hold to a cluster of other core attributes and beliefs, such as simplicity, immutability, impassibility, timeless eternality, and *actus purus* (pure act or pure actuality). Most classical theists have held to the belief that God created the world *ex nihilo* and denied that the world is eternal. Some classical theists have held to the belief that God creates by necessity instead of a free act by God. Modern defenders of classical theism include Paul Helm, Katherine Rogers, William Mann, Brian Leftow, and Eleonore Stump, just to name a few.

Modified or Neo-Classical Theism

Following classical theists, modified or neo-classical theists believe that God is omnipotent, omniscient, omnibenevolent, omnipresent, necessary, and *a se*. Generally, modified classical theists qualify or reject certain core tenets of classical theism, namely, divine timelessness, simplicity, impassibility, and immutability. Instead of divine timelessness, modified classical theists will

---

[20] R. T. Mullins, "Classical Theism," in *T&T Clark Handbook of Analytic Theology*, ed. James M. Arcadi and James T. Turner Jr., paperback ed. (New York: T&T Clark, 2022), 85.

often defend God as everlastingly eternal or omnitemporal. Some embrace immutability and impassibility but believe classical theists have taken these doctrines too far, going beyond what the Bible warrants. As for divine simplicity, most jettison the doctrine in favor of something like divine unity, though some will want to affirm a weaker version still. God has exhaustive foreknowledge of the future, whether by means of something like simple foreknowledge or middle knowledge. Defenders of modified classical theism deny that God and creation are coeternal, opting for creation *ex nihilo* and the belief that the universe came into existence at a definite time in the past. Moreover, they deny that creation is necessary. Finally, defenders of neo-classical theism advocate for theistic personalism and theological essentialism. Key defenders include John Feinberg, William Lane Craig, Alvin Plantinga, Ryan T. Mullins, and John Peckham.[21]

Open Theism

Open theists agree with both classical theists and modified classical theists that God is omnipotent, omniscient, omnibenevolent, *a se*, and necessary. However, they generally reject certain core tenets of classical theism, emphasizing especially God as temporal and passible (that God is in some way affected by the world). Some may hold to a version of immutability, but they emphasize that God is immutable only in the sense of the divine character or essential nature. A key distinction is that, while God is omniscient, knowing perfectly the past and the present, God does not have exhaustive foreknowledge of the future. In this case, passages in the Bible that speak of God as changing his mind or regretting are not merely anthropomorphic or a matter of divine accommodation. Furthermore, open theists maintain that humans have libertarian freedom. Open theists hold to the belief that God created the world *ex nihilo* and that God

---

[21] While "Modified-Classical Theism" is our label, we recognize some on this list may not agree with this label and would prefer to label themselves as classical theists.

in no way depends on the creation for divine existence. Current defenders include William Hasker, Gregory Boyd, Richard Rice, Dean Zimmerman, Alan Rhoda, and Richard Swinburne.

Essential Kenosis Theism

God is maximally powerful, maximally knowing, and maximally loving, and the creator of all things. Like open theists, this view says that God does not have exhaustive foreknowledge of the future; rather, the future is open and free. God does, however, have perfect knowledge of the past and present. Though God has maximal power, he does not (cannot) act or operate providentially in the world through divine causative power. Rather, out of love, God essentially "gives up" or "empties" the divine self of any causative power to cooperate with creatures who have libertarian freedom. God's love, which shapes all of God's divine action, is uncontrolling and others-empowering. Finally, according to this view, God has always created out of love and out of response to divine creativity. The key defender of this view is Thomas J. Oord.[22]

Eternalism vs. Theistic Personalism

Each model of God, whether classical theism, neo-classical theism, open theism, or essential kenosis theism, has differing beliefs on what is meant by "God," and each has different starting points. We believe these models fit into two broader categories: Eternalism and Theistic Personalism.

---

[22] Thomas Jay Oord, *The Uncontrolling Love of God: An Open and Relational Account of Providence* (Downers Grove: IVP, 2015), 94. For similar views, see Philip Clayton, *Adventures in the Spirit: God, World, and Divine Action* (Philadelphia: Fortress, 2008). John C. Polkinghorne, "Kenotic Creation and Divine Action," in *The Work of Love: Creation as Kenosis*, ed. John C. Polkinghorne (Grand Rapids: Eerdmans, 2001), 102.

Eternalism

In recent years, there has been something of a resurgence among classical theists to embrace a view called "eternalism," which teaches that creation is eternal or everlasting and that God timelessly and tenselessly sustains the four-dimensional space-time universe. Eternalism rests on the classical theist's affirmation of the strongest senses of divine simplicity, immutability, and impassibility, coupled with the doctrines of divine timelessness and *actus purus*. This view reinterprets creation *ex nihilo* to mean that creation only has a boundary; there is no temporal beginning. Not all who call themselves classical theists affirm the eternal or everlasting nature of the world. Instead, they affirm the classical understanding of creation *ex nihilo*. But we doubt this option is feasible for two reasons. First, not only do these doctrines entail one another (apart from qualification), but they stand or fall together. Second, as we'll argue in a later chapter, the doctrine of divine simplicity ultimately leads to modal collapse, requiring creation to be necessary.

Theistic Personalism

A good number of theologians and philosophers today reject eternalism and fall under the category of what is called "theistic personalism." Brian Davies coined the phrase in response to the views of philosophers such as Richard Swinburne and Alvin Plantinga, who "think it important to stress God is a person."[23] If that's all that one means by "theistic personalism," then all well and good. A few classical theists might agree. But there's more to the story. Davies continues,

> What do Plantinga and Swinburne mean by "person"? Their writings, and the writings of those who share their view of God, proceed from the assumption that, if we want to understand what

---

[23] Brian Davies, *An Introduction to the Philosophy of Religion* (New York: Oxford University Press, 2020), 11.

persons are, we must begin with human beings. Yet Plantinga and Swinburne, and those who broadly agree with them about God, do not want to suggest that God is just like a human being. So they also think that there can somehow be a person who, while being like human beings, is also decidedly different from what people are. In particular, and as Swinburne's phrase "person without a body" indicates, they think that there can be a disembodied person.[24]

Beyond taking God to be something like a disembodied person like us, theistic personalists also deny most of the tenets of classical theism, claims Davies. For instance, with respect to God's knowledge, unlike the classical theists who affirm that God knows all history by virtue of being Creator, "theistic personalists are more likely to assert that God's knowledge of history may partly be acquired by him as history unfolds," and that "God's knowledge of the world, especially the world of human affairs, is capable of increase."[25] Davies lists other notable differences between classical theists and theistic personalists. For example, theistic personalists deny that God is atemporal/timeless, simple, active in all things, immutable, and impassible. Finally, he takes it that theistic personalists believe "God is a being among beings" and is "seriously comprehensible."[26]

Davies is not alone. James Dolezal, Ed Fesser, and David Bentley Hart all join in on critiquing this view. Dolezal prefers the term "theistic mutualism," whereas Hart prefers the term "monopolytheism." Consider the words of Hart:

It seems to involve a view of God not conspicuously different from the polytheistic picture of the gods as merely powerful discrete entities who possess a variety of distinct attributes that lesser entities also possess, if in smaller measure; it differs from polytheism . . .

---

[24] Davies, 11.
[25] Davies, 11.
[26] Davies, 18.

solely in that it posits the existence of only one such being. It is a
way of being that suggests that God, since he is only a particular
instantiation of various concepts and properties, is logically dependent on some more comprehensive reality embracing both him and
other beings.[27]

How should the theistic personalist respond?

We find these critiques a bit surprising, especially coming from such
prominent philosophers as Hart and Davies. Besides being pejorative (e.g.,
Hart's "monopolytheism"), they often lack the kind of nuance that one
might expect when critiquing an interlocutor's position. Theistic personalism as a category encapsulates a wide range of views. Yet, modified classical
theists, open theists, essential kenosis theists, and process theists are often
lumped together in these critiques as believing the same kinds of things. But
these models of God are quite distinct. A model such as modified classical
theism affirms much of what classical theists affirm, whereas process theists
deny most, if not all, of classical theism's major claims. Open theists and
essential kenosis theists fall somewhere in between the extremes. We should
think of these models on a spectrum rather than lumping them altogether.

We agree with Davies that theistic personalists emphasize God as a personal being, but it doesn't follow that we begin with our thoughts on human
persons and then work our way to God. If we take Scripture as revelation
from God—God's communication to us—then why not think we can work
our way to an understanding about the nature of person beginning with that?
Certainly, there are hermeneutical issues at play, and all of Scripture needs
to be interpreted; but that cuts both ways, and the defender of classical theism is not exempt from having to make interpretive decisions. Furthermore,
theistic personalists are quite aware that Scripture is neither a theological
or philosophical textbook, nor does it provide a proper definition of what

---

[27] David Bentley Hart, *The Experience of God: Being, Consciousness, Bliss* (New
Haven, CT: Yale University Press, 2013), 127–28, quoted in James Dolezal, *All
That Is in God* (Grand Rapids: Reformed Heritage Books, 2017), 2.

it means to be a person. Yet, like any other doctrine (Trinity, incarnation, etc.), Scripture provides the reflective context for thinking deeply about the nature of persons.

Finally, what of the claims that "God is a being among beings" and that "God is seriously comprehensible"? Theistic personalists need not think of God as just one being among others. God is *sui generis*, necessary, *a se*, and incorporeal, as we'll argue below. Moreover, that God is a triunity of persons makes God quite unique, something that no created being can claim. Yet, we find the doctrine of the Trinity as having serious explanatory power for how we're to understand humanity, relationships, and morality—not the other way around. Though some theistic personalists (e.g., process theists, essential kenosis theists) believe that God needs a world for self-actualization, others (e.g., modified classical theists, open theists) like ourselves, believe God created out of freedom, denying God needs a world at all.

Do theistic personalists think God is comprehensible? If by this it is meant that one can know things about God because God has revealed things about himself in Scripture, then we'd happily agree. But hardly any theistic personalist believes that a human can have comprehensive understanding of God. How could that even be possible? What's really at play is the role of religious language, whether we can speak of God in univocal or analogical terms. Theistic personalists are divided on the use of religious language. Some affirm analogical language, whereas others find serious difficulties with such a view, opting for some form of univocal language.[28] We agree with those who affirm the use of analogical language. In our estimation, while there is similarity that corresponds between our language used of God and our language used of humanity, there are also important dissimilarities, and this is because of God's uniqueness as the transcendent Creator of things. Here, we agree with John Peckham, "to know precisely what the

---

[28] For an important discussion, see William P. Alston, *Divine Nature and Human Language: Essays in Philosophical Theology* (Eugene, OR: Wipf & Stock, 1989).

extent of similarity and dissimilarity is would require an understanding of God and of language that transcends human language."[29] Yet, the use of analogy shouldn't provide theists with a free pass to proclaim mystery every time they're confronted with a supposed contradiction in their understanding of God.

Let's now turn to the divine attributes.

---

[29] John C. Peckham, *Divine Attributes: Knowing the Covenantal God of Scripture* (Grand Rapids: Baker Academic, 2021), 36.

PART 2

3

God the Creator: Immaterial, Necessary, Free, and Present

At this point, we have only mentioned the attributes and have given little attention to defining or analyzing them. In the following chapters we will consider the biblical, theological, and philosophical basis for each, following our Anselmian approach, giving preference to biblical normativity when conflict arises.[1] In this chapter specifically, we consider God as Creator and examine four divine attributes: incorporeality, aseity, necessity, and omnipresence. Though not without controversy, these attributes are more widely agreed upon than others we will consider in later chapters. But before examining the various perfections, it would first be helpful to consider God as Creator to set the stage for our understanding of the divine perfections.

---

[1] Given the nature and size of our project, it will be impossible to discuss all of the divine perfections. Our purpose here will be to examine only the most significant perfections playing out in recent discussions in philosophical theology.

Creator of Heaven and of Earth

One of the central tenets of monotheism is the belief that God is the Creator of the heavens and of the earth (Gen 1:1), a biblical idiom meaning the whole of created reality. This needs qualification. Christians embrace the Creator/creature distinction, recognizing that there is a qualitative distinction between God the Creator and his creatures. God the eternal Creator is infinite in nature, whereas creatures are finite and limited.[2] God's power and wisdom are inexhaustible, whereas any power or wisdom that creatures have is limited and derivative in nature. It is through God's inexhaustible power and wisdom that he created the world.

Christians dispute about what is meant by "creation." Traditionally, Christians have held to the concept of *creatio ex nihilo* (creation out of nothing or from no preexisting matter), in contrast to other conceptions of creation, such as *creatio ex Deo* (creation out of God), *creatio ex materia* (creation out of preexisting materials), or *creatio divinia emanatio* (creation by divine emanation). Though some Christians, such as Aquinas, have held to the belief that it was possible for the world to have always existed (though not his actual position), this was by far the exception and not the norm.[3] Most Christians have held that creation is grounded in God's freedom and an act of divine volition, but some, as noted above, have embraced creation by divine necessity.

Scripture is replete with passages on creation, most notably the first chapter and verse of the Bible, "In the beginning God created the heavens and the earth" (Gen 1:1). Christians have long taken this passage to refer

---

[2] There are different ways of speaking of "infinite." When we speak of infinite with respect to God, we do not mean it regarding the mathematical concept of an infinite, in the sense that there is no beginning or end to a set of numbers as found in set theory; rather, we mean infinite with respect to the qualitative nature of God's perfections, which has to do with God's maximal greatness or God's being a perfect being.

[3] Thomas Aquinas, *On the Eternality of the World* (De Aeternitate Mundi), trans. Robert T. Miller, https://sourcebooks.fordham.edu/basis/aquinas-eternity.asp.

to creation *ex nihilo*, but that is not the only interpretation. Process theists have challenged the *ex nihilo* doctrine and have argued instead that God created out of already preexisting materials.[4] Certain biblical scholars have also argued that Gen 1:1 does not demand that God created *ex nihilo*.[5]

Regardless of what one does with Gen 1:1, there are other passages that imply creation *ex nihilo*.[6] As theologian Millard Erickson explains, such passages go beyond speaking of a mere fashioning and making of preexisting materials, emphasizing the very beginning of the existence of created reality.[7] Even more so, such passages were not written within the context of speaking about the nature of creation itself; yet that's what makes them all the more significant. As John Feinberg explains, "The fact these passages speak of a beginning of creation leads one to ask what preceded that beginning. From the biblical authors' viewpoint, it seems that nothing did, except God."[8] Other key passages indicating creation *ex nihilo* include John 1:1–3; Rom 4:17; 1 Cor 8:6; Col 1:16; Heb 1:2; and Heb 11:3. Each of these passages demonstrates that creation itself came from God. Note the all-encompassing language of John 1:3 (e.g., "all things") and Col 1:16. Some might retort that passages such as Heb 11:3 imply God created "visible" things (matter) from "invisible" things (e.g., invisible material). But there are two problems with

---

[4] John B. Cobb Jr. and David Ray Griffin, *Process Theology: An Introductory Exposition* (New York: Westminster, 1976), 65.

[5] Take, for example, Old Testament scholar John Walton, who believes that Genesis 1 has less to do with material origins and refers instead to functional creation. On this view, the Hebrew author of this text was more interested in God's assigning functions and roles to the created order than the material coming-into-being of creation. John H. Walton, *The Lost World of Genesis One: Ancient Cosmology and the Origins Debate* (Downers Grove: IVP, 2009), 22–24.

[6] Consider Matt 13:25; 19:4, 8; 24:21; 25:34; Mark 10:6; 13:19; Luke 11:50; John 1:24; Rom 1:20; Eph 1:4; Heb 1:10; 4:3; 9:25; 1 Pet 1:20; 2 Pet 3:4; Rev 3:14; 13:8; 17:8.

[7] Millard J. Erickson, *Christian Theology*, 3rd ed. (Grand Rapids: Baker Academic, 1998), 341.

[8] John S. Feinberg, *No One Like Him: The Doctrine of God* (Wheaton: Crossway, 2001), 555.

this line of thinking. First, the chief aim of the author of Hebrews is not to make metaphysical claims about the types of matter that exist; rather, his focus is on the nature of faith. Second, such an interpretation doesn't square with Paul's teaching in Col 1:16, which suggests that all things were created by Christ, including those things "visible" and "invisible."

Another reason for affirming creation *ex nihilo* stems from Scripture's emphasis on God's eternal nature. Take, for example, Ps 90:2:

> Before the mountains were brought forth, or ever you had formed the earth and the world, from everlasting to everlasting you are God. (NRSV)

and Ps 102:25–27,

> Long ago you laid the foundation of the earth, and the heavens are the work of your hands. They will perish, but you endure; they will all wear out like a garment. You change them like clothing, and they pass away; but you are the same, and your years have no end. (NRSV)

Here we see an emphasis on God's own eternal nature as "everlasting to everlasting," standing in contrast to creation, which was "brought forth" and "formed," and which "will wear out like a garment." Finally, as William Lane Craig and Paul Copan explain, "The clear implication of Yahweh's title 'the first and the last' (Isa. 44:6)—or, as the NT puts it, 'the Alpha and the Omega' (Rev. 1:8)—is that he is the ultimate originator and only eternal Being."[9]

Another reason Christians hold firmly to the doctrine of creation *ex nihilo* has to do with the desire to preserve the doctrine of divine aseity. According to the doctrine of aseity, God is self-sufficient and does not need a world for divine self-actualization. God is complete in and of the divine

---

[9] Paul Copan and William Lane Craig, *Creation out of Nothing: A Biblical, Philosophical, and Scientific Exploration* (Grand Rapids: Baker Academic, 2004), 65.

self. Consider the following passage: "The God who made the world and everything in it—he is Lord of heaven and earth—does not live in shrines made by hands. Neither is he served by human hands, as though he needed anything, since he himself gives everyone life and breath and all things" (Acts 17:24–25). Here we see the apostle Paul proclaiming to the Athenians that God doesn't need our worship. He doesn't need human beings at all! Rather, Paul tells us that God "made the world and everything in it." Furthermore, God is "Lord of heaven and earth" and "gives life and breath and all things."

Finally, there are powerful philosophical and scientific reasons for holding to the doctrine of creation *ex nihilo*. One such argument that brings together both philosophical and scientific reasons for holding to creation *ex nihilo* is the Kalam Cosmological Argument (KCA), most ably defended by William Lane Craig, Paul Copan, J. P. Moreland, and Andrew Loke.[10] This argument posits that the universe had a beginning—a finite time in the past. The basic form of the argument goes as follows:

1. Everything that begins to exist has a cause.
2. The universe began to exist.
3. Therefore, the universe has a cause.[11]

The extended KCA establishes philosophically the impossibility of traversing an actual infinite either backward or forward in time and appeals to scientific evidence for the finite existence of the universe grounded in Big Bang cosmology. Such evidence includes red shifting found in distant

---

[10] Given space, we can at best provide some highlights of KCA and point readers to some of its ablest defenders. William Lane Craig and James D. Sinclair, "The Kalam Cosmological Argument," in *The Blackwell Companion to Natural Theology*, ed. William Lane Craig and J. P. Moreland (Oxford: Wiley-Blackwell, 2009), 101–201; Andrew Ter Ern Loke, "*Creatio Ex Nihilo*," in *T&T Clark Handbook of Analytic Theology*, ed. James M. Arcadi and James T. Turner, Jr., paperback ed. (New York: T&T Clark, 2022), 297–324; Copan and Craig, *Creation out of Nothing*.

[11] Loke, "*Creatio Ex Nihilo*," 301.

galaxies, background radiation in the universe, and the second law of thermodynamics.

Beyond creation *ex nihilo*, Scripture also speaks of God's work in conservation. Regarding conservation, in his letter to the Colossians, the apostle Paul proclaims that the Son is the "image of the invisible God," that "everything was created by him" and "by him all things hold together" (1:15–17). Similarly, the writer of the book of Hebrews declares concerning the Son of God that he is "sustaining all things by his powerful word" (1:3). In other words, the Son of God sustains and keeps all things in existence through the power of his word. Strikingly, Job tells us that if God "withdrew the spirit and breath he gave, every living thing would perish together and mankind would return to the dust" (Job 34:14–15). This resonates with the creation narrative of Genesis, especially the Spirit's work in creation (Gen 1:2) as well as God's creation of humanity from the dust of the earth (Gen 2:7; cf. Gen 3:19). But here Job emphasizes God's power in giving life and breath to creatures. Interestingly enough, Thomas Aquinas says something similar about God's conservation. In responding to the charge of whether God could annihilate anything, Thomas had this to say: "If God were to annihilate anything, this would not imply an action on God's part; but a mere cessation of His action."[12] In other words, if God were to remove his sustaining power, the creature would cease to be. In light of these passages, God's creative power sustains and upholds the whole of creation, keeping it in its being. The import of the doctrine of divine conservation demonstrates three things: (1) creation's lack of self-sufficiency, (2) God's work in creation is ongoing and doesn't end with his initial work in creating the heavens and the earth, and (3) the initial creation and preservation of creation are a matter of God's will and power.[13]

---

[12] Thomas Aquinas, *Summa Theologiae*, I, Q. 104. A. 3 Reply to Objection 3.

[13] Erickson, *Christian Theology*, 360.

Based on our survey of biblical data, we believe there's good reason to hold to the traditional view of creation *ex nihilo*. Not only did God create the universe from no preexisting material or things, but God also sustains and holds all of creation together. Our understanding of creation has significant ramifications for a variety of divine perfections, such as divine necessity, incorporeality, aseity, eternality, immutability, impassibility, power, knowledge, and simplicity, just to name a few.

Incorporeality: The Immaterial God

Of the divine perfections we're considering in this chapter, the first is incorporeality. Incorporeality teaches that God is essentially without a body. To put it positively, God is spirit. Certain religious systems, such as Mormonism, teach that God has a body that is corporeal in nature. After all, they say Scripture teaches that God created humanity in his own image (Gen 1:27), that the Lord spoke to Moses face to face (Exod 33:11), that Moses saw God's *back* side (Exod 33:23), and so on. How are we to take such passages? Unlike the Church of Latter-day Saints, orthodox Christianity has long understood such passages as anthropomorphic depictions of God's actions. When the writers of Scripture use physical depictions of God, such as God's having hands or eyes, they mean something more akin to the power of God ("hand of God") or God's knowledge and wisdom ("eyes of God"). Such physical depictions are natural uses of language, as John Feinberg rightly suggests, "We have no other language to depict a nonmaterial thing acting in the world."[14]

Certainly, the doctrine of incorporeality does not mean that God cannot, if God so chooses, manifest in bodily form (known as theophanies or Christophanies), as certain instances in the OT indicate, nor does it mean that God cannot "add" or "take on" a human nature, as affirmed by the NT and early church regarding the incarnation. What the doctrine teaches is

---

[14] Feinberg, *No One Like Him*, 215.

that in God's essential nature, God is without a body.[15] Consider the words of Jesus to the Samaritan woman in John 4:21–24:

> "Believe me, woman, an hour is coming when you will worship the Father neither on this mountain nor in Jerusalem. You Samaritans worship what you do not know. We worship what we do know, because salvation is from the Jews. But an hour is coming, and is now here, when the true worshipers will worship the Father in Spirit and in truth. Yes, the Father wants such people to worship him. God is spirit, and those who worship him must worship in Spirit and in truth."

What's striking about this passage is that the Jews and Samaritans had stark differences of where true worship took place. Jesus reminds the woman that true worship is not bound by physical location and that believers are to worship God in "Spirit and in truth." Jesus grounds his reasoning in the belief that "God is spirit" and is not bound to any place or location. Against Mormon teaching, this passage teaches clearly that God the Father is incorporeal in nature.

But this is far from the only passage that teaches that God is incorporeal. John 1:18 teaches that no one has ever seen God, but it is God the Son who reveals to us the Father. This has led some to believe that any physical manifestations of God in the OT may have indeed been Christophanies—manifestations of the preincarnate Christ. Colossians 1:15 affirms that it is Christ who is the "image of the invisible God." Similarly, the book of Hebrews says that the Son is "the radiance of God's glory and the exact expression of his nature, sustaining all things by his powerful word" (Heb 1:3). First Timothy 6:16 says of God's metaphysical nature that it is "unapproachable" and that "no one has seen or can see." Finally, creation itself

---

[15] Some theists take God's incorporeality as essential to God's nature; however, they hold that the world is of sorts God's body. See T. J. Mawson, *The Divine Attributes* (New York: Cambridge University Press, 2019), 22.

motivates a teaching on God's incorporeality. Notice what Paul says in Colossians 1 about all that the Son of God created: "For everything was created by him, in heaven and on earth, the visible and the invisible" (Col 1:16). In other words, God is the creator of everything that exists, whether it is material or immaterial in nature.[16]

Aseity: The Self-Existent God

Having considered incorporeality, let's now turn to the doctrine of aseity, which we've touched on briefly already. The doctrine in its most basic sense refers to God's self-existence, or to the idea that God does not depend on or need anything outside of himself for his existence.[17] Alvin Plantinga refers to it as God's "uncreatedness, self-sufficiency, and independence of everything else."[18] James Beilby defines it as follows: "God is independent, self-existent, and fully self-sufficient. He does not need anything outside of himself to exist, be satisfied, be fulfilled, or (to borrow an overused phrase from contemporary psychology) be 'self-actualized.'"[19]

Beilby further differentiates between two senses of divine aseity: *ontological aseity* and *psychological aseity*. Ontological aseity refers to God's being

---

[16] While the doctrine of aseity has significant theological and biblical support, there remains a powerful objection to it from Platonism that centers on the problem of universals and abstract objects, which we'll touch on briefly below. For further exploration, we refer readers to the following works: Lindsay K. Cleveland, "Divine Aseity and Abstract Objects," in *T&T Clark Handbook of Analytic Theology*, ed. James M. Arcadi and James T. Turner, Jr., paperback ed. (New York: T&T Clark, 2022); William Lane Craig, *God Over All: Divine Aseity and the Challenge of Platonism* (New York: Oxford University Press, 2018).

[17] Cleveland, "Divine Aseity and Abstract Objects," 165; Feinberg, *No One Like Him*, 239.

[18] Alvin Plantinga, "Does God Have a Nature?" in *The Analytic Theist: An Alvin Plantinga Reader*, ed. James F. Sennet (Grand Rapids: Eerdmans, 1998), 225.

[19] James Beilby, "Divine Aseity, Divine Freedom: A Conceptual Problem for Edwardsian-Calvinism," *Journal of the Evangelical Theological Society* 47, no. 4 (2004): 647.

"uncaused, without beginning, not dependent on an external person, principle, or metaphysical reality for his existence."[20] Psychological aseity, on the other hand, refers to God's being "fully self-satisfied."[21] In this latter case, God is without need or want and fully fulfilled within himself. Christians affirm aseity in both the ontological and psychological sense of the word.

Perhaps one of the clearest passages about aseity is found in Acts 17:24–25, as examined earlier. The doctrine of aseity also finds theological motivation from the doctrine of creation. In Acts 17:24, Paul says that God "made the world and everything in it." Similarly, in John 1:3 we're told that "all things were created through him, and apart from him not one thing was created that has been created." Colossians 1:15–17 makes clear that it was through the agency of the Son that all things were created, things "visible and invisible," that these things were created "for him," and that "by him all things hold together." Moreover, we're told in Col 2:2–3 that in Christ "are hidden all the treasures of wisdom and knowledge." Reflection on creation posits the idea that God created everything else other than God.

Aseity is closely linked to God's life. A number of passages link God's life and divine self-existence. Perhaps, one of the clearest is found in Exodus 3:14. When God called Moses to deliver the Israelites from the clutches of their Egyptian captors, he tells Moses to tell the Israelites that "I AM WHO I AM" sent him. God's name "I AM" implies that he is the living God.[22] Jesus understood this when he confronted the Sadducees over their unbelief in the resurrection. When God tells Moses, "I am the God of Abraham and the God of Isaac and the God of Jacob," Jesus said he's referring to the God of the living and not the dead (Mark 12:24–27). This is also reminiscent of what Jesus says of himself at the raising of Lazarus from the dead, "I am the resurrection and the life. The one who believes in me, even if he dies, will live. Everyone who lives and believes in me will never die" (John 11:25–26).

---

[20] Beilby, 648.
[21] Beilby, 648.
[22] Erickson, *Christian Theology*, 240.

Not only is God's life in and of himself, but he's also the source of eternal, unending life for others, which has immense implications for the Christian doctrine of the resurrection from the dead. John 5:26 tells us that "just as the Father has life in himself, so also he has granted the Son to have life in himself." Finally, in 1 Thess 1:9 Paul commends his readers for turning from idols to serving "the living and true God."[23]

One central difficulty for the doctrine of aseity centers on the problem of God and abstract objects. Platonism taught the existence of an eternal realm of unchanging entities, such as eternal forms and immortal souls. This eventually led to a debate among medieval theologians on whether there are universals (i.e., characteristics or qualities that exist independent of one's mind). In recent discussions, the debate moved on to whether abstract objects exist.[24]

Though not fully agreed upon by philosophers just what an "abstract object" is, there is some consensus. On this, Paul Gould says, "It is generally agreed to be immaterial, nonspatial, necessary (setting aside sets with contingent numbers), and eternal (again, setting aside sets and perhaps fictional objects) non-agents."[25] Those in the debate generally fall into one of three camps: realists, nominalists, and conceptualists. Platonic realists affirm universals exist and that such entities are mind-independent. Aristotelians, too, are realists. Instead of having their own independence, universals are exemplified in a particular entity (e.g., the universal "blue" is exemplified in a blue hat or "goodness" is exemplified in a good man).[26] One other realist option is known as absolute creation, a modified form of Platonism, which teaches mathematical objects, like other concrete objects, are creations by

---

[23] Erickson, 242.

[24] Paul Gould, "Christian Metaphysics and Platonism," in *Four Views on Christian Metaphysics*, ed. Timothy M. Mosteller (Eugene, OR: Cascade, 2022), 1–2.

[25] Gould, "Christian Metaphysics and Platonism," 2.

[26] James S. Spiegel, "Christian Metaphysics and Idealism," in *Four Views on Christian Metaphysics*, ed. Timothy M. Mosteller (Eugene, OR: Cascade, 2022), 76.

God.[27] Nominalists, on the other hand, deny universals altogether. Only the particulars exist. There is no universal "blue," but only some blue entity, say, that blue hat or that blue bird. Conceptualists fall somewhere in between realists and nominalists, affirming the reality of universals and abstract objects, but also denying that these things are somehow mind-independent. Conceptualists fall into two camps: *subjective* and *theistic*. Subjective conceptualism places abstract objects and universals in the human mind, which is much closer to nominalism. Theistic conceptualism places them in the mind of God, which aligns more with realism.[28]

Where does this leave the Anselmian theist? We believe some form of realism, such as absolute creation or theistic conceptualism, best preserves the doctrine of divine aseity. Of the two, perhaps the most promising is theistic conceptualism, which was the view of the early church.[29] On this view, things like mathematical objects and other universals are concrete entities that are real, existing within the mind of God. Any view, such as Platonic realism, that claims abstract objects exist apart from and are independent of God is problematic. Such a view would indicate that something other than God is eternal and necessary. Theistic conceptualism affirms both God's unique self-existence and eternal existence, while maintaining the reality of abstract objects, grounding them in God.[30]

Necessity: The Necessary Existing God

Just as there is more than one way to understand divine aseity, there is also more than one way to understand divine necessity. Philosophers distinguish

[27] J. P. Moreland and William Lane Craig, *Philosophical Foundations for a Christian Worldview* (Downers Grove: IVP, 2003), 514.

[28] Spiegel, "Christian Metaphysics and Idealism," 76–77.

[29] For an important discussion on the biblical and historical warrant of theistic conceptualism, see William Lane Craig, *God and Abstract Objects: The Coherence of Theism: Aseity* (Cham, Switzerland: Springer, 2017), ch. 2.

[30] Moreland and Craig, *Philosophical Foundations*, 514.

between *de dicto* and *de re* necessity. The former, *de dicto* necessity, has to do with certain conceptual claims or propositions about God's nature, such as, *necessarily, God is good* or *necessarily, God is omnipotent*. When we speak of God having some property or attribute in the *de dicto* sense of the word, we mean that no being can properly count as God who does not instantiate that property or attribute. Goodness, omnipotence, and omniscience, so to speak, count as conceptual requirements for something to be called "God."

When we speak of *de re* necessity, on the other hand, it has to do with an expression of one of God's essential properties, say, divine omniscience, omnipotence, or goodness. In other words, if God did not have such-and-such property, then God could not be God.[31] God has such properties essentially or necessarily; God himself essentially is all-powerful, holy, etc. As Thomas Morris points out, "*De re* necessities tie goodness, omnipotence and omniscience to the very existence of the divine being."[32]

So, employing possible world semantics, when we speak of some entity E as having such-and-such property P essentially, we mean that E has that property in any possible world that E exists. Perhaps an example would help. There are some possible worlds in which I (Ronnie) become a rockstar or barista and not a theologian. Such properties are not essential to my being; they are accidental or contingent. In other words, things could have been other than they are. Yet, in any world in which I were to exist, there are some properties that I would have necessarily or essentially, such as the potentiality of my being conscious or my having a mind.[33] The same, then, is true of God. God has certain properties necessarily or essentially, such as God's being omniscient, omnipotent, and omnibenevolent.

But theists want to say something even stronger than God has certain properties necessarily or essentially; they want to say that God has *necessary*

---

[31] Thomas V. Morris, *Our Idea of God* (Vancouver, BC: Regent University Press, 2002), 106–7.

[32] Morris, 106.

[33] Morris, 108.

existence. Contingent beings—like you and me, the trees in the forest, amoeba, angels, and even the universe—owe their being and essence to something other than themselves.[34] However, that's not the case with God. When we speak of God existing necessarily, we mean it's impossible for God not to exist. It is necessary existence that sets God apart from all his creatures. If God exists necessarily, then God would exist in every possible world. In other words, there is no possible world in which God does not exist.

What we have been arguing for is what T. J. Mawson calls "metaphysical necessity." Not everyone, admittedly, is satisfied with the idea of God's metaphysical necessity. Some deny the category altogether. Against such denials, Mawson raises a *reductio* style argument. Let's suppose, he says, there are other kinds of necessities, say, logical, physical, moral, or aesthetic, but no metaphysical necessities. Eventually, we'll need to come to grips with why that's the case—that is, why it is necessary that there are no metaphysical necessities. But what could explain that? Mawson believes that the obvious choice among those who challenge it is logical necessity, that is to say, "it's a logical necessity that there are no metaphysical necessities" or, to put it differently, "metaphysical necessities are logically impossible."[35] In other words, proponents of this view must show that there's a contradiction "implicit in the claim that there are metaphysical necessities."[36] Mawson isn't sure how one could show this, as one examines the other necessities, it becomes clearer that those necessities face even greater obstacles for explaining why it's necessary that there are no metaphysical necessities.[37] Eventually, one concludes that the only proper explanation that there are no metaphysical necessities is by metaphysical necessity. But those claims are logical contradictions.

---

[34] Ronald H. Nash, *The Concept of God: An Exploration of Contemporary Difficulties with the Attributes of God* (Grand Rapids: Zondervan, 1983), 107.

[35] Mawson, *The Divine Attributes*, 55.

[36] Mawson, 56.

[37] Mawson, 56.

What biblical and theological grounds do Christians have for believing that God is a necessarily existing being and that God has certain attributes necessarily? No small number of biblical and theological reasons come to the fore. First, Scripture speaks of God as having always existed (Ps 90:2; Heb 1:10–12). Second, as mentioned earlier, there is good reason to take it that God himself is the transcendent creator of all things. Everything that is not God owes its being and existence to him (John 1:1–3; Acts 17:24; 1 Cor 8:6; Col 1:15–16; Heb 1:2–3, 10–12). Third, the doctrine of divine aseity tends toward the idea that God is a necessary being, since aseity affirms that God is the source of his own existence (Exod 3:14; John 5:26) and that God does not need anything outside of himself for his existence or self-actualization (Acts 17:24–25). Fourth, and finally, Scripture teaches that God has some attributes eternally and unchangeably. For example, in Rom 1:20, Paul speaks of God's power as "eternal." Malachi 3:6 and Jas 1:17 speak of God's character as unchanging. Scripture also speaks of God's truthfulness (Num 23:19), honesty (Heb 6:17–18), and mercy (Num 23:19) as constant and unchanging.

Taken together, these philosophical, theological, and biblical ideas produce a portrait of what philosophers and theologians mean when they speak of God as a necessary being. As John Feinberg rightly points out, "If God is not created, has life in himself so that he depends on no one for his existence, and has always and will always exist, then God qualifies as a necessary being in the philosophical sense of the term."[38]

Omnipresence: The Wholly Present God

Two words are often used to express God's infinitude with respect to space: *omnipresence* and *immensity*. The former, classically understood, refers to God's "presence in the totality of his being at each point in space," and the latter refers "to the fact that God transcends all spatial limitations and is

---

[38] Feinberg, *No One Like Him*, 212.

everywhere at once."[39] In regard to God's immensity, though God is not bound by space, he nevertheless "fills all of space."[40] One way to think of the distinction is that immensity is concerned with God's transcendence as it relates to space and omnipresence more with God's immanence. Though we'll consider both God's immensity and omnipresence, our focus in this section is on God's presence as it relates to space.

Scripture clearly affirms God's omnipresence. Take, for example, Ps 139:7–12:

> Where shall I go from your Spirit? Or where shall I flee from your presence? If I ascend to heaven, you are there! If I make my bed in Sheol, you are there! If I take the wings of the morning and dwell in the uttermost parts of the sea, even there your hand shall lead me, and your right hand shall hold me. If I say, "Surely the darkness shall cover me, and the light about me be night," even the darkness is not dark to you; the night is bright as the day, for darkness is as light with you. (ESV)

There is nowhere that the psalmist can go to escape the presence of God, even into the depths of Sheol! Beyond this passage, the Bible is replete with language that refers to God's "watching" or "seeing" or being aware of his creatures. As Prov 15:3 says, "The eyes of the LORD are everywhere, observing the wicked and the good." Obviously, the "eyes" in this verse do not refer to God having physical anatomy as you and I have, since God is incorporeal; rather, the language is anthropomorphic in nature. As John Peckham reminds us, "This is figurative language using 'eyes' to signal divine awareness *analogous* to physically seeing everything."[41] He continues, "While texts depicting God as 'all-seeing' indicate *at least* God's comprehensive awareness of all places, other texts indicate God's power extends to every location,

---

[39] Feinberg, 249.
[40] Feinberg, 249.
[41] Peckham, *The Divine Attributes*, 82.

'sustain[ing] all things' (Heb 1:3)."[42] Yet, on the other hand, Scripture also affirms God's immensity, teaching that God cannot be contained by anything (1 Kgs 8:27; Isa 66:1; Acts 17:24).

There are other passages which speak of God's presence but indicate that God is (seemingly) spatially present or located in special ways, such as God's presence with the Israelites in the tabernacle and the temple (Exod 19:16–20). Likewise, in 1 Kings 8, after Solomon had finished building the temple, and after the priests had taken the ark of the covenant "to its place in the inner sanctuary" (v. 6) and had come out of the Holy Place, "the cloud filled the LORD's temple, and because of the cloud, the priests were not able to continue ministering, for the glory of the LORD filled the temple" (1 Kgs 8:10–11).

The Bible also speaks of God's presence with us, specifically through the indwelling presence of the Holy Spirit in the lives of believers (John 14:17; Rom 8:11; 1 Cor 3:16; 6:19) and in the incarnation. Regarding the latter, John 1:14 says, "The Word became flesh and dwelt among us. We observed his glory, glory as of the only Son from the Father, full of grace and truth." Regarding the words "dwelt among us," Millard Erickson points out, "The term is a strong one, which literally means 'tabernacled among us' or 'pitched his tent among us,' which would have harkened back to God's indwelling presence in the wilderness tabernacle and in the temple."[43]

Some Christians have taken God's presence to mean that God permeates all of creation. Some have even suggested that God is the "soul of the world." This understanding of divine presence is often found in forms of pantheism (i.e., God is identical to the world) or panentheism (i.e., God is radically immanent within creation), but should Christians affirm this language when used of God? Certainly, Christians have held to the belief that God is immanent and near to creation, but they reject such notions of

---

[42] Peckham, 82.

[43] Millard J. Erickson, *The Word Became Flesh: A Contemporary Incarnational Christology* (Grand Rapids: Baker, 1991), 27.

God as radically or fully immanent. After all, as we've seen in earlier discussions on both God's aseity and necessity, in no way does God depend on creation for his existence. God has life and existence independent of the created world. Moreover, creation itself is distinct from and dependent on God for its existence. In other words, Christians hold to a form of dualism, recognizing God's ontological distinctness from the world, which stands behind the Creator/creature distinction.

Interestingly enough, the medieval theologian Anselm uses permeation language when discussing God's existing in everything:

> The supreme nature exists in everything that exists, just as much as it exists in every place. It is not contained, but contains all, by permeating all. This we know. . . . Locational language is often applied unobjectionably to things that are neither locations nor contained by locational circumscription. Thus I would say that where rationality is in the soul, there is the intellect. "There" and "where" are locational words, but the soul does not contain anything, nor are the intellect and rationality contained, by locational circumscription. "Everywhere," then, in the sense of "in everything that exists" is, as regards the truth, the more appropriate thing to say of the supreme nature. . . . Necessarily, therefore it is in all things that exist in such a way that it is in each individual thing as a whole, as one and the same, perfectly and simultaneously.[44]

On the one hand, Anselm claims that God "permeates" everything and that "the supreme nature exists in everything" and "in every place." Yet God is in no way contained; rather he contains everything. Strikingly, Anselm suggests that not only is God in all things that exist, but that the whole of his being is in everything.

Anselm is not alone in this belief. Aquinas fleshes out three ways that God is said to be in all things: presence, power, and substance. How is this

---

[44] Anselm, *Monologion*, 14.

the case? On this, Aquinas explains: "Therefore, God is in all things by His power, inasmuch as all things are subject to His power; He is by His presence in all things, as all things are bare and open to His eyes; He is in all things by His essence, inasmuch as He is present to all as the cause of their being."[45] Yet there is another way in which God is in all things, namely, through his grace. On this, Aquinas takes it that God is in the rational creature because the rational creature has the prerogative to know and love God. It is in this sense that God is "in" the saints by grace.[46]

Anselm and Aquinas take what R. T. Mullins expresses as the traditional view of omnipresence, which "holds that the entire being of God is wholly located in every point or region of space."[47] But what shall we make of the classical view of omnipresence? First, it's unclear what Anselm means by "permeating all" or how something can be said to "permeate" without also being temporally and spatially located or extended. If all that he means by this is something similar to Aquinas, that God is in all things by his power, knowledge, and causation, then we could happily agree, and he would be on good footing biblically and theologically. But modern believers might find it quite odd to think of the whole of God's being present and existing at every place. Let's see if we can flesh this out a bit more.

Ross Inman distinguishes between three modes of presence: circumscriptively, definitively, and repletively. The first mode of presence, circumscriptively refers to the mode that is common to material beings, say a cat, a tree, or a building. Material beings are composed of parts. Because of their material composition, they extend through space and are not mereologically simple (i.e., without parts). On this understanding, a person's body may be extended at a particular and singular place; yet, each of the person's body

---

[45] Aquinas, *Summa Theologica*, V. I, Pt. 1, q.8, a.3.

[46] Aquinas, q.8, a.3.

[47] R. T. Mullins, *The End of the Timeless God* (Oxford: Oxford University Press, 2016), 38.

parts are part of a particular place.[48] As Inman puts it, "That which is circumscriptively present at a place is *circumscribed by* and *contained in* the place in question: while my body can be *partly* present at distinct places at the same time, it is incapable of being *wholly* present (without remainder) at distinct places at one and the same time (it cannot simultaneously be *wholly* multi-located)."[49]

Definitive presence, on the other hand, refers to the mode of presence related to things that are spiritual in nature, such as the human soul or angels. Spiritual things like the human soul or angels are noncomposite (without proper parts); they are limited in nature. Unlike material beings, says Inman, they can be "*wholly* present at distinct places at the same time."[50] However, he continues, like material beings, immaterial entities like souls and angels "are *bound* and *contained* by the places where they are present insofar as their natures are finite and limited."[51] A soul, for example, as an immaterial thing can be wholly present in each part of a person's body at some specific location, but it cannot be present at some location distant from the person's body (much of this, however, rides on what one means by soul, of course).

Finally, repletive presence refers to something only God has in his divine essence. Because God is "spiritual, infinite, and immense," the divine essence "is capable of being *wholly present at each and every place at the same time*."[52] Because God is mereologically simple, that is, God is without parts, we can speak of God in neither the circumscriptively nor the definitively present senses.[53]

---

[48] Ross D. Inman, "Retrieving Divine Immensity and Omnipresence," in *T&T Clark Handbook of Analytic Theology*, ed. James M. Arcadi and James T. Turner, Jr., paperback ed. (New York: T&T Clark, 2022), 130.

[49] Inman, 130.

[50] Inman, 130.

[51] Inman, 131.

[52] Inman, 131.

[53] Inman, 131.

Inman goes on to distinguish between two modern perspectives on divine omnipresence—derivative omnipresence and functional omnipresence. Derivative omnipresence refers to God's being present derivatively at every place and location; that is to say, God is present to every place and location because God causally sustains the whole of creation and because God is aware of it by divine omniscience. In other words, God is present to every place due to causal and epistemic relations. According to Inman, this is the view often falsely conveyed upon classical theists like Anselm and Aquinas and is defended by some modern adherents today, such as Richard Swinburne, Charles Taliaferro, Edward Wierenga, William Lane Craig, and J. P. Moreland. Functional omnipresence, on the other hand, takes it that God could indeed be both epistemically and causally present to all things, but there seems to be something more to God's omnipresence, that is, that God's very being or nature or essence is in some sense present everywhere and to all places. According to defenders of functional omnipresence, derivative models reduce to divine omniscience and omnipotence. For them, omnipresence should be its own attribute, something distinct from either divine power or knowledge. In his constructive defense of omnipresence, Inman believes that though omnipresence and immensity are closely linked, the two attributes should remain distinct. Immensity provides the ground for divine omnipresence.[54] On this he says, "It is precisely *because* the divine essence is infinite and immense *ad intra* that the divine essence is repletively present to each and every place *ad extra*."[55] He continues, "On this classical picture, then, divine immensity is *explanatorily prior* to divine omnipresence; divine immensity is the principle *metaphysical ground* of God's repletive presence in creation.[56] Historically, then, the doctrine of functional omnipresence rests on three theological grounds:

---

[54] Inman, 132–34.

[55] Inman, 134.

[56] Inman, 134.

"divine simplicity, immediate divine causal action at every place, and divine immensity."[57]

A number of modern theists find the repletive view of omnipresence a tough pill to swallow and opt for the derivative view instead, taking it that God is present predominately epistemically and causally. Defenders of derivative omnipresence maintain with the classical tradition that God is spaceless, recognizing that space itself came into existence with creation (whether one takes a relational or substantival view of space). As J. P. Moreland and William Lane Craig emphasize,

> Without creation, therefore, God exists spacelessly. But the creation of space would do nothing to "spatialize" God, that is to say, to draw him into space. The creating of space is not itself a spatial act (as is, say, bumping something). Hence there is just no reason to think that divine spacelessness is surrendered in the action of creation. If not, then omnipresence should be understood in terms of God's being immediately cognizant of and causally active at every point in space. He knows what is happening at every spatial location in the universe, and he is causally operative at every such point, even if nothing more is going on there than quantum fluctuations in the vacuum of "empty" space.[58]

Where, then, does this land us? Certainly, we can feel the pull of arguments like Inman's, which emphasizes that divine omnipresence should be its own attribute and not reduced to omnipotence and omniscience. Though we're inclined toward derivative omnipresence, we would agree with John Peckham that in the end Scripture is inconclusive on whether divine omniscience is repletive or derivative.[59] Furthermore, we concur with Peckham that any conception of omnipresence should reflect biblically warranted

---

[57] Inman, 135–36.

[58] Moreland and Craig, *Philosophical Foundations*, 517.

[59] Peckham, *Divine Attributes*, 85–86.

images of God's relatedness to the world through divine presence. Consider a few summary points from Peckham's analysis: (1) God's manifestation of his presence to particular people at particular places (Gen 18:33; Exod 3:4–5; 33:11–23; John 1:14); (2) God dwelling in holy places such as the tabernacle and temple (Exod 25:8; Num 5:3; 1 Kgs 8:11; 1 Cor 3:16); (3) God's presence can "come" and "go" in some sense and that his presence to creatures is somewhat contingent on their relationship with him (Gen 4:16; 2 Chron 15:2; Ezek 11:22–23; John 1:3); and (4) the Word's presence in the incarnation (John 1:1, 14).[60] Finally, along with Peckham, we affirm the following points: (1) that divine presence at times does not seem uniform, given Scripture's depiction of God as spatially present at certain locations to certain individuals; (2) that God cannot be contained by creation; and (3) that God remains incorporeal.[61] Any model of omnipresence should consider these key points.

Having thus far argued for a God who is the Creator of all things *ex nihilo*, who is incorporeal, *a se*, necessary, and omnipresent, we now turn to divine eternity, immutability, simplicity, and impassibility. Our work in the previous two chapters laid the groundwork for how we think of the following attributes in the next two chapters, which are more contentious among philosophers and theologians.

---

[60] These points are adapted from Peckham, *Divine Attributes*, 84. Peckham gives ten major areas for consideration. For our purposes, we only highlighted a few.

[61] Peckham, 87–91.

4

Eternality, Immutability, Impassibility, and Simplicity

The doctrines of eternality, immutability, simplicity, and impassibility are among the more contentious attributes of God. After all, hardly any Christian theist denies that God is omnipotent, omniscient, or all-good (which we will consider in the next chapter), though there are different understandings of these doctrines. Yet, when it comes to the doctrines of eternality, immutability, impassibility, and simplicity, things get a bit dicey. As with the previous attributes, we'll consider the biblical data, as well as historical and contemporary expressions of each attribute, followed by an overall assessment, since these perfections are often taken together under a view known as "eternalism."

Ultimately, we deem eternalism to have significant problems. Instead, we argue for God's temporal mode of existence as everlastingly eternal. We take it that God is immutable, impassible, and simple, but we deny the stricter versions of these doctrines, offering what we take to be biblically and theologically appropriate qualifications. Finally, we affirm that if God undergoes any suffering, such suffering is voluntary.

Eternal God: Timeless or Everlasting?

All Christians believe that God is eternal. One can hardly escape the pages of the Bible without seeing references to his eternal nature (Pss 9:7; 93:2; 102:25–27). Consider the following passage from the Psalms: "Before the mountains were brought forth, or ever you had formed the earth and the world, from everlasting to everlasting you are God" (Ps 90:2 ESV). In Gen 21:33, Moses tells us that the Lord is the "everlasting God." Isaiah speaks of God as the one who "inhabits eternity" (Isa 57:15 ESV). Elsewhere he speaks of the Lord as the one who brings "everlasting salvation" to Israel (Isa 45:17) and that he is the "Everlasting Father" (Isa 9:6 ESV).

Beyond these Old Testament passages, the apostle Paul, in his letter to the Romans, speaks of God's "eternal nature" (Rom 1:20) and the "command of the eternal God" (Rom 16:26 ESV). Similarly, in 1 Timothy, Paul writes of God "only" as "immortal," which speaks to God's having always existed (1 Tim 1:17; 6:12). Finally, several passages in both the Old and New Testaments speak on God's endless existence (Gen 21:33; Deut 32:40–41; Job 36:26; Pss 41:13; 92:8; 102:24–27; 100:5; 103:15–18; 106:48; Isa 9:6–7; 40:28; 57:15; Jer 10:10; and Dan 4:34).[1]

From such passages, it's clear that the Bible teaches that God is eternal. The more troublesome issue centers on what Christians mean by divine eternity. Unfortunately, the Bible does not define divine eternity for us, so philosophical theologians must extrapolate an understanding of God's temporal mode of existence based on the data from Scripture and by considering other philosophical and theological truths (e.g., creation *ex nihilo*, cosmological arguments, etc.) to arrive at a coherent doctrine. At bare minimum,

---

[1] John S. Feinberg, *No One Like Him: The Doctrine of God* (Wheaton: Crossway, 2001), 260.

all parties agree that God has always existed and that he will never cease to exist. Beyond this, there is a sharp dispute among contemporary theologians on whether God is timelessly eternal or everlastingly eternal.

As mentioned earlier, classical theists, such as Paul Helm, Eleonore Stump, and Brian Leftow,[2] follow Augustine, Boethius, Anselm, and Aquinas in taking God's temporal mode of being to be timeless or atemporal.[3] By "timeless," they mean that God is without temporal location or extension.[4] As Leftow explains, "God bears no temporal relation to any temporal relatum—God does not exist or act earlier than, later than, or at the same time as any such thing. If God is timeless, such truths as 'God exists' are timeless truths; though they are true, they are not true at any time."[5]

In contrast, some theists hold to God's temporal mode of existence as being "in time" or "temporal" or "everlasting." They claim divine timelessness entered Christian thought through Greek philosophical reflection on the concept of eternity and does not properly reflect the biblical view of God.[6] When speaking of God "in time," divine temporalists do not mean

---

[2] For contemporary defenders of divine timelessness, see Paul Helm, *Eternal God: A Study of God without Time*, 2nd ed. (New York: Oxford University Press, 2011); Eleonore Stump and Norman Kretzmann, "Eternity," *The Journal of Philosophy* 78, no. 8 (August 1981), 429–58; Brian Leftow, *Time and Eternity* (Ithaca, NY: Cornell University Press, 1991).

[3] Augustine, *Confessions*, Book 11; Boethius, *The Consolation of Philosophy*, Book V; VI; Anselm, *Monologium,* Books XVIII-XXIV; *Proslogium*, Book XIII, XIX-XX; Aquinas, *Summa Theologica*, Question 10; *Summa Contra Gentiles*, Book 1:15.

[4] Nash, *The Concept of God: An Exploration of Contemporary Difficulties with the Attributes of God* (Grand Rapids: Zondervan, 1983), 73; Nelson Pike, *God and Timelessness* (New York: Schocken Books, 1970), 15.

[5] Leftow, *Time and Eternity*, 20.

[6] Oscar Cullmann, *Christ and Time: The Primitive Christian Conception of Time and History*, 3rd ed, trans. Floyd V. Filson (Philadelphia: The Westminster Press, 1962), 61–68; Richard Swinburne, *The Christian God* (New York: Oxford University Press, 1994), 138. Nicholas Wolterstorff, "God Everlasting," in *Contemporary Philosophy of Religion*, ed. Steven M. Cahn and David Shatz (New York: Oxford University Press, 1982), 78; Clark Pinnock, "Systematic Theology," in *The Openness of God* (Downers Grove: IVP, 1994), 121. Interestingly enough,

that God came into being at some point in time, nor do they mean that God is bound up or restricted by created space or time. Rather, they mean that God's nature or being is in some sense "temporal." Some theists prefer to speak of God as "omnitemporal" or of God as having "metaphysical time," which, as Garrett DeWeese puts it, "would be equivalent to God's time."[7]

In recent years several models have emerged seeking to provide a coherent view of God's temporal mode of existence. Perhaps the most well-known alternative view is William Lane Craig's model, which is something of a "hybrid" between the divine timeless and everlasting views. This model espouses that God is timeless *sans* creation but becomes temporal with the creation of time.[8]

Others like Richard Swinburne, Alan Padgett, Garrett DeWeese, and Ryan Mullins argue for God's essential temporality.[9] Unlike Craig, for them there is no transition from timelessness to temporality. Instead, God is essentially temporal, either as the ontological ground for time or time is (in some sense) an aspect of God's being. Regarding the former, divine temporalists like Swinburne, Padgett, and DeWeese believe God grounds time through divine causation. Padgett even calls his view "relative timelessness," since God is neither measured by time nor is God affected by or contained by time.[10] DeWeese, on the other hand suggests that "the causal succession

---

Eleonore Stump and Norman Kretzmann agree with the temporalists when they claim that the Greek concept of eternity "would not be out of keeping with the tradition that runs through Parmenides, Plato, and Plotinus into Augustine, Boethius, and Aquinas." Stump and Kretzmann, "Eternity," 445.

[7] Garrett J. DeWeese, *God and the Nature of Time* (Burlington, VT: Ashgate, 2004), 10. For a defense of omnitemporality, see chapters 9–10.

[8] For a fuller defense, see William Lane Craig, *Time and Eternity: Exploring God's Relationship to Time* (Wheaton: Crossway, 2001); *God, Time, and Eternity* (Dordrecht, NL: Kluwer Academic, 2001).

[9] Richard Swinburne, *The Christian God*, 137–44; Alan G. Padgett, *God, Eternity, and the Nature of Time* (Eugene, OR: Wipf & Stock, 2000), 122–46; DeWeese, *God and the Nature of Time*, 239–76; Ryan Mullins, "The Divine Timemaker," *Philosophia Christi* 22, no. 2 (2020): 211–37.

[10] Padgett, *God, Eternity, and the Nature of Time*, 126.

of mental states in God's conscious life grounds the flow and direction of metaphysical time," and because "God is creator and sustainer of the contingent order, his causal sustenance of every world will ground the time of that world."[11] Regarding the latter, R. T. Mullins, following Samuel Clarke, Isaac Newton, and Thomas Torrence, holds to the "identification" view of God's relationship to time, arguing for time as identical to or an aspect of God's nature or being.[12]

Changing or Constant?

The doctrine of immutability means that God is without change. But why accept this? After all, the kinds of things we see God doing in Scripture—hearing and answering prayers, rescuing his people from their enemies, working miracles—require a being who changes, or so it seems.

One reason is because Scripture affirms that God does not change. In the *Summa Theologica*, Thomas Aquinas cites Mal 3:6 (ESV)—"For I the LORD do not change," and he infers from this that God is "altogether immutable."[13] Other passages that emphasize God's unchanging nature include Heb 1:11–12 (cf. Ps 102:26) and Jas 1:17. But what is true of God is also true of Jesus Christ, who the writer of Hebrews says "is the same yesterday, today, and forever" (Heb 13:8). Scripture also indicates that God does not change his mind (Num 23:19).

A second reason stems from the belief that only a God who is immutable can perform the kinds of actions attributed to him in Scripture. Paul Helm, a contemporary defender, argues that it preserves other qualities of God, such as divine timelessness, divine fullness, or divine self-sufficiency. He also believes it preserves the Creator/creature distinction.[14]

---

[11] DeWeese, *God and the Nature of Time*, 253.

[12] Mullins, "The Divine Timemaker," 230.

[13] Aquinas, *Summa Theologica*, Q. 9, Art. 1.

[14] Helm, *Eternal God*, 19.

The kind of immutability that classical theists like Aquinas and Helm have in mind is the strongest variant possible. According to Helm, an individual who is immutable experiences no temporal or spatial changes, not even so-called "merely Cambridge" changes.[15]

Process and open theists have long criticized the classical theist's view on the doctrine, as have many contemporary biblical, systematic, and philosophical theologians.[16] One of the key objections to the doctrine is that the immutable God of classical theism is not the God we see in Scripture, a God who hears and answers prayers, delivers his people from bondage, and the like. These actions require a God who can act and change.

Process theologians argue that though he is the greatest conceivable being, God is not "absolute" or unchanging. Rather, God, who is in process, is deeply affected by creatures. They reject Aquinas's position that God isn't really related to the world. Instead, relatedness to the world is central to their understanding of God. According to process theists, the God of classical theism is more akin to the Greek philosophers' understanding than that of the Bible.

---

[15] Philosophers often distinguish between a "real" change and merely "Cambridge" changes. When we speak of a real change within a substance, we mean that some change has occurred intrinsically with respect to one of its properties. For example, if a person's hair changes from blond to brown, then we can speak of that person having experienced a real change. Cambridge changes, on the other hand, denote no real (intrinsic) changes within the substance; rather, we can speak of a change occurring only in some relation to that substance or thing. For example, it may be the case that Socrates is being thought about by Plato at time t_1 but not at t_2. Here, we would say that Socrates experiences no real change. Instead, the real change occurs in Plato. A relational or Cambridge change may be defined as follows: "a substance x changes if some predicate 'ϕ' applies to a substance x at one time but not at another time without that substance having 'changed' in the ordinary sense of the word." Richard Swinburne, *The Coherence of Theism*, 2nd ed. (Oxford: Oxford University Press, 2016), 232.

[16] See Cobb and Griffin, *Process Theology*, 8–9; Feinberg, *No One Like Him*, 264–76; Nash, *The Concept of God*, 99–105; Stephen T. Davis, *Logic and the Nature of God* (Grand Rapids: Eerdmans, 1983), 41–51.

Not all critics of the classical doctrine of immutability want to deny that Scripture speaks of God as unchanging, nor do they want to take the position of process theologians and say that God is always in process and mutable. They question whether Scripture justifies such a strong or absolute understanding of the doctrine. For example, the nineteenth-century theologian Isaak August Dorner defended immutability in his important monograph, *Divine Immutability*, specifically ethical immutability.[17] Richard Swinburne distinguishes between what he calls "strong" and "weak" immutability. The strong version suggests that God cannot change in any sense at all. The weak version suggests that God is immutable only with respect to divine character and essential properties.[18] Swinburne rejects the strongest version because such a view does not mesh with the picture we gain of God from the Old Testament.[19] Jay Richards takes it one step further, distinguishing between immutability "in every respect, in some respects or in no respects."[20] Richards argues for a God who is strongly immutable, but rejects the view that God is immutable "in every respect." Such a view goes too far, since Scripture indicates God has some accidental properties, such as being Lord of Israel or being creator of the world. Like Swinburne, Richards takes it that God is immutable with respect to essential properties and character.[21]

Impassible or Impassioned?

Closely linked to the doctrine of immutability is the doctrine of impassibility. If God is immutable in the strongest sense, as eternalists and classical theists believe, then it would only stand to reason that God is also impassible in the strongest sense. There is no monolithic view on impassibility

---

[17] Isaak August Dorner, *Divine Immutability: A Critical Reconsideration*, trans. Robert R. Williams and Claude Welch (Minneapolis: Fortress, 1994), 161–81.

[18] Swinburne, *The Coherence of Theism*, 232.

[19] Swinburne, 233.

[20] Richards, *The Untamed God*, 197.

[21] Richards, 195–212.

within the Christian tradition;[22] however, Christians from the Patristic era up through the Medieval and Reformation periods have affirmed it.[23] It came to the forefront in theological discussion during the nineteenth and twentieth centuries. In contemporary discussion, the doctrine of divine impassibility remains a significant disputed issue.[24]

Discussions on the doctrine of impassibility often center on two questions: (1) Does God suffer? and (2) Does God have emotions?[25] Classical theists have emphatically said "no" to the first question, though there has been debate on the second one, particularly with respect to the extent we can speak of God having emotions. Regarding the second question, a common charge by passibilists is that God on the classical conception has no emotions whatsoever. However, that is not the case, as R. T. Mullins and Paul Gavrilyuk have shown.[26]

---

[22] Richard E. Creel, *Divine Impassibility: An Essay in Philosophical Theology* (Eugene, OR: Wipf & Stock, 2005); Paul Gavrilyuk, *The Suffering of the Impassible God: The Dialectics of Patristic Thought* (New York: Oxford University Press, 2004).

[23] R. T. Mullins, *God and Emotion* (New York: Cambridge University Press, 2020), 1.

[24] Cobb and Griffin, *Process Theology*, 3–9, 43–48; Charles Hartshorne, *The Divine Relativity* (New Haven, CT: Yale University Press, 1964), 54–59; Richard Rice, "Biblical Support for a New Perspective," in *The Openness of God: A Biblical Challenge to the Traditional Understanding of God* (Downers Grove: IVP, 1994), 22–38; William Hasker, *Providence, Evil and the Openness of God* (New York: Routledge, 2004), 133–34, 160–61, 182–83; Pinnock, *Most Moved Mover: A Theology of God's Openness (The Didsbury Lectures)* (Grand Rapids: Baker Academic, 2001), 85–92; Jürgen Moltmann, *The Crucified God* (Minneapolis: Fortress, 1993); Jürgen Moltmann, *The Trinity and the Kingdom* (Minneapolis: Fortress, 1993), 21–60; Terence E. Fretheim, *The Suffering of God: An Old Testament Perspective* (Philadelphia, PA: Fortress, 1984); Alvin Plantinga, "Self-Profile," in *Alvin Plantinga*, ed. James Tomberlin and Peter van Inwagen (Dordrecht, NL: Kluwer Academic, 1985), 36; John C. Peckham, *The Love of God: A Canonical Model* (Downers Grove: IVP, 2015), 147–89; Millard J. Erickson, *The Word Became Flesh: A Contemporary Incarnational Christology* (Grand Rapids: Baker, 1991), 599–624; Feinberg, *No One Like Him*, 277; Mullins, *God and Emotion*, 15.

[25] Mullins, 15.

[26] Mullins, 19–25; Gavrilyuk, *The Suffering of the Impassible God*, 47–63.

According to Mullins, the core of the doctrine of divine impassibility rests on three claims: (1) "it is metaphysically impossible for God to suffer"; (2) "it is metaphysically impossible for God to be moved, or acted upon, by anything outside of God"; and (3) "God lacks passions."[27] Regarding this last claim, God's lacking passions does not imply, necessarily, that God is without emotions. But how is it that classical theists discern which emotions literally apply to God? Mullins gives three criteria. First, God cannot have any emotions that are inconsistent with his moral nature. Second, God cannot have any emotions that are inconsistent with his perfect rationality. Third, God cannot have any emotions that disrupt his eternal blessedness.[28] Moreover, classical theists will often ground the doctrine of impassibility in other doctrines, such as immutability and simplicity. After all, a God who is immutable and simple is a God who never changes, nor are there any real distinctions within God.

Those who reject the doctrine of divine impassibility do so for several reasons. Again, some see the doctrine of impassibility as a holdover and influence from Greek philosophy, what Gavrilyuk calls "the theory of theology's fall into Hellenistic philosophy."[29] However, most who deny the doctrine do so because it stands in tension with what the biblical narrative teaches about God.[30]

---

[27] R. T. Mullins, "Classical Theism," in *T&T Clark Handbook of Analytic Theology*, ed. James M. Arcadi and James T. Turner Jr., paperback ed. (New York: T&T Clark, 2022), 91.

[28] Mullins, 91.

[29] Gavrilyuk, *The Suffering of the Impassible God*, 21–46.

[30] John C. Peckham, "Qualified Passibility," in *Divine Impassibility: Four Views of God's Emotions and Suffering*, ed. Robert J. Matz and A. Chadwick Thornhill (Downers Grove: IVP), 88. "[A] cursory reading of Scripture," claims Peckham, "manifests that God is depicted therein as profoundly emotional in a way responsive to the actions of creatures." Some of those depictions include God's pleasure or displeasure (Gen 6:6; Deut 9:7; Ps 78:40–41; Prov 15:8; Col 1:10), a "desire for exclusive relationship with his people" (Hos 1–3; Isa 62:4; Jer 2:2; 3:1–12;

Others deny impassibility because they believe God genuinely suffers along with his creatures. Suffering is required for God to relate with and redeem his creatures and to overcome evil in the world. Consider the words of philosopher Alvin Plantinga:

> God's capacity for suffering, I believe, is proportional to his great-ness; it exceeds our capacity for suffering in the same measure as his capacity for knowledge exceeds ours. Christ was prepared to endure the agonies of hell itself; and God, the Lord of the universe, was prepared to endure the suffering in order to overcome sin, and death, and the evils that afflict our world, and to confer on us a life more glorious than we can imagine.[31]

Simple or Complex?

Ronald Nash said it best; "The doctrine of divine simplicity has a public relations problem."[32] Today, a good number of philosophers and theologians reject the doctrine because they see it as incoherent. But what does the doctrine affirm and how have classical theists understood it?

The doctrine of divine simplicity has a long history within the Christian tradition, beginning in the patristic era all the way up through Reformation.[33] According to James Dolezal, "The doctrine of divine simplicity teaches that (1) God is identical with his existence and his essence and (2) that each of his attributes is ontologically identical with his existence and with every other one of his attributes."[34] Moreland and Craig define it

---

Ezek 16; 23; Zech 8:2), passionate (Deut 4:24), and compassionate (Deut 1:31; 4:31; Ps 103:13; Isa 49:15; Jer 31:20; Hos 11:1–4).

[31] Plantinga, "Self-Profile," 36.

[32] Nash, *The Concept of God*, 85.

[33] Steven J. Duby, *Divine Simplicity: A Dogmatic Account* (New York: Bloomsbury, 2016), 7–25; James E. Dolezal, *God Without Parts: Divine Simplicity and the Metaphysics of God's Absoluteness* (Eugene, OR: Pickwick, 2011), 3–10.

[34] Dolezal, *God Without Parts*, 2.

as follows: "According to the doctrine of divine simplicity God has no distinct attributes, he stands in no real relations, his essence is not distinct from his existence, he just is the pure act of being subsisting. All such distinctions exist only in our minds, since we can form no conception of the absolutely simple divine being."[35]

What other reasons might a classical theist give for holding to belief in the doctrine of divine simplicity? James Dolezal suggests that the doctrine rests squarely in the affirmation that God is "most absolute" and in the Creator/creature distinction.[36] Despite claims that the doctrine has no support from Scripture,[37] Stephen Duby provides the following exegetical and theological reasons for affirming the doctrine: (1) God's divine singularity and oneness (e.g., Deut 6:4; John 5:20, 44; 17:3; 1 Cor 8:6); (2) divine life and aseity (Exod 3:14; 33:19; Rom 9:1–7); (3) divine immutability (Num 23:16; Mal 3:6; Jas 1:17); (4) divine infinity (Job 5:9; 9:10; 11:7–9; 1 Kgs 8:27; Ps 145:3; Isa 40:12–14, 26; 66:1–2; Acts 17:28; Col 1:17); and (5) creation *ex nihilo* (Gen 1:1; Ps 33:6; Acts 17:24; Rom 11:36; 1 Cor 8:6; Heb 11:3; Rev 4:11).[38]

---

[35] Moreland and Craig, *Philosophical Foundations*, 530. Thomas Aquinas begins his *Summa Theologica* with the five ways for knowing God's existence and moves straight away to the doctrine of divine simplicity. The doctrine of divine simplicity becomes strong support for other things that Aquinas believes and argues for about God, namely, God as timeless, immutable, and impassible. Standing behind Aquinas's view of divine simplicity is the Aristotelian notion that God is *actus purus*, the idea that God is always in act. Within God there can be no potentiality or accidents. Thomas Aquinas, *Summa Theologica*, Pt. 1, Q.3, Art. 7.

[36] Dolezal, *God Without Parts*, 1, 30.

[37] Moreland and Craig, *Philosophical Foundations*, 530.

[38] Duby, *Divine Simplicity*, 91–177. Despite this, we wonder how much of Duby's metaphysical commitments are smuggled into his conclusion on divine simplicity. Certainly, these theological points provide evidence for such a doctrine as divine simplicity; however, the evidence, in our view, does not demand such a conclusion.

Evaluation of Eternalism

What does all this mean for the Anselmian theist? Surely, we want a God who is perfect and worship-worthy. But we also want a God who properly reflects Christian Scripture. Does the God of eternalism fit that bill?

We've seen again and again the charge that the God of eternalism is not the God of the Bible and that such a view is more influenced by Greek than Hebrew thought. There may be some truth to that, but as emphasized in chapter 1, just because something is "Greek" doesn't make it wrong. God has revealed himself through special *and* general revelation. After all, a good many of the things we say about God are not explicitly stated in Scripture (e.g., the doctrine of the Trinity), so we must turn not only to the biblical reflective context, but other principles, such as the sovereignty-aseity conviction and principle of perfection.

In our view, there are significant problems with eternalism. Let's begin with the doctrine of divine simplicity. We agree with other critics on the incoherence of the stronger version of the doctrine. First, as Moreland and Craig point out, simplicity leads to agnosticism concerning God's nature. On this they write: "While we can say what God is not like, we cannot say what he is like, except in an analogical sense. But these predications must in the end fail, since there is no univocal element in the predicates we assign to God, leaving us in a state of genuine agnosticism about the nature of God. Indeed, on this view God really has no nature; he is simply the inconceivable act of being."[39]

Second, it goes beyond credulity to think that God's properties have no significant distinction and that God just is his properties. Certainly, God's attributes may entail one another, but omnipotence and omnibenevolence are not the same thing. If there are no significant distinctions within God, how can we even make sense of the Trinity? According to the doctrine of the Trinity, the Father, Son, and Spirit are really distinct from one another (even

---

[39] Moreland and Craig, *Philosophical Foundations*, 530.

if by divine relations, as Aquinas held), but how can we truly speak of the Persons being distinct if God is identical to his properties, act, and being? The divine Persons would collapse in on one another. It would only appear to us that the Persons are distinct.

Third, and more damaging, is the problem of modal collapse. According to eternalism, God is *actus purus*, which means that there is no potency within God. God can have no accidental properties. But affirming God's freedom raises a significant dilemma for the doctrine of simplicity. How so? To say that God is free means there is "unactualized potential" in God, since God may have refrained from creating the world in the first place, or he could have created a completely different world.[40] But if God is pure act, as eternalists believe, God only had one option—to create this world. He could not have done otherwise since his actions are identical with his being. But that also makes God dependent upon creation—one of the very problems divine simplicity seeks to avoid! If that's the case, what ultimately distinguishes the God of Christian theism from the God of panentheism?[41]

Are there any redeeming qualities to the doctrine of divine simplicity? In our estimation, Christian theists should avoid any view that implies that God created by necessity, ultimately resulting in a form of fatalism. However, if one were to take a modified view of divine simplicity, then, perhaps there is room within Christian theology. After all, we can fully agree that God is not a composite being, who is composed of various parts. We can also agree that the triune Persons are an undivided unity, and that God is *sui generis* and *a se* with respect to his being and nature.

What about the doctrines of divine timelessness, immutability, and impassibility? Given the difficulties of divine simplicity in the strictest sense, there is one less motivation for holding on to these doctrines. But we believe other problems ensue.

---

[40] R. T. Mullins, "Simply Impossible: A Case against Divine Simplicity," *Journal of Reformed Theology* 7 (2013): 194.

[41] Mullins, 197.

As mentioned, one motivation for holding to the doctrine of divine immutability centers on the argument from Scripture. We agree that the Bible speaks of ways in which God does not change. God does not change with respect to his eternal nature (Rom 1:20) and character (Mal 3:6; Jas 1:17), but we also agree with Moreland and Craig that the biblical writers, when speaking of God's immutability, did not have in mind the "radical changelessness contemplated by Aristotle."[42]

Another motivation for an absolute doctrine of immutability is God's perfection. Yet, there is an underlying assumption that all change is either for the better or for the worst. But how can the greatest conceivable being change for either the better or the worst? If God is already the greatest conceivable being, then how can he change for the better? Can he become more perfect? If he can change for the worse, wouldn't that imply that he's no longer the greatest conceivable being? But this is a false dilemma. Why think that all changes result in a change of value? Can't there be value-neutral changes that do not affect a being's metaphysical stature? If so, then it doesn't follow from the fact of God's not changing for the better or for the worse that God can't change in any sense whatsoever.[43]

In our estimation, the God of Scripture is constant in his nature, character, and responses to his creatures. Such a God is religiously available and personal, acting in the world, responding to his creatures. Thus we agree with Karl Barth that God is "immutable," but not in the sense of being "immobile" or "motionless;" rather, the biblical view of God is one whereby he is "the living God" who possesses "mobility" and "elasticity."[44]

Given the conceptual connection between divine timelessness and immutability, if God is not absolutely immutable, then neither can he be timeless, since timelessness entails that God cannot experience any

---

[42] Moreland and Craig, *Philosophical Foundations*, 532.

[43] Morris, *Our Idea of God*, 127.

[44] Karl Barth, *The Doctrine of God*, vol. 2.1 of *The Church Dogmatics*, ed. G. W. Bromiley and T. F. Torrance, 1st paperback ed. (London: T&T Clark, 2000), 495.

change whatsoever, not even "Cambridge" changes. But why think God is temporal?

First, the doctrine of creation provides a powerful reason for taking God to be temporal. If God is the creator and sustainer of the world, then it's implausible to see how God remains untouched by temporality of the world. Christians have long held to the belief that God created the world *ex nihilo*. God was arguably free to create or not to create. But by virtue of creating and sustaining the world, God now stands in a causal relationship with the world that he did not always have. We can imagine two episodes of God's life, one episode of God existing alone, apart from a world, and one episode whereby God brings creation into existence and sustains the world. Even if one maintains that God experiences no intrinsic changes by creating, it's hard to deny that God experiences at least an extrinsic change due to this now causal relationship with creation. But even if God was timeless before creation, at the moment of creation, God is drawn into time by his relationship to sustaining the world.[45]

Second, divine timelessness is hard to square with the doctrine of the incarnation. In the incarnation, the Second Person of the Trinity is united to a human nature—a belief known as the hypostatic union. The Chalcedonian Creed affirms that the Son is of "one substance with the Father" and that he is of "one substance with us as regards his manhood." He is like us in every way but without sin, which means that he's temporal with respect to his humanity. Yet, the union of the divine and human natures exist "without confusion, without change, without division, without separation." In other words, the natures remain distinct and are "no way annulled by the union."[46]

---

[45] William Lane Craig, "Timelessness and Omnitemporality," in *Philosophia Christi* 2, no. 1 (2000): 30.

[46] The Westminster Standard, "Chalcedonian Creed (451 A.D)," The Westminster Standard, Last modified 2023, https://thewestminsterstandard.org/the-chalcedonian-creed/.

The hypostatic union raises several perplexities if we are to take God as timeless. John 1:14 speaks of the Word becoming flesh. Most take this "becoming" language as the Son of God adding or taking on our humanity, which includes both a body and rational soul. We agree. Yet how does the timeless Son of God "add" or "take on" or "become" anything, since the timeless God can experience no change whatsoever. But that's not all. On pain of heresy, any of the predicates that apply to Jesus Christ must also apply to the Son of God, as Thomas Senor rightly argues:

P1) Jesus Christ read in the synagogue (at the start of his ministry)
C1) So, temporal predicates apply to Jesus Christ
P2) Jesus Christ = God the Son
C2) So, temporal predicates apply to God the Son
P3) Temporal predicates don't apply to timeless beings
C3) So, God the Son isn't timeless[47]

How is it that the Second Person of the Trinity is temporal, if the other two persons are timeless? As Garrett DeWeese points out, while this does not show atemporality as false, it does make it suspect.[48]

One possible escape for the defender of divine timelessness is simply to say that the Godhead has timelessly willed that at a specific point in time the Son of God becomes, takes on, or adds a human nature. But, again, in what sense is the Son of God really united to the human nature? If time is really in process and the present is all that exists (a view known as "presentism," which Augustine and other classical theists affirmed), then we can speak of two phases to the Son of God's life—the first phase, the Son without the human nature, and the second phase, the Son united to the

---

[47] Thomas Senor, "Incarnation and Timelessness," in *Faith and Philosophy* 7, no. 2 (April 1990): 150.
[48] DeWeese, *God and the Nature of Time*, 233.

human nature.[49] So, at t_1, t_2, t_3 . . . the world exists apart from the Son of God's being united to the human nature. But at, say, t_{10} the Son of God is united to the human nature. How can this be since there can be no "before" or "after" in the life of a timeless God? Moreover, there can be no temporal moments to God the Son's life, such as being born, healing the sick, resurrecting, ascending, etc.

To avoid this, some defenders of divine timelessness employ the qua (with respect to) move, that is, qua the Son's divine nature, the Son remains timeless; qua the Son's human nature, the Son remains temporal. While we believe at times employing the qua move is both beneficial and necessary, in the case of divine timeless and the incarnation it smacks of Nestorianism. Not only does such a move dissolve the union between the two natures, it leads to the Son being two distinct persons. The union between the two natures would simply be functionally causal. But why think that such a causal relation (which goes one way) between the divine and human nature of the Son is really any more distinct or unique from other causal activity that God performs. Might that not result in a form of adoptionism? We believe a better explanation for the incarnation requires indwelling and embodiment. Though God is not bound by created space-time, he is, as the Lord and Creator of space-time, free to enter the world that he's created in a real and present way. He does this without diminishing his omnipresence.

Others like Paul Helm avoid the incarnation problem by denying that time is in process and have opted for something like a tenseless or static view of time. All times exist as earlier than and later than relations and are in a sense metaphysically real. This requires us to believe that our births, deaths, and future resurrection all somehow co-exist. But such a view demands radical philosophical and theological commitments. First, this view redefines creation *ex nihilo* to mean that there is only a boundary to creation. There

---

[49] For a detailed defense that classical theism affirms presentism, see Mullins, *The End of the Timeless God*, 74–126.

is no temporal becoming of creation. God has eternally caused or tense-lessly produced the four-dimensional space-time universe (and anything else that exists contingently, such as angels, heaven, etc.).[50] Second, this view requires that the Son of God be eternally or tenselessly united to the human nature.[51] As with our own lives, the Son of God's death, resurrection, ascension, and second coming all co-exist and are ontologically real. But even more problematic, evil is never fully eradicated. It's just as real in one time slice as its defeat is in another. How can we proclaim that Christ has conquered sin and death through his work, death, and resurrection?

Third, and finally, in our view divine timelessness leads to diminished view of omniscience. Though the timeless God knows all true propositions, he could only know them tenselessly. Moreland and Craig are surely right when they say, "In order to know the truth propositions expressed by tensed sentences . . . God must exist temporally."[52] They continue, "Such ignorance is inconsistent with the standard account of omniscience, which requires that God know all truths, and is surely incompatible with God's maximally cognitive excellence."[53]

Finally, we turn to divine impassibility. Can the Anselmian theist affirm impassibility? Again, that depends on whether one takes impassibility in the strictest sense or not. It seems that the patristic fathers employed the term "impassibility" to distinguish between the God of Christian theism and the pagan gods of the pantheon. God is not fickle in how he responds to his creatures, swayed by every whim and giving into every passion. Instead, God remains steadfast in both his character and nature.[54] One's understand-

[50] Paul Helm, "Divine Timeless Eternity," in *God and Time: Four Views*, ed. Gregory Ganssle (Downers Gove: IVP, 2001), 49.

[51] Stump and Kretzman, "Eternity," 453.

[52] Moreland and Craig, *Philosophical Foundations*, 520.

[53] Moreland and Craig, 520.

[54] Thomas H. McCall, *Forsaken: The Trinity and the Cross, and Why It Matters* (Downers Grove: IVP, 2012), 68. For fuller discussion, see also Paul Gavrilyuk, *The Suffering of the Impassible God*.

ing of impassibility hinges on what one means by "suffering." If by suffering one means God becomes impoverished or is in some way not flourishing, we would certainly agree that God doesn't suffer in those respects. But if by suffering one means that God experiences the effects of evil, pain, and suffering from the world, then, as we've noted, the Bible indicates that he does.

At the heart of the question is whether God has emotions and whether he suffers. Scripture is replete with depictions of God as having emotions and responsive to the actions of his creatures. Scripture depicts God as having genuine love, long-suffering, compassion, and wrath, just to name a few.[55]

Certainly, the language used in Scripture includes anthropomorphism when it speaks of God's emotions and suffering, but we shouldn't think that such images have no import with respect to the divine nature. Any suffering that God partakes in is something that God endures voluntarily. God has often imposed limitations upon himself (e.g., creation, incarnation, or when he makes covenants with his people); yet such self-imposed limitations lead to no deficiency in the divine nature.[56] Perhaps, the clearest example of divine suffering is found in the cross of Christ, whereby God makes it possible for his creatures to be reconciled to himself. Through Christ's work on the cross, God has brought about our redemption and reconciliation. Yet, as Erickson reminds us, reconciliation comes at a great cost and with pain. To flesh this out, he gives the following example: if two people quarrel, harsh statements are often exchanged. To end the quarrel, it requires someone to give up on retaliating, "absorbing the pain into oneself."[57] This is what God has done for us through Christ. He has chosen to absorb the pain, which means that "God must in a sense suffer the consequences of human sin himself."[58]

---

[55] See Fretheim, *The Suffering of God*, chaps. 7–9 especially.
[56] Erickson, *The Word Became Flesh*, 609–10.
[57] Erickson, 616.
[58] Erickson.

In this chapter we have argued against eternalism. While we maintain such doctrines as immutability, impassibility, and simplicity, they need to be qualified in a way that aligns with the biblical data and with other central doctrines of the faith, such as creation *ex nihilo*, the Trinity, and incarnation. Regarding divine timelessness, we have argued that the biblical data and the deliverances of reason do not warrant such a view. In the end, though long-standing within Christian tradition, eternalism fails to provide an adequate understanding of the Christian God.

5

God, Providence, and Divine Action

In the previous chapter, we examined four of the more controversial attributes—divine timelessness, immutability, impassibility, and simplicity—often found in classical theism which, when taken together, form a view known as eternalism. We found eternalism wanting. In this chapter, we examine those attributes related to God's providential action in the world—power, knowledge, and goodness—and assess how well each model of God explains divine providence and divine action. In relation to God's providence and action, we argue for a form of modified classical theism.

Divine Providence and Sovereignty

No doubt God is sovereign, but Christians differ on just what that means. Providence refers to God's governance over the world. Scripture is replete with accounts of God's providential action.

We find God's general provision for nature and humans (Job 5:10; 38:41; Ps 147:9; Isa 43:20; Matt 5:45). We also find God's provision for the nations (Job 36:31; Acts 14:17), for his people Israel (Exodus 3; 12; 13:21; 16; Deut 7:17–24; Ezek 34:29), and for individuals (Gen 4:15; 6:14–17; 1 Sam 23:14; John 1:17; Acts 5:19; 12:6–11). In the life of believers, we see God's providential provision through offering redemption (Ps 111:9), giving a savior (John 3:16), providing the Holy Spirit to guide believers to truth (John 16:13), and giving the Scriptures for spiritual growth (2 Tim 3:16).[1]

The doctrine of divine providence intersects with God's divine plan and purposes for creation. Scripture affirms that God has plans for the universe (e.g., the new heavens and the new earth), different groups and nations (e.g., the inclusion of Gentiles in God's plan for salvation), and for individuals (e.g., the conversion of the apostle Paul). In the life of Abraham, we see God's plan to bring about a great nation, Israel, as well as the Messiah who will bring salvation to the world. We also see God's use of pagan leaders (Pharaoh, Nebuchadnezzar, and Cyrus) to fulfill his plans and purposes (cf. Exod 9:16; Isa 44:28).[2]

In addition to God's general provision and his action in carrying out his plans and purposes, God works through miraculous intervention. We see this not only through the lives of his prophets (e.g., Moses and Elijah), but also in the life of Jesus, who healed disease (Luke 4:40), restored sight to the blind (Mark 8:22–26; John 9:1–7), cast out demons (Matt 8:28–34), calmed storms (Matt 8:23–27; Mark 4:35–41; Luke 8:22–25), and raised the dead (Luke 7:11–17; 8:40–56; John 11). Central to the heart of the Christian gospel is a miraculous claim: the belief that God raised Jesus from the dead. As Paul declares in his first letter to the Corinthians, if Christ has not been raised from the dead, then "our preaching is useless," "we are then found to be false witnesses about God," our "faith is futile," and we're still in our sins" (1 Cor 15:14–17 NIV).

---

[1] Bruce R. Reichenbach, *Divine Providence: God's Love and Human Freedom* (Eugene, OR: Cascade, 2016), 2.

[2] Reichenbach, 2.

Power, Knowledge, and Goodness

We cannot think of divine providence and sovereignty apart from understanding God's nature, particularly God's power, knowledge, and goodness. In what follows, we consider each of these. Let's begin with divine power.

Divine Omnipotence

Often, when Christians discuss God's power, they have in mind the idea of divine omnipotence. In its most basic sense, omnipotence means that God is all-powerful and that he can do all things. The Bible has much to say about God's power, but does it teach omnipotence?

For starters, the first passage of the Bible speaks of God creating the heavens and the earth (Gen 1:1), a theme that reverberates throughout the entirety of Scripture (e.g., Ps 33:6; Rom 1:20). Not only does God create the world and everything in it, but we also see that God (the Son) sustains and upholds its existence (Col 1:16–17; Heb 1:2–3). God's work is also evident through his power over nature. Perhaps one of the clearest examples of divine power is found in God's deliverance of his people from the clutches of Egyptians through sending the ten plagues (Exod 7–12). In the Gospels, there are several nature miracles that Jesus performs, such as walking on water (Matt 14:22–33) and stilling a storm (Mark 4:35–41).[3] God even has power over the events of history (Acts 17:26).

Throughout the Bible we see God exercising his power through raising the dead (1 Kgs 17:17–24; Luke 7:11–17, 8:40–42, 49–56; John 11:38–44; Acts 20:7–12). Chiefly, God raised his Son from the dead, which is a foreshadowing for believers (Rom 8:11). The Bible speaks of Jesus as the "firstfruits" and "firstborn" from among the dead (1 Cor 15:20–22; Col 1:18).

---

[3] Millard J. Erickson, *Christian Theology*, 3rd ed. (Grand Rapids: Baker Academic, 1998), 247. John C. Peckham, *Divine Attributes: Knowing the Covenantal God of Scripture* (Grand Rapids: Baker Academic, 2021), 142.

Coinciding with the resurrection from the dead is the Jewish and Christian belief that God will bring about new creation. The book of Revelation emphasizes that God will create a new heaven and a new earth (Rev 21:1). It's not clear what that new heavens and the new earth will be like, but there is a correlation between our humanly resurrection and God's work in the liberation of creation from its current state of decay (Rom 8:18–23; Col 1:20).

Finally, we see God's power displayed in his defeat of the dark powers who have rebelled against his divine rule. Throughout the Gospels Jesus exorcised demons (Mark 1:21–28; Luke 8:2). In the case of the Gerasene demoniac, Jesus cast out a "legion" or many demons (Luke 8:2). Finally, the book of Revelation speaks of God's ultimate defeat over Satan (Rev 20:7–10), "the great dragon," who is called "the deceiver of the whole world" (Rev 12:9 NRSV).

The Bible also explicitly speaks of things that God cannot do. It is impossible for God to "deny himself" (2 Tim 2:13), "be tempted by evil" (Jas 1:13), "lie" (Titus 1:2), look favorably at sin (Hab 1:13), and fail to keep his promises (Heb 6:17–18). At times, God restricts the operation of his power due to commitments he makes (e.g., making covenants) or because of his character.[4]

Given the biblical data, how then should we understand the concept of God's power? René Descartes held to a view known as "absolute omnipotence," which understands omnipotence to mean that God can do anything, whether that's creating a square circle or making 2 + 2 =5.[5] But why affirm such a view? For Descartes, to claim otherwise would make God subject to the laws of logic or something outside of God. While admirable, this view is extremely problematic. First, it doesn't mesh with how we normally think about the world in which we live. It's not entirely clear how we could communicate God's actions in such a world or even participate in coherent discourse about reality, since divine actions are arbitrary, going beyond logical

---

[4] Peckham, *Divine Attributes*, 143–44.
[5] Peckham, 49.

restraints.[6] Second, it would require us to imagine absurd and nonsensical beliefs about God. As Moreland and Craig put it, Descartes's position "asks us to believe, for example, that God could have brought it about that he created all of us without his existing; that is to say, there is a possible world in which both God does not exist and he created all of us. This is simply nonsense."[7] Third and finally, as we have already shown, there are things that God simply cannot do, such as lie, deny himself, or break his promises due to his character.

Unsatisfied with idea of absolute omnipotence, most theists follow Thomas Aquinas, who emphasized the idea that God can do all things that are logically possible. But some have questioned whether the Thomistic view of omnipotence can stand against the so-called "stone paradox," which asks whether God can create a stone that not even he can lift. If God cannot make such a stone, then he's not omnipotent since there's something he cannot do. If God can make such a stone, then, again, he would not be omnipotent since he could not lift it. Peter Geach, for instance, finds the Thomistic view utterly problematic in responding to such paradoxes, leading to all sorts of logical contradictions. He prefers Scripture's language of God as "Almighty."[8]

But not all are as pessimistic as Geach. T. J. Mawson defines omnipotence as "having the most power-granting set of abilities that it is logically possible anyone might have."[9] This doesn't entail that God has all abilities, since "some abilities are liabilities."[10] In the case of the stone paradox, one cannot believe that God has both the ability to create such a stone so heavy

---

[6] Thomas V. Morris, *Our Idea of God* (Vancouver, BC: Regent University Press, 2002), 67.

[7] J. P. Moreland and William Lane Craig, *Philosophical Foundations for a Christian Worldview* (Downers Grove: 2003), 533.

[8] Peter Geach, "Omnipotence," in *Contemporary Philosophy of Religion*, ed. Steven M. Cahn and David Shatz (New York: Oxford University Press, 1982), 46–60.

[9] T. J. Mawson, *The Divine Attributes* (New York: Cambridge University Press, 2019), 41.

[10] Mawson, 41.

that he cannot lift it and the ability to lift any stone, since "having one logically entails not having the other."[11] For God to create such a stone that he could not lift would itself be a liability and hence should not be included as a "member of the most power-granting set of abilities that it's logically possible anyone might have."[12] Thus, he concludes, "An omnipotent being should be understood as having the power to lift any stone and therefore as not having the liability of being able to create a stone so heavy that He Himself could not then lift it."[13]

Moreland and Craig take a different approach. Instead of taking omnipotence to be about God's unlimited power (whether in quantity or power) we ought to understand it more akin to God's ability to "actualize certain states of affairs."[14] It's not enough to claim that an omnipotent being can actualize just any state affairs that is logically possible. After all, there may be states of affairs, due to the passage of time, that are no longer logically possible for God to actualize. Changing the past or backward causation will not do, since both are broadly logically impossible. The past is now necessary—locked in, so to speak.

Moreover, if human beings have libertarian freedom, given counterfactuals of creaturely freedom, God cannot actualize just any world.[15] For a person to genuinely perform some free action in the libertarian sense, this means those actions can in no way be caused by anything (e.g., law, agent, God) other than the one performing the action. Given libertarian freedom, Plantinga distinguishes between "strong" and "weak" actualization. To say that some agent *A* brings about or actualizes some state of affairs *S* in the

---

[11] Mawson, 41.

[12] Mawson, 41.

[13] Mawson, 41.

[14] Moreland and Craig, *Philosophical Foundations*, 533.

[15] Alvin Plantinga defines libertarian freedom as follows: "If a person *S* is free with respect to a given action, then he is free to perform that action and free to refrain; no causal laws and antecedent conditions determine either that he will perform the action, or that he will not." See *The Nature of Necessity* (New York: Oxford University Press, 1982), 165–66.

strong sense, means that *A* causally determines *S*'s obtaining. But the weaker sense of actualization suggests that rather than causally determining some state of affairs, God brings about the circumstances whereby a person freely performs or refrains from performing some action. This means, as it relates to omnipotence, that God cannot actualize just any state of affairs possible, without thereby also taking into account libertarian freedom.

Whichever way one goes, whether by following the Mawson or the Moreland and Craig model of omnipotence, it seems that the theist can escape the stone paradox and preserve God's maximal power. Let's now turn to divine omniscience.

Divine Omniscience

As Thomas Morris reminds us, knowledge is power.[16] And as with our discussion on divine power, the doctrine of divine knowledge carries with it a variety of perplexities, and, yet it is deeply connected to God's omnipotence. Christians take God's knowledge to be maximally great and infallible and have classically considered him to be "omniscient" or "all-knowing." But where they disagree is with respect to the extent of God's knowledge and whether God has exhaustive knowledge of the future. In what follows, we'll tackle both issues.

So what does Scripture say about God's knowledge? Quite a bit! In Rom 11:33–36 the apostle Paul reminds us that God's knowledge is not like ours, making a clear distinction between the Creator and the creature. There's a depth to God's knowledge that surpasses anything we finite humans can know. Furthermore, this description of God's knowledge reminds us of God's aseity, in that no one counsels God (cf. Job 12:13; 21:22; Isa 40:14), nor does God need our gifts or to be repaid, since he is himself the source and telos of all things. Furthermore, Job 37:16 describes God as being "perfect in knowledge" (ESV), and 1 John 3:20 tells us that he "knows everything"

---

[16] Morris, *Our Idea of God*, 83.

(ESV). The psalmist declares that God's "understanding is beyond measure" (Ps 147:4–5 ESV). Scripture also tells us that God has knowledge of the created order and that he used his knowledge in the creation of the heavens and the earth (Pss 136:5; 147:4–5; Jer 51:15). Moreover, God demonstrates his knowledge and providential concern even for the animals (Ps 50:11; Matt 10:29).

In relation to human beings, God knows all the peoples of the earth (Ps 33:13–15) and specific things about them (Job 14:16; 2 Kgs 19:27; Isa 37:28; Matt 10:30). God knows our innermost thoughts and the secrets of our hearts (1 Kgs 8:39; 1 Chron 28:9; Ps 44:21; Prov 24:12; Jer 20:12; Ezek 11:5; Mark 2:8; Luke 5:22; 16:15; Acts 15:8). God knows our needs before we ask (Matt 6:8) and he knows our righteous and evil deeds (Gen 3:22; 20:6; 2 Chron 16:9; Job 23:10; Prov 15:3, 11; Jer 29:23; Hos 5:3; Amos 5:12; Matt 25:31–40; 2 Cor 5:10). God also sees the afflictions of people and hears their cries and suffering (Gen 16:13; 18:2–21; Exod 3:7).

Perhaps, one of the more contentious problems surrounding God's knowledge centers on whether he knows the future, and if so, to what extent. After all, Scripture is replete with examples of what seems to be God's knowledge of the future. Take, for example, the following passages from Isaiah:

> "Submit your case," says the LORD. "Present your arguments," says Jacob's King. "Let them come and tell us what will happen. Tell us the past events, so that we may reflect on them and know the outcome, or tell us the future. Tell us the coming events, then we will know that you are gods. Indeed, do something good or bad, then we will be in awe when we see it. Look, you are nothing and your work is worthless. Anyone who chooses you is detestable." (Isa. 41:21–24; Cf. Isa 46:9–10)

In this passages God lays down the gauntlet. It is his ability to know the end from the beginning that sets him apart from the gods of the nations. Beyond such seemingly clear passages, the Bible speaks of God knowing the future generally (Isa 44:6–8; Matt 24, 25; Acts 15:8), details Daniel's prediction of the specific rise of kingdoms and nations (Dan 2, 7, and 8) and the rise of Cyrus (Isa 44:26–45:7), and foretells specific events related to Christ's life, such as his coming (Mic 5:2) and crucifixion (Acts 2:23; 3:18). Moreover, in the Gospels we see that Christ foretold his own death and resurrection (Mark 8:31; 9:31; 10:32–34).[17] Finally, the whole sweep of biblical prophecy depends on God's knowledge of the future.[18]

Classically, Christians have defended the belief that God has maximal knowledge as it pertains to the past, present, and the future. Open and free theists (e.g., process, essential kenosis) agree that God knows perfectly the past and the present; however, they deny that God has exhaustive foreknowledge of the future. They base this on two reasons. First, they argue it's impossible for God to know the future and for human beings to have libertarian free will.[19] Second, they believe that certain passages in Scripture depict God as lacking knowledge of how particular events will turn out, or, at least, that God seems surprised by the actions of his creatures. For instance, Gen 6:6 depicts God as regretting or feeling sorry for having created humanity. Let's consider these in reverse order, beginning with those Scriptures that depict God as ignorant or lacking knowledge.

Suppose defenders of open theism are right about God's being surprised or disappointed in the outcomes of the future free actions of his creatures. But wouldn't such beliefs render God as having false beliefs? How so? It would seem that before some event, say, the flood, God would have held to certain beliefs about his creatures; surely they would not have descended into the types and kinds and degrees of evil they did. God

---

[17] Henry C. Theisen, *Lectures in Systematic Theology*, rev. Vernon D. Doerksen (Grand Rapids: Eerdmans, 2000), 47.

[18] William Lane Craig, *The Only Wise God: The Compatibility of Divine Foreknowledge and Human Freedom* (Eugene, OR: Wipf and Stock, 1999), 27.

[19] Pinnock, "Systematic Theology," in *The Openness of God* (Downers Grove: IVP, 1994)," 121; William Hasker, "A Philosophical Perspective," in *The Openness of God: A Biblical Challenge to the Traditional Understanding of God* (Downers Grove: IVP, 1994), 147.

would have had certain expectations of his creatures; however, as Stephen Davis points out, when those expectations were not met, it would seem that God held to false beliefs.[20] If surprise and disappointment are true representations of God's mental states, it's hard to see how one can plausibly believe that God experienced such mental states and failed to have false beliefs.

But what of the first open theist objection that it's impossible for God to know the future? Just as there are limitations to divine power, open theists believe there are limitations to God's omniscience. God cannot know something that's logically impossible for him to know, and this is certainly true when it comes to those truths related to temporal indexicals. Consider the following proposition: "Jones mowed his lawn on Saturday." God knows that Jones mowed his lawn on Saturday *if and only if* Jones performed the action of mowing his lawn on Saturday. Moreover, God knows that this took place a week earlier. However, God could not have known this truth before the event of Jones mowing his lawn? Why not? Because there is nothing there yet for God to know. The future had not yet happened. Jones had not yet mowed the lawn. If humans have libertarian freedom, as open theists maintain, then performing or refraining from some action depends solely on the individual's choosing, and it is in no way coerced or caused by something internally (e.g., biology) or externally (God, other agents, etc.). But how could God have known what Jones would do without God bringing about the event or causing it? In such a case, there would be no free will.

But perhaps the open theist's argument is too hasty. First off, such an argument depends on a certain belief about God's temporal mode of existence and his relationship to time, namely, that God is temporal. Those who hold to God as timeless would say: "Of course God couldn't know

---

[20] Stephen T. Davis, "Three Views of God, Which Is Correct?" in *Disputed Issues: Contending for Christian Faith in Today's Academic Setting* (Waco, TX: Baylor University Press, 2009), 216.

that Jones will mow his lawn tomorrow, since certain indexicals such as 'now,' 'tomorrow,' and 'fifty years from now' don't apply to God's knowledge." God could know such truths tenselessly and without having to discover them. For example, God knows that on March 21, 2035, Jones mows the lawn. He knows the truth of Jones's mowing the lawn, but he doesn't know it in a temporal manner. He knows it innately and not through any perception (we shall return to this below). Now, the issue of God's timelessness brings with it a myriad of problems, which we saw in the previous chapter, and we're not convinced that affirming God's timelessness really solves the issue, since divine timelessness itself raises a further limitation to divine omniscience, namely, that God is incapable of knowing temporal indexicals.

Ultimately, the open theist's argument boils down to something like the argument from fatalism, which goes as follows:

1.   Necessarily, if God foreknows *x*, then *x* will happen.
2.   God foreknows *x*.
3.   Therefore, *x* will necessarily happen.[21]

But as William Lane Craig has noted, (3) does not logically follow from (1) and (2). It's "fallacious to infer that *x* will *necessarily* happen it just *will* happen," says Craig.[22] So (3) should be stated as follows:

3.   Therefore, *x* will happen.

Based on God's foreknowledge, we can be sure that some event *will* happen, but God's foreknowledge doesn't require that it *must* happen. But what if *x* fails to obtain? According to Craig, this isn't a problem. God would have foreknown differently, namely that *x* fails to obtain. In other words, God's

---

[21] Craig, *The Only Wise God*, 72; "The Middle Knowledge View," in *Divine Foreknowledge: Four Views*, ed. James K. Beilby and Paul R. Eddy (Downers Grove: IVP, 2001, 126.

[22] Craig, 73.

knowing that such and such will take place does not mean that God caused such and such. There's a difference between what "will" happen and what "must" happen.

But there remains the problem of God's knowledge of the future free actions of his creatures. Assuming that the future is not fixed or determined, and humans have libertarian freedom, how could God know what will happen in the future, particularly with respect to the counterfactuals of creaturely freedom?

One possible solution, as alluded to, is that God has innate knowledge. Attacks against the belief in God's foreknowledge often rest on a perceptual model, which suggests that God comes by way of genuine knowledge based either on an immediate perception or by way of causal inference.[23] But why think that? The theist is in no way obligated to such a view. She might instead prefer a conceptual model, as Craig suggests:

> A conceptualist model can come in different forms. One could maintain that God's knowledge of future-tense statements is simply innate and logically foundational. Or one could maintain that God's knowledge of future-tense statements is based on logically prior statements which he knows and which enable him to know the truth of future-tense statements. This latter form of the conceptualist model has a name of its own: middle knowledge.[24]

Given something like a conceptual model, God neither learns nor acquires knowledge; rather, the storehouse of God's knowledge of all true statements is eternal.[25] The open theist and other objectors might ask, "How is it that God can know these truths conceptually or innately?" In response, defenders of the conceptual model might suggest that such questions are on par with asking how God created the world *ex nihilo*. We need not know *how*

---

[23] Craig, 122.
[24] Craig, 122.
[25] Craig, 123.

God created the world *ex nihilo* to know *that* God created the world in such a fashion. In the same way, just because we can't explain *how* God has innate knowledge, that doesn't mean God can't have such knowledge.

Craig believes that a mere conceptual model is enough to stave off the objections raised by open theists; however, he thinks an even stronger case for the conceptualist model can be made by opting for divine middle knowledge—a term coined by the Jesuit priest Luis de Molina during the counter-Reformation.

Middle knowledge, or "Molinism" as it is often called, suggests that there exist three logical, but not temporal, moments to God's knowledge. The first moment is what Molina called "natural knowledge." Natural knowledge refers to God's knowledge of all logical possibilities, including the content of all possible worlds.[26] The third moment to God's knowledge is God's "free knowledge." This refers to God's knowledge of the world that has obtained—the actual world. So far, so good. No one denies God's natural and free knowledge. In between God's natural knowledge and God's free knowledge is God's middle knowledge, which, as Craig suggests, refers to "God's knowledge of what every possible free creature would do under any possible set of circumstances and, hence, knowledge of those possible worlds which God can make actual."[27] God's decision to create the world is grounded in divine middle knowledge and, according to Craig, is an "eternal decision." It is this second moment, God's middle knowledge, that is contentious.

Molinists use two key passages to support middle knowledge. They claim each passage demonstrates God's knowledge of counterfactuals of creaturely freedom. In both cases, God knows that things would have

---

[26] A possible world refers to the sum total, complete, or maximal collection of states of affairs. The actual world (the world in which we inhabit) is just one of many possible worlds but with the distinction that it has obtained. See Alvin Plantinga, *The Nature of Necessity* (Oxford: Oxford University Press, 1982), 45.

[27] Craig, *The Only Wise God*, 131.

turned out differently had the circumstances been different or if humans had so chosen differently than they did. In 1 Sam 23:9–13, if David had stayed in Keilah, God knew that the people would have turned him over to Saul. In Matt 11:20–24, Jesus knew that if the miracles he had performed had been performed in other cities, then the people in those cities would have repented.

But of course, not everyone is on board with middle knowledge, and like many theological issues, it is quite controversial. Perhaps, the strongest objection against middle knowledge is known as the "grounding objection." The grounding objection suggests that counterfactuals of creaturely freedom are false or have no truth value at all. Why is that? According to the objector, there is nothing in reality on which such counterfactuals statements correspond. But such thinking is confused. All that's required for grounding future-tense or counterfactual statements is that such statements either will exist (as in the case of future-tense statements) or that they would exist if such-and-such circumstances were to come about (as in the case of counterfactual statements).[28]

Some defenders of open theism persist in their belief that future-tense statements have no truth value. In so doing they deny the principle of bivalence, which affirms that for any proposition p, p is either true or false.[29] Such a denial, however, leads to several absurdities, as Craig has shown.[30]

In the end, it seems that the burden of proof is on defenders of open theism to show why God cannot know both future-tense statements about what free creatures will do and counterfactuals of creaturely freedom. Whether one takes a mere conceptualist view or the middle knowledge view, the Christian theist is on good grounds for thinking that God knows the future.

---

[28] Craig, 140.

[29] Craig, "A Middle Knowledge Response," in *Divine Foreknowledge: Four Views*, ed. James K. Beilby and Paul R. Eddy (Downers Grove: IVP, 2001), 56.

[30] Craig, 59–60.

Omnibenevolence

As with God's power and knowledge, the Bible tells us quite a bit about God's goodness. Scripture speaks of God's goodness in general ways, as expressed in the Psalms:

> Taste and see that the LORD is good! How happy is the person who takes refuge in him! (Ps 34:8)

> The LORD is good and upright; therefore he shows sinners the way. (Ps 25:8)

The Hebrew word *ḥĕ'·sĕḏ*, which carries the idea of "goodness," is often translated as "steadfast," "faithful," or "unfailing" love when used in reference to God's interactions with his people (cf. Exod 34:6, Pss 33:5; 52:1).

In the New Testament, Jesus proclaims to the rich young ruler that there is no one good except God (Matt 19:16–17; cf. Mark 10:17–18; Luke 18:18–19). James 1:17 tells us that "every good and perfect gift is from above, coming down from the Father of lights, who does not change like shifting shadows."

Scripture often speaks to God's general care and concern for his creatures. Consider Paul's words in Acts 14:17: "Although he did not leave himself without witness, since he did what is good by giving you rain from heaven and fruitful seasons and filling you with food and your hearts with joy." Jesus says something similar, highlighting God's general care and concern for both the righteous and the unrighteous alike (Matt 5:45). In Luke 6:35, Jesus instructs us to love our enemies, since God is himself "gracious to the ungrateful and evil." In Matt 6:28–30, Jesus reminds his hearers to not be anxious, since just as God cares for the lilies of the field, he will also provide for our needs.[31]

---

[31] John S. Feinberg, *No One Like Him: The Doctrine of God* (Wheaton: Crossway, 2001), 365–67.

Theologian Millard Erickson links three other categories of attributes to God's goodness: moral purity, integrity, and love.[32] God's moral
purity includes not only holiness but also divine righteousness and justice (Deut 7:9; Ps 19:7–9; Ezra 9:15; Neh 9:33; Isa 45:21; Jer 9:24).
On the one hand, divine holiness refers to God's unique, transcendent
otherness. Consider the words from Exod 15:11, "LORD, who is like
you among the gods? Who is like you, glorious in holiness, revered with
praises, performing wonders?" Other passages speak of God's exalted
and lofty nature (1 Sam 2:2; Isa 6:1–4; 57:15). Holiness also refers to
God's moral purity (Hab 1:13; Jas 1:13), as 1 John 1:5 tells us, "God is
light, and in him is no darkness at all" (ESV). God's holiness and moral
goodness becomes the grounds for "moral character" and "religious practice" (Lev 11:44–45). Concerning God's integrity, Scripture emphasizes
his genuineness (Jer 10:6–10; John 17:3), veracity (1 Sam 15:29; Titus
1:2), and faithfulness (Num 23:19; 1 Cor 1:9; 2 Cor 1:18–22; 1 Thess
5:24). Finally, regarding God's love, Scripture outlines God's benevolence (Matt 6:25–26, 28, 30–33; 10:30–31; Acts 14:17), grace (Exod
34:6; Eph 1:4–8; 2:6–9; Titus 2:11), and mercy (Deut 5:10; Pss 57:10;
86:5; 103:13).[33]

There are at least two senses by which we can understand God's goodness, namely, that God is "wholly good," and that God is "necessarily good."
God's being wholly good means that God is without defect or blemish in his
being or actions. God as necessarily good refers to something much stronger. Not only is God without defect or blemish in his being and actions,
but, God's being necessarily good means that, as Thomas Morris puts it,
"God is so firmly entrenched in goodness, or alternatively, that goodness
is so entrenched in God, that it is strictly impossible for there to be in him

---

[32] Erickson, *Christian Theology*, 256–67.

[33] Erickson, 256–67; Henry Clarence Thiessen, *Lectures in Systematic Theology*,
rev. Vernon D. Doerksen (Grand Rapids: Eerdmans, 2000), 85.

any sort of flaw or defect."[34] Or to put it another way, to claim that God is necessarily good means that "he is utterly invulnerable to evil."[35]

Some have questioned God's goodness based on the problem of evil or due to certain passages that seem to implicate God of doing evil actions. We will not consider those issues here since we will examine the problem of evil more specifically in a later chapter. For now, we will center our focus on God's necessary goodness.

Some Christians have raised concerns about God being necessarily good by leveling two arguments against it. The first kind of argument centers on whether God could be impeccable with respect to his moral character and yet be genuinely free. This is known as the "problem of moral freedom."[36] Another closely associated argument is known as the "problem of praiseworthiness."[37] We shall consider these two arguments in reverse, beginning with the praiseworthiness objection, followed by the argument of moral freedom.

Morris lays out the argument from praiseworthiness as follows:

1. A person is praiseworthy for an action only if he could have refrained from performing it.
2. A necessarily good being cannot refrain from performing good actions.

   So

3. A necessarily good being is not praiseworthy for any of his good actions.

   If

4. God is necessarily good,

   then

---

[34] Morris, *Our Idea of God*, 48.
[35] Morris, 48.
[36] Morris, 59.
[37] Morris, 56.

5. God is not praiseworthy for any of his good actions.

   But surely

6. God is praiseworthy for his good actions.

   So

7. It is not the case that God is necessarily good.[38]

That God is praiseworthy cannot be compromised (Ps 48:1), so how might the Christian move forward? The central premises under question are (1) and (2).

Premise (1) suggests that one requirement for praiseworthiness is for God to have freedom. However, if God cannot but act in a moral manner, and was therefore forced to perform such an action, then it is doubtful whether God has freedom, and hence he would not be praiseworthy. But Morris is doubtful that (1) is successful in capturing what freedom involves. On this Morris claims, "For an agent is praiseworthy for a good act he performs just in case (a) he intended to perform it, and (b) no causal conditions independent of his own character and decisions alone forced the action upon him, or rendered him such that he was unable to avoid it."[39] In other words, for an agent to act, he must be free from any outside compulsion. But why think that God was in some way compelled to perform the action by something external, that is, by something outside of his character or decision? As Morris explains, "If the necessity of his action in this situation just arises out of that feature of his character, we have no reason to think of it as having been forced on him by causal conditions independent of his character and decision."[40] If God performs the action intentionally, and if there is nothing externally causing or compelling him to perform the action, then it's hard to see how he was not responsible for the action, and thus praiseworthy for it.

---

[38] Morris, 56.

[39] Morris, 57.

[40] Morris, 57.

But (2) is just as problematic as (1). As stated, (2) is ambiguous and can be parsed out as follows:

(2′) A necessarily good being cannot refrain from ever performing any good action whatsoever.

And

(2″) A necessarily good being cannot refrain from performing any of the good actions he performs.[41]

(2′) doesn't produce the kind of conclusion the argument is going after. So (2″) is needed. However, says Morris, (2″) expresses a false proposition, resulting in an unsound argument. Why is that? While it is the case that a "necessarily good being cannot perform any evil actions," it doesn't mean that a necessarily good being must perform any or every good action. A necessarily good being may have the option to perform or refrain from a myriad of good actions, which are not required of him. Such actions are called supererogatory because, though they are good for God to perform, they are in no way obligatory.[42]

But what about the argument from moral freedom? Morris states the problem as follows: "Being a moral agent, a person capable of and engaging in morally assessable conduct, requires having a certain sort of freedom with respect to one's actions. A being who is not free in the requisite sense does not perform actions which are morally characterizable at all, as either morally good or morally bad."[43] Such objections rest on taking God's freedom too closely aligned to something like human libertarian freedom, by which the objector means that God has such genuine freedom to either perform or refrain from performing some morally significant action. God's being necessarily good means that God could have no other alternative than to perform

---

[41] Morris, 58.
[42] Morris, 58.
[43] Morris, 59.

some right action. If that's the case, then God would lack morally significant freedom. Thus, if God is not morally free, then neither is he a moral agent. Such a being, then, would not have moral goodness, if he has goodness at all. So much, then, for necessary goodness.[44]

But Morris believes that such an abandonment of necessary goodness is too hasty. After all, such a view rests on the belief that God has duties like you and I have duties. To flesh this out, Morris gives the example of God leading Moses out of Egypt. God promises Moses help and therefore he trusts God when the time comes to confront Pharaoh. But is God free to assist or refrain from assisting Moses? Must God keep his promise, or is he free to break it? If God is necessarily good, then it's impossible for God to break such a promise. Wouldn't this imply that God really doesn't have freedom and that God cannot but help Moses?

How, then, should the defender of God's necessary goodness respond? Morris believes that even if a person denies that God has moral duties, that doesn't mean such an objection nullifies the duty model of divine goodness. Why is that? God doesn't share the same ontological status as human beings, namely, being bound by moral principles and duties. That doesn't mean God can't act in accordance with such principles and duties in such relevant circumstances. As Morris explains, "He does so necessarily."[45] So, while it is the case that if God makes a promise to Moses he cannot break, the question we must ask is why God even made such a promise in the first place? Perhaps, such promises are a result of God's grace or mercy. God could have refrained from bringing about such a good. Yet, it is within supererogation, Morris believes, God exercises his freedom between alternatives, and thus can be said to act morally.

Morris believes that he has preserved God's being a morally necessary being, even if that means God does not have moral duties. Such a model, however, does not mean that God cannot act in morally significant ways,

---

[44] Morris, 59.
[45] Morris, 61.

nor does that mean that God cannot act out of benevolence. God's actions, however, are ultimately supererogatory in nature and significantly out of his grace and, hence, free.

Models of God and Divine Action

In chapter 2 we gave an overview of four models of God: classical theism, modified/neo-classical theism, open theism, and essential kenotic theism. In chapter 4, we concluded that the God presented in Scripture is not the God of eternalism, a God who is timelessly eternal, immutable, impassible, and simple, as those perfections are often defined by classical theists. We found that there is good reason to take God to be temporal (at least in some sense), immutable with respect to God's nature and character, and simple in the sense that God is not a composite being. We take it that God is really related to his creatures and that any suffering that God partakes in is of his own volition. Furthermore, in chapter 3 we argued that God is a necessary being, who is *a se*, incorporeal, and the creator of all things. God created the world *ex nihilo*, that is, apart from any preexisting materials. Moreover, we argued against the idea that God created by divine necessity. The world that God created was out of divine freedom. God could have freely refrained from creating the world. Because we hold to divine freedom, we must affirm that God has accidental properties, such as being the creator of the world or Lord of Israel, thus rejecting the Aristotelian notion of God as *actus purus*. Though we resonate with much that is found within classical theism, we find that classical theism, especially those forms of it that hold to eternalism, makes for an inadequate model of God.

In this chapter, we argued for a God who is maximally great with respect to his power, knowledge, and goodness. We have examined specific ways in which God acts in the world through his divine providence, both with respect to his divine power and divine knowledge. Regarding divine knowledge, we argued for a God who not only knows the past and present perfectly, but who also has exhaustive knowledge of the future, whether one takes a conceptualist view of divine knowledge or something like divine middle knowledge. We also sought to defend God's goodness, arguing for God's impeccability and God as a morally necessary being.

Where, then, does this leave us? It would seem that both open theism and essential kenotic theism are ruled out. First, concerning open theism there are some tenets within this model with which we can agree. We agree that God created the world *ex nihilo* and that God was free to refrain from creating a world. Moreover, we concur that God is providentially active in the world, though God at times limits divine action in relation to free creatures. Yet, based on our understanding in this chapter, we find any model that denies God's knowledge of the future difficult to maintain. Though open theists affirm that God is sovereignly active in the world, we believe that such a model severely limits God's sovereignty, especially in light of the problem of evil. We can see how defenders of open theism may think that God's ignorance of the future would have the upper hand as a theodicy. After all, if God has created creatures with libertarian freedom (whether angels or humans), and if God does not know what will take place in the future, then he would not be responsible for the choices he did not know they would make. But this also sheds light on one of the significant weaknesses of the open theist view. God took a great risk in creating a world such as ours, since there was no guarantee that even one person would have accepted his offer of salvation. In contrast, the Bible is clear that God does know who will be saved in the end, and he knew this before the foundation of the world (Rev 13:8).

But what about essential kenosis theism? We find this view significantly more problematic than either classical theism or open theism. As with open theism, the essential kenosis view denies God's knowledge of the future. This we take to be problematic, for the reasons already expressed.

But beyond this, Thomas J. Oord's essential kenosis view denies the doctrine of creation *ex nihilo*, which stands in stark contrast to tradition and Scripture.[46] Rejection of creation *ex nihilo* goes against other deeply held doctrines such as divine aseity. Why is that? According to Oord's own view, God is essentially loving—it is the chief among God's attributes. God's love directs God's power, yet it also limits what God can do. Since God is essentially loving, there must be some other for God to love. Hence God has always been creating. But if there must be some other for God to love, then God is not, nor could God ever be, independent of creation. But as we have argued in chapter 3, there is good reason to take God as *a se*. Moreover, the doctrine of the Trinity provides the necessary resources to maintain God's absolute freedom as touched on in chapter 1.

Finally, the essential kenosis view severely limits God's providence. At the heart of essential kenosis is self-limitation, which Oord believes "makes it possible to solve the problem of evil."[47] Because God must give freedom to creatures, and because God cannot override the gift of freedom that's been given to them, then we shouldn't blame God for those instances when creatures misuse their freedom. "An uncontrolling God is not culpable when creatures oppose what this loving God desires"; instead, says Oord, the blame is entirely with the creature.[48]

But we cannot help but wonder what kind of eschatological payoff such a view holds. Certainly, on Oord's view, God cooperates with his creatures, encouraging them to do the right thing. Yet can we have any confidence that there will be ultimate justice for the world? Will God ever put the world's wrongs to rights? Given Oord's model, it is difficult to see how God could do this.

---

[46] Thomas Jay Oord, *The Uncontrolling Love of God: An Open and Relational Account of Providence* (Downers Grove: IVP, 2015), 169; Thomas Jay Oord, "God Always Creates out of Creation in Love: *Creatio ex Creatione a Natura Amoris*," in *Theologies of Creation: Creatio ex Nihilo and Its New Rivals*, ed. Thomas Jay Oord (New York: Routledge, 2014), 109–22.

[47] Oord, *Uncontrolling Love of God*, 169.

[48] Oord, 171.

Beyond evil, miracles present a problem under Oord's model. He takes it that even in miracles, God does not unilaterally override creaturely freedom. God cooperates with creatures to bring about an intended outcome.

We agree that God often cooperates with individuals when performing a miracle. We can also agree that miracles often involve "creaturely contribution."[49] We also agree that we should avoid language that speaks of a violation of nature. Yet, fundamentally, it's not clear to us that such miracles always involve creaturely cooperation, particularly in miracles that involve demonic possession or nature miracles. Regarding demonic possession, often the person is not in her right mind and cannot freely cooperate. Those around her may cooperate, but it's not at all clear that the individual herself will cooperate. Moreover, though the demons cooperate, they cooperate not because they are willing, but because they know either who (e.g., Jesus) is casting them or by what authority they are being cast out. Cooperation is out of fear because they understand the power that stands behind their being cast out.

Regarding natural miracles, Oord holds to a form of panpsychism (or panexperientialism), the belief that the basic constituents of reality have some kind of mental element or experience to them. Those entities that are true individuals (e.g., animals, trees, etc.) also cooperate with God, in some sense. There are difficulties with the essential kenosis view on this point. First, panpsychism is deeply controversial. Though panpsychism is a rising view among Western thinkers who want to avoid either naturalistic reductionism or some form of dualism, it runs up against the combination problem, which questions how these primitives or atomic simples combine to form a unified field of consciousness.[50]

Beyond the combination problem, again, it is not clear that individuals (as Oord means them here) always cooperate with God. Consider again

---

[49] Oord, 202.

[50] J. P. Moreland, *Consciousness and the Existence of God: A Theistic Argument* (New York: Routledge, 2008), 128.

the idea of demon exorcism. In the case of the Gadarene demoniac, Jesus cast the legion of demons into a herd of swine (Matt 8:28–34). How, in this case, were the swine cooperative? Moreover, according to the book of Revelation, God will raise all people, some to eternal life and some to eternal destruction. It's hard to think that those raised for eternal destruction are raised in cooperation with God. While we're not inclined to speak of the final resurrection as a miracle (based on our understanding of miracle), we do believe it is a display of God's might and strength and, to a large extent, a unilateral action of God, particularly in the case of the raising and judging of unbelievers (Rev 20). Ultimately, we find such a view as divine kenosis is riddled with difficulties and bucks against, not only much of Christian tradition, but also what we find to be true of God's nature and work in Scripture.

At the end of the day, we find ourselves landing in the modified classical theism camp. We recognize that this camp is widely cast, including a diversity of soteriological and theological viewpoints. Nevertheless, we believe that this view on God, as argued thus far, is faithful to Scripture and the deliverances of reason.

PART 3

6

Trinity, Human Freedom, and Ethics

Trinity and Perichoresis

Since the Enlightenment, the doctrine of the Trinity has fallen on hard times. But in recent years, there has been a renewed interest in the doctrine by both philosophers and theologians. Perhaps, part of the reason for a renewed interest in the doctrine of the Trinity has to do with postmodernity's interest in "the relatedness of all things"[1] and emphasis on community.

For Karl Barth the Trinity is no mere "footnote" to Christian theology—it is at its heart and center.[2] God has most fully revealed himself through the person and work of Jesus of Nazareth, the second person of the triune God. It is the doctrine of the Trinity that sets Christianity apart from various other monotheistic religions, in that God is a plurality of persons.

---

[1] John S. Feinberg, *No One Like Him: The Doctrine of God* (Wheaton: Crossway, 2001), 439.
[2] Karl Barth, quoted in Feinberg, *No One Like Him*, 439.

According to J. P. Moreland and William Lane Craig, "God is a triad of persons in eternal, self-giving love relationships."[3] Similarly, Stanley Grenz argues that "the essence of God is love," and that love best characterizes the eternal divine life itself.[4] If that's the case, we find within the Trinity the deepest loving relationship in all of reality—the perichoretic relationship between the Father, Son, and Holy Spirit. But what is meant by perichoresis?

Gregory of Nazianzus coined the term in connection to Christology.[5] John of Damascus later employed it to describe "the mutual indwelling" or "mutual interpenetration" between the Father, Son, and Spirit.[6] According to Verna Harrison, perichoresis was an important theological concept expressing "the conjunction of unity and distinction, stability and dynamism, symmetry and asymmetry," illuminating three key areas: the Trinity, the incarnation, and life in the kingdom.[7]

Karl Barth describes perichoresis as "a definite" or "complete participation of each mode of being in the other modes of being."[8] As a corrective measure, Barth used "mode" instead of "person," due to the modern understanding of a person as an autonomous, isolated self.[9] In his view on the Trinity, he emphasized "fellowship" and "complete participation" among each of the "persons."[10]

---

[3] J. P. Moreland and William Lane Craig, *Philosophical Foundations for a Christian Worldview* (Downers Grove: IVP, 2003), 595.

[4] Stanley J. Grenz, *Theology for the Community of God* (Grand Rapids: Eerdmans, 1994), 71.

[5] Verna Harrison, "Perichoresis in the Greek Fathers," *St Vladimir's Theological Quarterly* 35, no. 1 (1991): 55.

[6] S. M. Smith, "Perichoresis," *Evangelical Dictionary of Theology*, 2nd ed., ed. Walter A. Elwell (Grand Rapids: Baker Academic, 2001), 906–7.

[7] Harrison, "Perichoresis in the Greek Fathers," 63–65.

[8] Karl Barth, *Church Dogmatics*, vol. I.1 *The Doctrine of the Word of God*, ed. G. W. Bromiley and T. F. Torrance, 1st paperback ed. (New York: T&T Clark International, 2004), 370.

[9] Barth, 370.

[10] Barth, 370.

Daniel L. Migliore describes the inner life of the triune God as "an activity of mutual self-giving, a community of sharing, a 'society of love' (Augustine)."[11] Migliore believes that it is God's inner relationship of love which provides the basis for God's "history of love for the world narrated in Scriptures."[12] He suggests that we ought not speculate, then, how God is in eternity, and then seek to understand how God relates and interacts with his creatures, but we must, rather, see how God has revealed himself to us from the "history of revelation and salvation attested by Scripture, and experienced by Christians from the beginning of the church."[13] He continues by asserting, "The logic of trinitarian theology moves from differentiated love of Father, Son, and Holy Spirit in the economy of salvation (the economic Trinity) to the ultimate ground of this threefold love in the depths of the divine being (the immanent Trinity)."[14] In other words, we come to understand how God is in the ontological Trinity through reflection on how God has revealed himself to us through salvation history.[15] What we see taking place in the economic Trinity is a unified plan and outworking of the persons of the Trinity. All that the Son does is for the Father. All that the Father does is for the Son. All that the Spirit does is for the Father and the Son.[16]

---

[11] Daniel L. Migliore, *Faith Seeking Understanding: An Introduction to Christian Theology* (Grand Rapids: Eerdmans, 1991), 61.

[12] Migliore, 61.

[13] Migliore, 61.

[14] Migliore, 62. We think Migliore's basic approach is right. We all come to Scripture with our concepts of God, whether we recognize them or not. Our ideas, thoughts, and concepts affect how we interpret Scripture. Yet it should not be left at that. Our reflection on Scripture should influence our concept of God, just as much as our reflection on the nature of God influences our Scripture reading. See our discussion in chapter 2.

[15] One may, happily, take the first part of Rahner's rule, that is, that the economic Trinity is the ontological Trinity. However, we must be careful, since the reverse is not true. To suggest that the ontological Trinity is the economic Trinity would lead to panentheism, since the economic Trinity, to some extent or another, would require the existence of the world. Such an understanding goes against orthodoxy.

[16] For a detailed discussion and biblical analysis on idea of "divine giving," see J. Scott Horrell, "Toward a Biblical Model of the Social Trinity: Avoiding

In our estimation, central to the doctrine of perichoresis is the dynamic love relationship among the divine Persons. Not only do the Persons share a common substance and nature, but the divine Persons are one through self-giving love toward the other—the deepest love possible—whereby the Father, Son, and Spirit eternally give of themselves toward the Others in interpenetrating love. Each Person is fully opened up toward the Other in complete and utter transparency.

Perichoresis, however, is not merely a theological concept, but one deeply grounded in the language of Scripture. The Gospel of John gives us a glimpse of the internal relationship of God, when it tells us that the "Word was *with* God" (John 1:1). Elsewhere, Jesus speaks of being "in the Father" and the Father being in him (John 10:38).[17] Jesus also tells Philip, "Anyone who has seen me has seen the Father. . . . Don't you believe that I am in the Father, and that the Father is in me? . . . Believe me when I say that I am in the Father and the Father is in me" (John 14:7–11). The Father's presence in Jesus is such that Jesus can declare to his disciples that seeing him is the same as seeing the Father.[18]

By examining the doctrine of perichoresis, it becomes clear why John says, "God is love" (1 John 4:8). "God is love" is an ontological claim about the inner life of God—a life of mutual indwelling and interpenetration between the persons of the Trinity. On perichoresis, Stephen Davis writes that "the core of God's inner being is the highest degree of self-giving love. The Persons are fully open to each other, their actions *ad extra* are actions in common, they 'see with each other's eyes', the boundaries between them are transparent to each other, and each ontologically

---

Equivocation of Nature and Order," *Journal of the Evangelical Theological Society* 47, no. 3 (September 2004): 410–11.

[17] Cf. John 14:20; 17:11, 21–23.

[18] Horrell, "Toward a Biblical Model of the Social Trinity," 407. For a further discussion, see Ronnie P. Campbell, *Worldviews and the Problem of Evil: A Comparative Approach* (Bellingham, WA: Lexham Press, 2019), 183–86.

embraces the other."[19] At the core of all of existence is a dynamic "loving relationship among persons."[20]

Reflection on the doctrine of perichoresis sheds light on the metaphysical ground for Christian ethics. To see this, it will be necessary to take into consideration several important Christian teachings, particularly the *imago Dei*, human worth and freedom, sin, incarnation, redemption, and communion.

Foundation for Christian Ethics

Imago Dei *and Human Worth*

According to Christian theology, humans were made in the image and likeness of God (Gen 1:26–27). It is the *imago Dei* which sets humans apart from all other creatures. Theologians do not agree as to what the *imago Dei* includes, but they nevertheless recognize its importance. Passages such as Psalm 8 indicate the greatness of human creatures in that humans were made "a little lower than the heavenly beings." These creatures are such that God is "mindful" of them. In comparing humans with animals, Jesus says, "Are you not much more valuable than they?" (Matt 6:26 NIV).

Many Christian moral philosophers and theologians believe human rights, value, and worth are grounded in the *imago Dei*. One such advocate of this approach is Robert Merrihew Adams. In *Finite and Infinite Goods*, Adams suggests that regardless of whether a person is a believer or not, he wants to recognize that humans have greater worth than animals do. Often, the reason for this comes by way of arguing that humans are more rational than other creatures. However, as Adams rightly suggests, such an answer falls short, since not all are on the same par rationally. He agrees with most moralists in that what distinguishes people morally, from, say,

---

[19] Stephen T. Davis, *Christian Philosophical Theology* (New York: Oxford University Press, 2006), 72.

[20] Stephen T. Davis, "God's Action," in *In Defense of Miracles*, ed. R. Douglas Geivett and Gary Habermas (Downers Grove: IVP, 1997), 176.

sheep, "Should be something that grounds an *equal* regard for persons as persons."[21] He finds his answer essentially in our having been made in God's image. Having the image of God itself is a kind of excellence. A person's value, then, is not found in that person sharing in some kind of generic humanity or in her individual contribution to the whole, but rather in value that is intrinsic to each individual person. On this point he comments:

> It is a value of persons, rather than of sums of value that they help to compose. It is, I think, a sort of excellence, and imaging of God. It is wonderful that you exist, because *you* are wonderful, in the way that parents rightly perceive their infant children as wonderful. And while this sort of value of persons can indeed be a good reason for wanting to procreate and raise a child, it is not a reason for wanting there to be more persons rather than fewer. It is primarily a reason for loving persons and, more imperatively, for respecting them, given that they exist.[22]

People are valuable because people are sacred. Sacred objects are the kinds of things that "we have reason to treat and not to treat in certain ways."[23]

Adams rejects the notion of "rank" among such human capacities or features—e.g., the ability to reason, having certain personality traits, etc.—as the sole feature of human excellencies as image bearers. He argues:

> [W]e may reasonably believe that human persons are globally more like God than sheep are, while resisting any attempt to rank individual persons on their global resemblance to God, since so many dimensions of comparison are relevant, and the resemblance is so distant, though still of the greatest importance. On the other hand, the very multidimensionality of this resemblance makes it a richer

---

[21] Robert Merrihew Adams, *Finite and Infinite Goods: A Framework for Ethics* (New York: Oxford University Press, 1999), 115.

[22] Adams, 120.

[23] Adams, 121.

and more significant resemblance to God than that of particular abilities, actions, and achievements—more significant too, for our imaging God, than the excellences that add to our happiness or well-being. This grounds a qualitative superiority of the excellence of persons as such, the excellence of persons as the sort of individual beings they are, over the much narrower excellences with regard to which we can clearly excel each other. Thus it grounds egalitarian application of the concept of the value, or sacredness, of persons as such.[24]

Adams's proposal seems to indicate that human value, or the sacredness of humanity because of humanity's having been made in the image and likeness of God, depends, to some extent or another, on the whole conglomerate of capacities found within human persons, or, at least, that humans in some respect deeply "resemble" God. Adams may have given us an option for considering a framework for human value.

Traditionally, theologians have distinguished between a *structural* and *functional* understanding of the *imago Dei*. They've often pitted one over the other. We take it that the *imago Dei* includes *both* structural and functional aspects, rather than having one over the other. Here we agree with Anthony A. Hoekema:

> One cannot function without a certain structure. An eagle, for example, propels itself through the air by flying—this is one of its functions. The eagle would be unable to fly, however, unless it had wings—one of its structures. Similarly, human beings were created to function in certain ways: to worship God, to love the neighbor, to rule over nature, and so on. But they cannot function in these ways unless they have been endowed by God with the structural capacities that enable them to do so. So structure and function are both involved when we think of man as the image of God.[25]

---

[24] Adams, 117–18.

[25] Anthony A. Hoekema, *Created in God's Image* (Grand Rapids: Eerdmans, 1994), 69.

By *structural* we have in mind something like the full range of capacities that enable humans to function properly, whether in performing various tasks ascribed by the Creator or by engaging others relationally, namely God, humans, and creation. These capacities—our rational, moral, and volitional powers, the ability to recognize beauty or to make aesthetically pleasing things, or the capability of carrying out certain intentions—image those of our Maker. While these capacities are limited, they nevertheless exemplify, in an analogous way, many of the same abilities of God himself. The *functional* aspect of the *imago Dei* refers to humanity's carrying out of God's original intentions in actions or relationships. The functional aspect of the *imago Dei*, says Hoekema, "means man's proper functioning in harmony with God's will for him."[26] In other words, humans were designed to *be* and *function* a certain way.

Loving God and Neighbor

When asked by a teacher of the law which of the commandments is the most important, Jesus responded by saying that the most important one is to love God with all that one has, and closely tied to it is the command to love one's neighbor as one's self (Matt 22:37; Mark 12:28–31; Luke 10:27). But as 1 John reminds us, one cannot properly claim to love God without also loving one's brother. If one hates one's brother, then one does not love God (1 John 4:20). If this is the case, then the reverse is true: if one truly loves God, then one will have love for one's brothers and sisters, and presumably, one's neighbors.

Love for God and for neighbor became a central theological motif for fourth-century theologian, Augustine. These commandments permeated all of Augustine's theology. For him, they served as an important interpretive principle for understanding Scripture. This is evident from the following passage:

---

[26] Hoekema, 72.

But I cherish a hope in the name of Christ, which is not without its reward, because I have not only believed the testimony of my God that "on these two commandments hang all the Law and the Prophets;" but I have myself proved it, and daily prove it, by experience. For there is no holy mystery, and no difficult passage of the word of God, in which, when it is opened up to me, I do not find these same commandments: for "the end of the commandment is charity, out of a pure heart, and of a good conscience, and of faith unfeigned;" and "love is the fulfillment of the law."[27]

For Augustine, the commandments to love God and neighbor should be at the forefront of one's thought. Again, regarding these two commandments, Augustine claims:

For they ought to be thoroughly familiar to you, and not merely to come into your mind when they are recited by us, but they ought never to be blotted out from your hearts. Let it ever be your supreme thought, that you must love God and your neighbor: God with all thy heart, and with all thy soul, and with all thy mind; and thy neighbor as thyself. These must always be pondered, meditated, retained, practiced, and fulfilled. The love of God comes first in the order of enjoying; but in the order of doing, the love of our neighbor comes first.[28]

The order is important, here, as Augustine notes. Love for God comes first with respect to the "order of enjoying"; whereas love for neighbor comes first with respect to the "order of doing." Augustine's first point seems to coincide with C. S. Lewis's emphasis on God's not having to receive anything from us, since God is complete in and of himself. He lacks nothing.[29]

---

[27] Augustine, *Letter LV*, 21.
[28] Augustine, *Homilies on the Gospel of John*, XVII.8.
[29] C. S. Lewis, *The Problem of Pain* (New York: HarperOne, 1996), 44–45.

Yet loving God is our enjoying him above all other things. With respect to doing, loving our neighbors is something that we are commanded to do.

Modern Western culture often associates love with feelings or an emotion, which C. S. Lewis took to be inadequate. Love is not found in the emotions but in "the state of the will."[30] Yet loving one's neighbor seems to be more than a matter of the will or a sheer benevolence, as the apostle Paul explains: "If I give all I possess to the poor and give over my body to hardship that I may boast, but do not have love, I gain nothing" (1 Cor 13:3 NIV). Our disposition toward the others is equally important, as Frances Howard-Snyder explains,

> The second great commandment is like the first. It is fair to assume that the love we owe our neighbor is of the same kind as the love we owe God. Our love for God ought to include an appreciation of him and a desire for union with him, in addition to a desire that his will be done. If our love for our neighbor is to be like the love we owe God, this suggests that the love we have for our neighbors should involve the same elements. Indeed, it makes sense that our love for other people should not be simply benevolence or sheer concern for their well-being, but should also involve desires to be related to them, and an appreciation of what is valuable in them, and enjoyment of them. For if one's attitude toward others was solely that of benevolence, it would seem that one wouldn't want anything they have to offer. Sheer benevolence looks like a kind of arrogance, an attitude of independence and inequality vis-á-vis our neighbors.[31]

"Love your neighbor as yourself" should serve as a blueprint for how we ought to respond to others. Though we find ourselves having greater

---

[30] C. S. Lewis, *Mere Christianity* (New York: HarperSanFrancisco, 1980), 129.

[31] Frances Howard-Snyder, "Christian Ethics," in *Reason for the Hope Within*, ed. Michael J. Murray (Grand Rapids: Eerdmans, 1999), 387–88.

love for those we have deep affection for or deem deserving of our love, self-love is not quite so temperamental. The object of our focus in self-love often shifts (e.g., moving from a state of being upset at our performance to a state of gladness by an accomplishment), yet our overall concern, no matter the state, remains targeted toward our own well-being, pointing toward the same ultimate desire.[32] Though, some may see it as vain or nihilistic to appreciate one's self, it's important to realize that the self's identity is found in relationship with God and with others.

The biblical view of love is unconditional. The parable of the Good Samaritan demonstrates this unconditional nature of love, whereby the Samaritan looks out for the good of the other, ultimately an enemy, and asks nothing in return (Luke 10:25–37). Unconditional love is an overall attitude and movement toward the other, not looking out for one's best interest. Instead, it looks out for the good and best for the other person, while also seeking union with the person, even if that means the other doesn't respond in the same manner.[33]

Sin and Human Freedom

According to Stephen T. Davis, "Human beings were created out of the dynamic relationship for the sake of that relationship."[34] If Davis is correct, human existence is grounded *in* and *for* relationship with God. God didn't need to create, since he is *a se* and complete through intra-trinitarian love. Yet, God created out of freedom to share life with something other than the Godhead.

Perhaps, what God desired to bring about in his creatures is something akin to what we see in the perichoretic relation of the divine persons, creatures who have the capacity for deep love—the same kind of deep love

---

[32] Howard-Snyder, 388.

[33] Howard-Snyder, 388.

[34] Davis, "God's Action," 177.

found within the Trinity. We don't mean the kind of love that is "self-seeking" or "boastful" (1 Cor 13:4–7), but one that is actively moving toward, seeking union with, and looking out for what's best and good for the other. Humans were created with the ability to relate with and love other persons on the deepest levels possible. It is this capacity for deep love and relationship that separates humans from other creatures. A Trinitarian grounding for relationship means that humans can be relational like God—a relationality with the capacity for sharing deep love toward others. More specifically, it's the capacity for reciprocating or abstaining from reciprocating love toward the other. As Marilyn Adams put it, "God made human beings to enter into nonmanipulative relationships of self-surrendering love with himself and relationships of self-giving love with others."[35]

Christians disagree on God's intentions for creating humans. John Feinberg makes the following claim regarding the kind of being that God intended to create:

> At a minimum, he intended to create a being with the capacity to reason (that capacity obviously varies from individual to individual), a being with emotions, a will that is free (compatibilistically free . . .), a being with desires, intentions (formed on the basis of one's desires), and the capacity to live and function in a world that is suited to beings such as we are.[36]

The kind of freedom Feinberg advocates for is compatibilism, which suggests humans are free to perform or refrain from some morally significant act so long as they want to. Some action is not brought about by compulsion or states of affairs extrinsic to the person; rather, it is a matter of a

---

[35] Marilyn M. Adams, "Redemptive Suffering: A Christian Solution to the Problem of Evil," in *The Problem of Evil: Selected Readings*, ed. Michael L. Peterson (Notre Dame, IN: University of Notre Dame Press, 1992), 173.

[36] John S. Feinberg, *The Many Faces of Evil: Theological Systems and the Problems of Evil* (Wheaton: Crossway, 2004), 168.

psychological state (e.g., a wish, desire, or intention). The person could have done differently if she had wanted to.[37] Compatibilist freedom is a basic part of the metaphysical structure of humans. Before the first humans sinned against God, they had compatibilist freedom.

Feinberg recognizes a potential criticism of this view, so he endeavors to answer, How it is possible that our first ancestors fell into sin? "Moral acts, then, ultimately begin with our desires," says Feinberg.[38] He continues, "Desires alone are not evil, but when they are drawn away and enticed to the point of bringing us to choose to disobey God's prescribed moral norms, we have sinned. Desires aren't the only culprit, for will, reason, and emotion, for example, enter into the process."[39] He sums up his argument as follows:

> As to how an evil action comes to be, an individual has certain basic desires or needs which aren't evil in themselves. He initially doesn't purpose to state these desires in a way that disobeys ethical norms. However, a desirable object comes before him, and he is attracted to it. He forms the intention to have it, even though acquiring it is prohibited by moral precept. Then, when the allurement becomes strong enough, he wills to acquire to do the thing he desires. At that point sin is committed. Then, bodily movement (whatever it might be) to carry out the decision occurs. Once the act is done, it is public knowledge that the moral law has been broken. As to the willing of the action, I hold that it is done with compatibilistic free will, for there are causally sufficient non-subsequent conditions that decisively incline the will without constraining it to choose. Some of the conditions surrounding the decision may involve God's bringing about the state of affairs in which the decision is

---

[37] William Hasker, *Metaphysics: Constructing a World View* (Downers Grove: IVP, 1984), 34.

[38] Feinberg, *The Many Faces of Evil*, 170.

[39] Feinberg, 170.

made. However, temptation to evil and the actual willing of evil stem not from God but from man.[40]

Feinberg's position is quite telling about the compatibilist's view of freedom. On the one hand, it seems reductionistic. Beyond this, if humans were compatibilistically free from the beginning, they were set to fail at the go. They had no option but to sin. Here's why: In order for the first humans to have not sinned, the states of affairs that brought about the desirable objects—to obey God or to disobey God—must have been (1) such that they produced equal attraction between the two desirable objects, which would have ended in a stalemate of sorts, or (2) such that to obey God was slightly more attractive than the attraction not to have obeyed God. Since from the Genesis text we see that our first ancestors chose to disobey God, then it would seem the states of affairs which brought about the one desirable object—disobeying God—was slightly more attractive than the states of affairs which brought about the other desirable object—obeying God. Therefore, it would follow that the first humans were at an unfair disadvantage.

Further, it seems that, for our first parents to have had a fair chance to do what was right, they would have had to arrive at some kind of threshold in their desire to either obey or disobey—a point of no return. In other words, the object of desirability became too unbearable to resist. Yet, if one grants a point of no return, then it would seem that there was also a point at which they could have refrained from the lure to disobey God. But where might we draw the line on such a threshold? Suppose we place desirability on a scale between 0–100. Would the threshold be somewhere between 1–25 or between 25–50? Perhaps the threshold is somewhere after the 50 percent mark. Who knows? Regardless of where the threshold is, having a threshold that transitions between little or no desirability to perform some action to unbearable desirability to perform it suggests that various other factors are involved. Feinberg seems to agree with this. However, he doesn't

---

[40] Feinberg, 170.

demonstrate how this could be. He only attempts to show how a person may be lured into sin. But where do these other capacities, such as "will, reason, and emotion," come to bear on doing or restraining from some action? Feinberg does not tell us.

It seems to us that if a threshold of sorts is involved, the agent must be, in the words of Roderick M. Chisholm, a "prime mover unmoved" of sorts.[41] But this is exactly what compatibilist freedom does not allow. *There can be no threshold*, nor can the agent be a *prime mover unmoved*. There could be no point where one can do one act over the other, since, psychologically, one's desires or intentions are determined by a set of prior conditions and circumstances or causal chain. Adam and Eve would have been prone to desire disobedience over obedience (or whatever the object was of their desires). But where did this desire come from? It seems that there are only two options—from God or from their own nature.[42] But if humans were created without a sinful nature, then it would seem that the only option is put the blame on God. But such a position is untenable for Christians who hold to the goodness of God. Ultimately, from the perspective of compatibilism, it seems that Adam and Eve could not help but to have sinned.

Perhaps, the compatibilist might respond by pointing to the influence of the Tempter in the formation of the desire of Adam and Eve to prefer disobedience to obedience. Suppose that is the case, but that would only push the issue back one step further. Why is it that the Tempter fell? Either the Tempter had libertarian freedom or he had compatibilistic freedom. If compatibilistic freedom, then what brought about the change in the Tempter? We could raise all of the same issues addressed above in our discussion on Adam and Eve and apply those to the Tempter. In our estimation, punting

---

[41] Roderick M. Chisholm, "Human Freedom and the Self," in *Metaphysics: The Big Questions*, ed. Peter Van Inwagen and Dean W. Zimmerman (Malden, MA: Blackwell, 1998), 362.

[42] Chisholm, 24.

to the Tempter does not solve the issue; rather, it muddies the waters, further complicating the issue.

Among other problems with compatibilistic freedom, we can only stress two here. First, compatibilism, if true, seems to make moral responsibility nonsensical. As expressed elsewhere, "duties tell us what we ought to do, and *ought* implies *can*."[43] However, if humans are determined by prior causes and circumstances, all of which are out of their control, how can one meaningfully say that one can do otherwise?[44] A second argument, especially important to the thesis of this chapter, is that it is difficult to make sense of love relationships if compatibilism is true. Love, in its very nature, requires volition—a choice to reciprocate.[45]

Based on the arguments presented so far, the tenable position for the Christian understanding of human freedom best aligns with that of libertarianism. If humans have the capacity to love God, then it would also imply that the opposite is true. That's what we see in the biblical narrative. Instead of choosing to love God, humans sinned and rebelled against him.

Sin is rebellion against God, but there's more to the story than that. At its core, sin is violent opposition to love. Instead of looking out for the best interest of the other, sin exalts the self at the expense of the other. Sin brings division, separation, and alienation, breaking harmony between humans and God, one another, and nature. Thankfully, God doesn't leave it at that, as Stephen Davis suggests:

> Cosmically, the relationship between God and human beings was severed by the entrance of sin into the world. Personally, it is broken whenever we separate ourselves from God by sin. All of God's actions in history are expressions of the personal relationship that

---

[43] David Baggett and Jerry L. Walls, *Good God: The Theistic Foundations of Morality* (New York: Oxford University Press, 2010), 69.

[44] Baggett and Walls, 69; William Hasker, *The Triumph of God over Evil: Theodicy for a World of Suffering* (Downers Grove: IVP, 2008), 153.

[45] Baggett and Walls, *Good God*, 71.

is at the center of reality. God is attempting redemptively to restore human beings to the splendor of that relationship. Christians affirm that the relationship is fully restored through the action of God in the world and preeminently through God's action in Jesus Christ. Its essence is summed up sublimely by the prophet Jeremiah: "I will be your God, and you shall be my people" (Jer 7:23). At the center of the universe is a personal relationship and a God who acts on its behalf.[46]

God desires humans to have abundant life, which is found in knowing him (John 17:3) and living in accordance to his commands. The kind of life that God desires for his creatures can only come about through Christ's work on the cross and in his resurrection, and through the empowering work of the Holy Spirit in the lives of those who believe. Because of God's work, humanity can be set free from the power, corruption, and effects of sin. The kind of freedom God offers overturns sin that results in alienation from God, others, and creation.

Incarnation, Redemption, and Communion

One of the great truths of Christianity is the belief that God became flesh and dwelt among us (John 1:14). God the Son became flesh for the redemption of our humanity. In working out their understanding of God's work in salvation, church fathers such as Irenaeus and Athanasius employed the term "*theosis*," which means something like "deification" or "becoming God."[47] The idea of *theosis* is less radical than it sounds, pointing to something like God's work in redeeming our humanity and our being brought into the life of God—the biblical concept of communion with God.

---

[46] Davis, "God's Action," 177.

[47] Robert V. Rakestraw, "Becoming Like God: An Evangelical Doctrine of *Theosis*," *Journal of the Evangelical Theological Society* 40, no. 2 (1997): 260.

In his *Against Heresies,* we find Irenaeus employing the concept of *theosis* in connection to the Son's work in our redemption and union with God. It was through incarnation that Christ took upon our human nature, giving up both soul and body for our behalf. It is by the blood of the Lord that humans are redeemed. In so becoming incarnate we receive "immortality." Intricately connected to Christ's work is the work of the Spirit. In giving us the Holy Spirit, humans receive God, and thus share in "union and communion" with God.[48]

Like Irenaeus, Athanasius affirmed the doctrine of *theosis,* linking it closely to his anthropology. Following other Greek fathers, Athanasius affirmed a clear ontological distinction between God and creation. For him, the eternal, immortal, and incorruptible God created all things *ex nihilo.* The belief that God created out of nothing stood in stark contrast to the Platonic idea of the artificer bringing form and function to the cosmos out of preexisting matter.[49] In the same way, humanity was created out of "nonexistence." God is the giver of life, and humans were created in a state of innocence, that is, a state of "incorruption." Athanasius saw evil as "nonbeing, the negation and antithesis of good," and thus, turning away from God, humanity became corrupted and, as a result, they were "in process of becoming corrupted entirely."[50] It was the Word who "had called them into being," but through rebellion they "lost the knowledge of God," and "they lost existence with it." The reason for sending the Word, says Athanasius, "was for our sorry case."[51] The beauty of the incarnation is that the very God who brought all things into existence, who fashioned in the virgin the very body that he would take on, died on our behalf through his great love for us:

---

[48] Irenaeus, *Against Heresies,* 3.10.2.
[49] Athanasius, *On the Incarnation,* 1.2.
[50] Athanasius, 1.4.
[51] Athanasius, 1.4.

Thus taking a body like our own, because all our bodies were liable to the corruption of death, He surrendered His body to death instead of all, and offered it to the Father. This He did out of sheer love for us, so that in His death all might die, and the law of death thereby be abolished because, having fulfilled in His body that for which it was appointed, it was thereafter voided of its power for men. This He did that He might turn again to incorruption men who had turned back to corruption, and make them alive through death by the appropriation of His body and by the grace of His resurrection. Thus He would make death disappear from them as utterly as straw from fire.[52]

Toward the end of his work on the incarnation of the Word of God, Athanasius says something surprising and startling: the Word "assumed humanity that we might become God."[53] This may sound strange to our modern ears, but it was a common thought among the Greeks of Athanasius's time. His readers would have understood the implications. The Son took on our human nature that we might "perceive the Mind of the unseen Father" and that he "endured shame from men that we might inherit immortality."[54] In so doing, he did not cease being who he was, that is, he remained "impassible and incorruptible" in his divine nature; nevertheless, it was through his impassibility "He kept and healed the suffering men on whose account He thus endured."[55]

Found in the works of such fathers as Clement of Alexandria, Gregory of Nazianzus, Gregory of Nyssa, Cyril of Alexandria, and Maximus the

---

[52] Athanasius, 2.9.

[53] Athanasius, 8.54. cf. Athanasius, *Letter 60, to Adalphius*, 4 "For He has become Man, that He might deify us in Himself, and He has been born of a woman, and begotten of a Virgin, in order to transfer to Himself our erring generation, and that we may become henceforth a holy race, and 'partakers of the Divine Nature,' as blessed Peter wrote." Also, *Against the Arians*, 2.59.

[54] Athanasius, *On the Incarnation*, 8.54.

[55] Athanasius, 8.54.

Confessor, the doctrine of *theosis* never meant to teach that humans "become God" ontologically; rather, it points the way to new creation. In the eschaton, humans will be transformed and brought into a state of "maturity and perfection through the regenerative grace of God and become not only sinless but also incapable anymore of falling into sin."[56]

According to Eastern Orthodox theologians, there are key Scriptures that point to the doctrine of *theosis* (2 Pet 1:4; Ps 82:6; John 10:34–35; 17:21–23).[57] Perhaps the strongest verse is 2 Pet 1:4, which informs us that believers "may become partakers of the divine nature, having escaped the corruption that is in the world on account of lust" (NASB). Because of their becoming "partakers of the divine nature" and because they have "escaped corruption," believers are to apply diligence "in" their "faith," adding spiritual qualities (virtues), which include "moral excellence," "knowledge," "self-control," "perseverance," "godliness," "brotherly kindness," and "love" (2 Pet 1:5–7 NASB). These qualities should belong in the life of believers and they should be "increasing" in measure (v. 8 NASB). When a believer lacks such qualities, he is "blind" and has "forgotten his purification from his former sins" (v. 9 NASB). Note the comparison between "having escaped the corruption that is in the world by lust" and having received "purification." Thus, believers have been purified and are to practice such qualities—qualities that are consistent with becoming "partakers of the divine nature." Believers are capable of such qualities because God's "divine power has granted to us everything pertaining to life and godliness" (v. 3 NASB). And, in so doing, believers are being *like* God, "who called us by His own glory and excellence" (v. 3 NASB).

---

[56] Vladimir Kharlamov, "*Theosis* in Patristic Thought," *Theology Today* 65, no. 2 (2008): 166.

[57] For a dissenting view that Ps 82:6 and John 10:34–35 refer to *theosis*, see Michael S. Heiser, "Monotheism, Polytheism, Monolatry, or Henotheism: Toward an Assessment of Divine Plurality in the Hebrew Bible," *Bulletin for Biblical Research* 18, no. 1 (2008): 2–4.

Another significant passage is John 17, where Jesus prays that all those whom he has been given by the Father "may all be one; just as You, Father, are in Me and I in You, that they also may be in Us, so that the world may believe that You sent Me. . . . I in them and You in Me, that they may be perfected in unity, so that the world may know that You sent Me, and You loved them, just as you loved Me" (John 17:21, 23 NASB). This unity that Jesus prays for is a unity that he and the Father share, and, yet, it seems that in some way believers will also be "in" both the Father and Son. This instance in John 17 is not, however, an anomalous thought in the New Testament.

Throughout the New Testament, especially in the Pauline letters, believers are said to be "in Christ" (Eph 1:3–4, 26; 2:10; 4:12–16; 5:23–32; Col 1:27; Gal 2:20). Because believers are "in Christ," they are a "new creation" and "the old has passed away, and . . . the new has come" (2 Cor 5:17). This new status comes about through God's work in reconciliation. As Paul reminds us in Colossians, though we were alienated from God, Christ has reconciled us through "his physical body through his death, to present" us as "holy, faultless, and blameless before him" (Col 1:21–22). As those who are "in Christ" and who have been reconciled, the church has been charged with the task of being ministers of "reconciliation" (2 Cor 5:18–20) and taking the "good news," the gospel of Christ, to the uttermost ends of the world.[58]

Central to the gospel message is the deity, death, and resurrection of Jesus. Through his death and resurrection, Jesus secured our salvation, and his resurrection is a foreshadowing of our own resurrection, when our bodies will be made new. For believers, there is an already/not yet aspect to their salvation. As we long for the redemption of our bodies (not yet), we have been granted the Holy Spirit who is the "firstfruits" or "deposit," serving as a guarantee for our future redemption (Rom 8:23; 2 Cor 1:22; Eph 1:13–14;

---

[58] For a clear discussion of the "in" passages in relation to *theosis*, see Gannon Murphy, "Reformed *Theosis*," *Theology Today* 65 (2008): 194–95; Rakestraw, "Becoming Like God," 258.

4:30). Though saved by grace through faith (Eph 2:8–9), believers reap the spiritual benefits of the already aspect of their salvation. Believers are justified (Rom 4:3), adopted as sons and daughters (Rom 5:15; Eph 1:5), sanctified (1 Cor 1:2), and regenerated by the Holy Spirit (Titus 3:6). Peter tells us that God has given us "new birth into a living hope" through Christ's resurrection, "an inheritance that is imperishable, undefiled, and unfading" (1 Pet 1:3–4). Moreover, through "his divine power" God has "given us everything required for life and godliness" (2 Pet 1:3).

Contrary to what some might think, the doctrine of *theosis* in no way implies pantheism or panentheism. Humans remain what they are and God remains who he is. There is no ontological union between God and humanity. Instead, when understood properly, *theosis* refers to the entire matrix of human salvation—justification, sanctification, and glorification—whereby God seeks to restore fallen humanity, bringing them back to a state of wholeness. As Myk Habets rightly puts it, *theosis* refers to "the recreation of our lost humanity in the dynamic, atoning interaction between the divine and human natures within the one person of Jesus Christ, through whom we enter into the triune communion of God's intra-trinitarian life."[59] Humans participate *in* God through the work of the Son and the Spirit, a union Habets describes as a "thoroughly personal and relational experiencing of the triune relations."[60]

Ultimately, *theosis* is the bringing about of God's original intentions for humans from the beginning, the capacity to share in the life of God, but not only that, to obtain ultimate human fulfillment. It points to our future hope and to the new creation, where humans will fully receive their final redemption and ultimately obtain human fulfillment. Yet this is not something that believers wait for in the eschaton. It begins now through the empowering work of the Holy Spirit, who works in us to bring us into a right

---

[59] Myk Habets, "Reformed *Theosis*?: A Response to Gannon Murphy," *Theology Today* 65 (2009): 491.

[60] Habets, 494.

relationship with God, and who also gives believers the energy and ability to live out Christian lives. Furthermore, the doctrine of *theosis* helps to redirect the proclamation of the Christian gospel. There is no doubt that Scripture expresses God's wrath against sin and the sinner. Nevertheless, there is much more to the proclamation of God's love, the gospel, and salvation than this. Again, in the words of Habets, "The ultimate goal of salvation is no longer to appease the wrath of an angry God but to attain to participation in the divine life through the Son by the Holy Spirit. This still necessitates judgment on sin and justification of the sinner, but it does not end there."[61] The church must continue to preach a gospel, which reflects "good news," that is, a gospel grounded in the death and resurrection of Jesus Christ, which brings hope of new life to a lost and dying world.

---

[61] Habets, 496–97.

7

Human Dignity, Moral Transformation, and the Holy Spirit

Having considered the metaphysical and theological foundation in the previous chapter, we now examine the resources within Christian theology to undergird human value, dignity, and worth, while also exploring the relationship between moral transformation and the empowering work of the Holy Spirit in the life of the individual and the church.

Human Dignity

When the great poet W. H. Auden arrived in the United States with Christopher Isherwood in January 1939, he was not religious, and he had not been since he was thirteen at Gresham's School in England. Os Guinness says that two experiences stood out among those that jolted Auden into rethinking the matter of faith. The first had been earlier in 1933, when he was a schoolmaster at the Downs School in the Malvern Hills. Sitting with three fellow teachers, he was suddenly overwhelmed by the sense that all their existence somehow had infinite value and that he loved them for themselves. Years later he described this experience as a "Vision of Agape" (Love).

The second experience came in New York two months after he had written the poem "September 1, 1939." He was in a cinema in Yorkville on the Upper East Side of Manhattan, which, unknown to him, was still largely a German-speaking area. Eager to follow news of the course of the war, he went to see *Sieg in Poland* ("*sieg*" means victory), a documentary of the Nazi invasion and conquest of Poland, in which SS Storm Troopers were bayoneting women and children, and, to Auden's horror, members of the audience cried out in support of their fellow-countrymen, "Kill them! Kill them!"

One thread had always linked Auden's successive convictions: a belief in the natural goodness of humankind. Whether the solution of the world's problems lay in politics, education, or psychology, he believed that once the problems were addressed, the world would be happy because humanity was basically good. Suddenly, however, as Auden watched the SS savagery and heard the brutal response of the audience, he knew he had been wrong. As Guinness puts it, "With everything in him he knew intuitively and beyond any doubt that he was encountering absolute evil and that it must be judged and condemned absolutely. There had to be a reason why Hitler was 'utterly wrong.'"[1]

These two experiences helped him realize that he needed a better understanding of the value of persons and the existence of evil. He also had to rethink this idea that people are good if his beliefs were going to align with reality. Aligning our beliefs to correspond with reality, especially as revealed by the unshakeable truths of morality, is key to thinking theologically. Take the examples from Auden: human beings are valuable, perhaps infinitely valuable; at the same time, we are not intrinsically good; there is something morally broken about us; and some things are just flat wrong, even evil.

---

[1] Os Guinness, *Fool's Talk: Recovering the Art of Christian Persuasion* (Downers Grove: IVP, 2015), 132.

Intrinsic Value of Persons

This is by no means an exhaustive list of moral realities on which to base our thinking about nature and existence, but it is a fruitful start. For time constraints, let's focus in even more and choose just one of these moral facts to think about for now: the intrinsic value of people, perhaps even something like the infinite value of people. Again, this is not to suggest that we are morally good, but we are valuable. Immanuel Kant had a way of talking about this issue: he said people have worth and value and dignity, but not a *price*.[2] There is an inherent dignity to persons that we deeply recognize, and it cannot be quantified or reduced to a dollar amount; there is something about it that is intangible, literally priceless. And somehow we know this, down deep, though we can forget it, or perhaps intentionally repress it. We can forget that it is true of others, and we can forget that it is true of ourselves.

What we find especially exciting about this particular piece of moral evidence is that many of our unbelieving friends themselves intuitively recognize its truth. At least at moments they are often able to see that people have great intrinsic value and dignity. They may not know why—just as they may not know why we have moral obligations, or that people are of equal moral worth, or that basic human rights obtain—but they can recognize the truths themselves. God has made all of us as human beings able to apprehend such truths.

Think about the Nazi depiction of Jews, the ugly history of American chattel slavery, and, more recently, the intellectual contortions required to deny the humanity of unborn children in order to justify their wholesale slaughter. In such paradigmatic instances of reprehensible mistreatment, we see on ready display the perceived need to deny the humanity of the victims. This is thought to make it okay; we would otherwise know the behavior is beyond the

---

[2] Immanuel Kant, *Foundations of the Metaphysics of Morals with Critical Essays*, trans. Lewis White Beck, ed. Robert Paul Wolff (Indianapolis: Bobbs-Merrill, 1969), 60.

moral pale. Even at our worst, we somehow recognize the value of humans, and to rationalize our behavior we deny the humanity of the victims—just as Goebbels's propaganda did the same of the Poles. We suspect general revelation alone gives us reason to think human beings are intrinsically valuable, sacred, and the legitimate bearers of human rights. What such recognitions should then lead us to do is ask what it is about reality that explains such truths. Why is it that people have such great intrinsic dignity and value?

Now, its very obviousness might be thought to imply that we need not search for a more ultimate explanation. If it is that obvious, why ask why? But this is to confuse the matter of the truth of the thing with our knowing it to be true. We may be able to recognize that something is true without being able to explain why. This is the difference between something being *self-evident* and something being *self-explaining*. Or philosophers might say it is confusing metaphysics (what is real) with epistemology (our knowledge of what's real). Even unbelievers can often grasp that people have mysteriously great intrinsic value, but this piece of moral evidence cries out for explanation.

This is a useful juncture to harken back to a point of methodology to lend clarity to our analysis. In this book we have focused considerable time on how best to understand God from a Christian perspective. Anselm, recall, was a Christian, and Nicholas Wolterstorff makes mention of an overlooked aspect of Anselmianism: "Anselm assumed the acceptability of engaging in a practice of reflection that presupposes the existence of God without first having proved the existence of God."[3] In moral apologetics we are inclined to start with moral evidence and argue toward theism; in theology the order is often reversed. We begin with who God is, and then show how it sheds light on various matters, including morality. This is more our approach here; we've taken a more apologetic tack elsewhere.[4]

---

[3] Nicholas Wolterstorff, *Justice: Rights and Wrongs* (Princeton, NJ: Princeton University Press, 2008).

[4] For example, see David Baggett and Jerry L. Walls, *Good God: The Theistic Foundations of Morality* (New York: Oxford University Press, 2010)

Mark Murphy distinguishes between explanandum-based approach and an explanans-centered approach. The former starts with the moral evidence and argues on that basis to God's reality; this is a standard apologetic approach. But the latter does not start with the moral evidence, but rather with God himself.[5] Then one can point out why God, as understood in terms like theistic personalism, is such a good candidate for answering the moral questions and accounting for moral realities furnished by our experiences. Murphy suggests that such an approach carries no apologetic significance since God's existence is presupposed.[6]

We demur, however, unconvinced that an explanans-centered approach lacks evidential significance.[7] Recall where we are in our dialec-

---

[5] Nicholas Wolterstorff dubs a similar approach "Anselmian" in this specific sense: "Anselm assumed the acceptability of engaging in a practice of reflection that presupposes the existence of God without first having proved the existence of God." This is Wolterstorff's modus operandi in his *Justice: Rights and Wrongs*.

[6] This bears some resemblance, too, to Eleonore Stump's effort through the use of Franciscan (rather than Dominican) second-person knowledge to make the case that in, say, Job there is a sort of answer to the problem of evil provided, though it speaks to the believer more so than the unbeliever. Some of this is reminiscent, too, of C. S. Lewis's *Till We Have Faces*. See Stump's *Wandering in Darkness: Narrative and the Problem of Suffering* (Oxford: Oxford University Press, 2012), and David and Marybeth Baggett's "Self-Knowledge, Who God Is, and a Cure for Our Deepest Shame: A Few Reflections on *Till We Have Faces*," *Perichoresis* 20, no. 3 (2022). There is a relevant distinction in this vicinity, of course, between unbelievers having *less* of an ability to glean the relevant insights and having *none*.

[7] In this *NDPR* analysis of Murphy's relevant work (*God and Moral Law: On the Theistic Explanation of Morality*), Mike Almeida writes, "If an explanans driven approach has no apologetic value in the sense Murphy describes, then it is hard to see how taking such an approach could, as described above, move us ultimately to a theistic account of morality. If consideration of the distinctive features of God in relation to morality does not at least increase the likelihood of the hypothetical explanans, then the explanans driven approach is not particularly well-suited to at least one goal (admittedly, not the most pronounced goal) of the book. But further, if Murphy is right about the lack of apologetic value in the explanans driven approach, then presumably there would be no corresponding decrease in the likelihood of the hypothetical explanans even if the distinctive features of God in

tic: we are considering the question of explanation. If we see that the God of theistic personalism is powerfully or even uniquely able to provide an impeccable explanation of important aesthetic phenomena, then that can arguably play a part in an evidential case for God's existence, a commitment at the heart of what has been called *explanationism*.[8] So the work we are currently doing, though primarily (philosophical) theology, is hardly bereft of apologetic value, exactly because of the existential centrality and powerful implications of the character of the God who loves us and made us in his image.

As Christians we have terrific reasons to think it is indeed true that human beings, each and every one of them, have great value, perhaps even infinite value, as Auden sensed that day in the Malvern Hills. Austin Farrer was a friend of C. S. Lewis who, in his own work, had for one of his main points of emphasis the value of persons. In one of his books, he asked readers to consider the way we normatively ought to think about other people. It is of great importance, he argued, that we value them rightly, that we think about others in such a way as to regard them properly. Such regard should be at once so pure and so entire that it leads to a sort of frustration. This frustration derives from the incompleteness of our definition of those we so regard.

---

relation to morality yielded a moral picture broadly and deeply inconsistent with the moral explananda. But then the explanans driven approach so described would amount to an odd exercise in determining what morality might look like under the assumption of a hypothetical explanans whose nature makes it an essential explainer of morality.

"I think it is good news for the project that Murphy is probably mistaken about the apologetic value of the explanans driven approach. There is really no reason not to believe that consideration of the distinctive features of God in relation to morality either increases or decreases the likelihood of the hypothetical explanans." See "Review of *God and Moral Law: On the Theistic Explanation of Morality*," Notre Dame Philosophical Reviews, https://ndpr.nd.edu/reviews/god -and-moral-law-on-the-theistic-explanation-of-morality/.

[8] Kevin McCain and Ted Poston, eds., *Best Explanations: New Essays on Inference to the Best Explanation* (Oxford: Oxford University Press, 2018).

Thinking of our neighbors in too casual a way cannot sustain the esteem we intuitively think they deserve. The conclusion to which Farrer felt compelled is that what deserves our regard is not simply our neighbor, but God in our neighbor and our neighbor in God.

This gets us to the heart of why we know as Christians that people are of infinite value. They are creations of God, made in his image, fashioned after his likeness, and they are loved by God, perhaps each of us differently, but all of us infinitely. There is nothing so revolutionary, for each of us, as coming into a deep understanding of God's love.

We have both taught a lot of seminary students and found on numerous occasions that these same folks willing to get up and preach God's love on Sunday can harbor doubts about God's love *for themselves*. Others find it hard to believe in a loving heavenly Father because they lacked a loving earthly father, taking to heart this line from *Fight Club*: "Our fathers were our models for God. If our fathers bailed, what does that tell you about God? . . . You have to consider the possibility that God does not like you. He never wanted you. In all probability, he hates you."[9]

Sadly, many children and young adults today lack a loving father in their lives, and tragically many of them may doubt God even likes them, much less loves them. But of course this is deeply confused, giving bad earthly fathers far too much power: power to condition our theology rather than good theology correcting our mistakes. Coming to apprehend the love of God is vitally important. It is who he is, and the right view of God can help us understand ourselves and others as we ought.

Understanding God's love is a process. Recall Paul's prayer for the Ephesians: that if Christ dwells in their hearts through faith, then they, being rooted and grounded in love, will have power, together with all the saints, to comprehend the length and width and height and depth of the love of Christ, and to know this love that surpasses knowledge, that they may be filled with all the fullness of God (Eph 3:17–19).

---

[9] *Fight Club*, directed by David Fincher (1999, 20th Century Studios).

We find it most instructive that when we think about the deepest reasons for the value of persons, it ends up invariably pointing us past humans to the real source of their value: God himself. And not just that—it points to *who God is*. God is love; in the triune relationship God is by his nature love—perfect, eternal, necessary love. The matter of *who God is* is just as important, if not more important, than merely *that God is*. The good news of the gospel is never merely that God exists, but that God loves us, even likes us, has made provision for our salvation, and wants us to experience abundant life and fruitful service and the deepest fulfillment imaginable. The better we understand the love of God, the better able we will come to understand the value of those made in his image. A low view of God results in a low view of people; a high view of God results in the right view of people. Our theology inevitably conditions our anthropology. This is one of the reasons why theology matters a great deal—and not just to appreciate the concepts in our head, but to appropriate them in our hearts.

With this in mind, listen to these words of C. S. Lewis: "There are no ordinary people. You have never talked to a mere mortal. . . . [I]t is immortals whom we joke with, work with, marry, snub and exploit—immortal horrors or everlasting splendors. This does not mean that we are to be perpetually solemn. We must play. But our merriment must be of that kind (and it is, in fact, the merriest kind) which exists between people who have, from the outset, taken each other seriously—no flippancy, no superiority, no presumption."[10]

---

[10] The full passage from Lewis's *The Weight of Glory* (New York: HarperOne, 2017):. "It is a serious thing to live in a society of possible gods and goddesses, to remember that the dullest most uninteresting person you talk to may one day be a creature which, if you saw it now, you would be strongly tempted to worship, or else a horror and a corruption such as you now meet, if at all, only in a nightmare. All day long we are, in some degree helping each other to one or the other of these destinations. It is in the light of these overwhelming possibilities, it is with the awe and the circumspection proper to them, that we should conduct all of our dealings with one another, all friendships, all loves, all play, all politics. There are no ordinary people. You have never talked to a mere mortal. Nations,

We, all of us, have been made in God's image; in this there is solidarity. At the same time, each of us is unique, in the true sense of the word, unrepeatable, *sui generis*. Every one of us is called to inhabit a particular portion of the body of Christ; each of us is called to do good works that God prepared beforehand for us to do (Eph 2:10). And those who avail themselves of God's overtures of love are reconciled to him and will be saved to the uttermost. We are told in Rev 2:17 that one day on a white stone our true name will be revealed—a secret between each of us and God. That name will be no merely arbitrary moniker but the deepest reflection of who God intended us to be: our deepest and most distinctive identity. We live in a time when issues of identity are much discussed, often in the most simplistic and superficial of ways, but our deepest sense of identity can be found only in our God-given callings and vocation. We look for it elsewhere in vain.

A few quotations come to mind that drive home this point about the uniqueness of each person. First, in his 1940 novel *The Power and the Glory*, Roman Catholic author Graham Greene charges his readers to recognize and respond rightly to the intrinsic value of each person: "When you visualized a man or woman carefully, you could always begin to feel pity—that was a quality God's image carried with it. When you saw the lines at the corners of the eyes, the shape of the mouth, how the hair grew, it was impossible to hate. Hate was just a failure of imagination."[11] And second, from the Christian novelist Marilynne Robinson: "Any human face is a claim on you, because you can't help but understand the singularity of it, the courage and loneliness of it."[12]

The face seems particularly important to our identity and personhood somehow. C. S. Lewis recognized this in his greatest novel *Till We Have Faces*. Interestingly enough, in more than one language, personality is tied

---

cultures, arts, civilizations—these are mortal, and their life is to ours as the life of a gnat. But it is immortals whom we joke with, work with, marry, snub, and exploit—immortal horrors or everlasting splendors."

[11] Graham Greene, *The Power and the Glory* (New York: Penguin, 1940), 131.

[12] Marilynne Robinson, *Gilead* (New York: Farrar, Straus and Giroux, 2004), 66.

to the face and sometimes even a mask. There is something ineliminably personalist about the face; it is far easier to be cruel to those who remain faceless. This is often, we suspect, why online activity can be so acidulous and vitriolic. No face, no humanity. In *Till We Have Faces*, to have a face in the full sense metaphorically means to acknowledge all of who we are—the good and the bad, the honorable and the shameful.

Once more, the way to authenticity and true identity is to grab hold of our identity as God's image-bearers, renouncing the works of darkness to which our sinful bent inclines us. This is the only path to the deepest fulfillment for which we were made, the most authentic self we can be. Kurt Vonnegut captured the moral of his novel *Mother Night* with these words: "We are what we pretend to be, so we must be careful about what we pretend to be."[13] In *Mere Christianity*, Lewis talked about putting on Christ as like putting on a mask that, by the time it's removed, the face has conformed to. This is the right form of pretending, you see; the right sort of mask, one that makes us more of what we were meant to be rather than less.

Before moving on, one word about special revelation. General revelation can show us that people have value, but the special revelation we have received through Scripture amplifies the message. This accounts for why the evolution in moral thought that enabled us to see the sacred and beautiful qualities in the Down syndrome child, the aged, and the exile was largely a function of Christian influence. Only a myopic view of history fails to see the revolutionary force of Christianity in generating such moral insight. Paul Copan writes about how this can add an important historical twist to the discussion of the moral sense God makes.[14]

---

[13] "This is the only story of mine whose moral I know," writes Kurt Vonnegut at the beginning of his 1962 novel *Mother Night*. "I don't think it's a marvelous moral; I simply happen to know what it is: We are what we pretend to be, so we must be careful about what we pretend to be." Kurt Vonnegut, *Mother Night* (New York: Doubleday, 1966), v.

[14] See Paul Copan and Thom Wolf, "Another Dimension of the Moral Argument: The Voice of Jesus and the Historical Fruits of the Christian Faith," in *A New Theist*

Just one quick corroborating word from atheist Jürgen Habermas from his *Time of Transitions*:

> Universalistic egalitarianism, from which sprang the ideals of freedom and a collective life in solidarity, the autonomous conduct of life and emancipation, the individual morality of conscience, human rights and democracy, is the direct legacy of the Judaic ethic of justice and the Christian ethic of love. This legacy, substantially unchanged, has been the object of continual critical appropriation and reinterpretation. To this day, there is no alternative to it. And in light of the current challenges of a postnational constellation, we continue to draw on the substance of this heritage. Everything else is just idle postmodern talk.[15]

Though Valuable, Not Good

We are each of us uniquely made in God's image and loved infinitely by God, but we are also sinners in need of grace. We are guilty: we both *feel* guilty for our wrongdoing, and we are *objectively* guilty. This is obviously a perfect prelude to proclaiming the gospel. A hopeful reminder in the face of our sinful state is this: Our having been made in God's image is *essential* to us, whereas our sinful state is merely *contingent*. In other words, more central to our identity is that we have been created by God in his image for reasons and purposes, than that we have fallen into sin and are in need of forgiveness. We can be forgiven and saved through and through so our sins need not define us; but we cannot help but be partially defined by having been made in God's image.

Response to the New Atheists, eds. Kevin Vallier and Joshua Rasmussen, Routledge New Critical Thinking in Religion, Theology, and Biblical Studies (London: CLC/Routledge, 2020), 131–52. Also Paul Copan, "Reinforcing the Moral Argument: Appealing to the Historical Impact of the Christian Faith" (Conference paper, Evangelical Theological Society, San Diego, November 20, 2014).

[15] Jürgen Habermas, *Time of Transitions*, ed. and trans. Ciaran Cronin and Max Pensky (Cambridge: Polity, 2006), 150–51.

Salvation from Start to Finish

All of us have three deep existential moral needs: to be forgiven our wrong-doing, to be changed, and ultimately to be changed to the uttermost, perfected, and this can set the stage for how Christianity meets each of these deep needs incredibly well. This is another piece of the cumulative case to show how the God of Christianity makes moral sense.

Forgiveness

Three deep moral needs we as human beings display: our need to be *forgiven*, our need to be *changed*, and our need to be *perfected*. Each of these profoundly existential needs corresponds to an important aspect of Christian salvation. And the fact that Christian theology so impeccably addresses each of these deep needs gives us moral reasons to take seriously both theism generally and Christianity specifically.

C. S. Lewis is well known for giving a popular version of the moral argument in Book 1 of *Mere Christianity*. There he writes of two truths that provide a clue to the nature of the world we live in. One is an objective moral law, and the other is that we inevitably fall short of it. As a result, we find ourselves experiencing not just subjective guilt, but objective guilt, for failing to meet the moral demand. There is a gap between what we are and what we feel called to become, something we can read about in Rom 3:9–20 but that we know experientially as well. These are the ingredients for one important version of the moral argument.

Something like our moral sense enables us to recognize that we have a problem. Even Charles Darwin thought that it is our moral sense that best distinguishes human beings from the animals. Indeed, he begins chapter 5 of *Descent of Man* with this admission: "I fully subscribe to the judgment of those writers who maintain that of all the differences between man and the lower animals, the moral sense or conscience is by far the most important." He even says he considers the moral sense, our sense of "ought," to be "humankind's finest quality." Elsewhere in the same book Darwin casts both "ought" and "disinterested love for all living creatures" as the noblest attributes of man.[16] For Sigmund Freud, too, the problem of guilt is so severe that he diagnosed it in *Civilization and Its Discontents* as the single most important development of civilization. Indeed, guilt is what is most responsible for our unhappiness.[17]

For both Darwin and Freud, the phenomenon of guilt was both interesting and important, even revelatory. But they mistook its import, embracing reductionist analyses and taking guilt itself as the essential problem, rather than the deeper malady of which guilt is but the symptom. Rightly construed, guilt is semiotic, pointing beyond itself to something else.

If we take our feelings of guilt as more than *mere* feelings, and something like a real objective condition of guilt, we are left wondering if there is a solution. Forgiveness is a basic and perpetual existential human need.

Unaddressed guilt can consume us. Sometimes people do have an overactive superego and feel guilty for all sorts of things that they are not really guilty of.[18] But at other times, our guilt is not a mistake, but a real insight into ourselves. We don't need our guilt merely rationalized, reduced, or explained away in those cases, but taken away.

Of course, this is one way that morality serves as the perfect pathway to the gospel of Christ—indeed we have fallen short and are in need of forgiveness. God has made provision by offering us forgiveness through the death and resurrection of Christ. Not only does God offer us forgiveness, but we can extend forgiveness to others, modeling the grace God has shown us. And many will recognize that all of this broaches the whole theological topic of *justification*.

---

[16] Charles Darwin, *Descent of Man* (Amherst, NY: Prometheus Books, 1997), chap. 5.

[17] Sigmund Freud, *Civilization and Its Discontents*, ed. and trans. James Strachey (New York: W. W. Norton, 2010).

[18] It goes without saying that sometimes people do not feel guilty when they should.

The good news that God's grace can forgive us of our moral wrong-doing functions as an ideal way to introduce the gospel. We have a problem of guilt but need not be permanently crippled by it. God offers a way out.

Sanctification

To be made right or reconciled with a holy God involves forgiveness for the many ways in which we all fall short, a gift of God's grace (Rom 3:21–26). More than forgiveness is needed, though. The next step is usually more explicitly associated with sanctification. After our conversion to Christ, we still have a long way to go. To be forgiven without being changed leaves too much undone. We need not just to become *better* people, but *new* people.

We need more than our sins to be forgiven; our sin problem itself needs to be taken away. Consider the distinction between pulling out a weed versus killing its root. The former is at best a temporary fix; the underlying problem will persist until the latter step is taken. A similar distinction holds in the arena of morality. One option is merely to deal with symptoms, but true acquisition of integrity, virtue, and holiness requires more.

Can we be transformed? This is a second great existential moral need, after forgiveness. Perhaps owing to his Lutheran upbringing, Immanuel Kant was quite sure that human beings have a deep moral problem, a tendency to be curved inward on themselves, an intractable ethical taint, a deeply flawed moral disposition in need of a revolution. Kant saw clearly that the moral demand on us is very high, while also recognizing that we have a natural propensity not to follow it.

Here, then, is a discursive formulation of the argument from grace from Kant:

1.   Morality requires us to achieve a standard too exacting and demanding to meet on our own without some sort of outside assistance.

2. Exaggerating human capacities, lowering the moral demand, or finding a secular form of assistance are not likely to be adequate for the purpose of closing the moral gap.

3. Divine assistance is sufficient to close the gap.

4. Therefore, rationality dictates that we must postulate God's existence.[19]

This argument pertains to the possibility of the moral life. If *ought implies can*, then the requirements of morality, if they are to be met, have to be within our reach. With God's help, and arguably only with God's help, they are.

Malcolm Muggeridge once said that the depravity of man is at once the most empirically verifiable reality but at the same time the most intellectually resisted fact. We have a problem, our "dear self," one too deep for us to solve on our own. Humans are not essentially good. We are deeply broken and need to be healed at the root. Like Clay Jones puts it, the people responsible for such unspeakable atrocities of history as the Holocaust were not, as human beings go, preternaturally bad people. They were, sober truth be told, garden-variety human beings who, when certain circumstances presented themselves, behaved deplorably. All of us have that hideous potential. Moral ugliness lurks in each of our hearts. There is something in need of radical fixing deep within us. We need major moral surgery.

Augustine offered the crucial insight: God bids us to do what we cannot, in order that we might learn our dependence on him. We cannot live as we ought in our own strength alone, but we can by God's grace, with divine assistance.

So, without sugarcoating our brokenness, there is great hope. Christianity teaches that the needed resources for radical transformation are available. Although we cannot meet the moral demand on our own, God

---

[19] This is John Hare's formulation of Kant's argument. See John E. Hare, *The Moral Gap: Kantian Ethics, Human Limits, and God's Assistance* (Oxford: Clarendon, 1997).

himself has made it possible, if we submit and allow him to do it through us. It may well require a painful process, but it is possible.

Having started his book *Mere Christianity* with talk of the moral gap between what we are and what we ought to be, Lewis then explained his reason for doing so. His explanation is telling:

> My reason was that Christianity simply does not make sense until you have faced the sort of facts I have been describing. Christianity tells people to repent and promises them forgiveness. . . . It is after you have realized that there is a real Moral Law, and a Power behind the law, and that you have broken that law and put yourself wrong with that Power—it is after all this, and not a moment sooner, that Christianity begins to talk. When you know you are sick, you will listen to the doctor. When you have realized that our position is nearly desperate you will begin to understand what the Christians are talking about. They offer an explanation of how we got into our present state of both hating goodness and loving it. They offer an explanation of how God can be this impersonal mind at the back of the Moral Law and yet also a Person. They tell you how the demands of this law, which you and I cannot meet, have been met on our behalf, how God Himself becomes a man to save man from the disapproval of God.[20]

God can do more than merely ameliorate the symptoms of our chronic moral malady. In the face of our urgent need to become not just *better* people, but *new* people, and our desperate need for a revolution of the will and for radical moral transformation, the death and resurrection of Christ is indeed "good news." This issue of transformation, again, is the Christian theological category of *sanctification*. Just as God answers our

---

[20] C. S. Lewis, *Mere Christianity*, in *The Complete C. S. Lewis Signature Classics* (New York: HarperCollins, 2002), 35.

need for forgiveness, God's grace in sanctification answers our need for radical moral transformation.

Having discussed our need for and God's gracious gift of both forgiveness and transformation, we can now discuss a third deep existential and spiritual need, namely, to be morally healed *completely*, saved to the uttermost.

Glorification

Having discussed our deep need for forgiveness and moral transformation—justification and sanctification, respectively—there is one more step: not just to be wholly forgiven and radically transformed, but for the process to culminate, for the work to be finished. We need the good work that has been begun within us to be completed, which God promises to do at the day of Christ Jesus for those who trust him. This is the Christian category of *glorification*, by which we are entirely conformed to the image of Jesus, morally beautified to the uttermost, every last vestige of sin having been excised and expunged (1 John 3:2).

This answers a deep intuitive recognition of a third basic moral drive or need: the hunger to be perfected, turned into the best versions of ourselves, delivered entirely from the power and consequences of sin. Christianity assures us, and we have principled reasons to believe, that this is no Pollyannaish pipe dream but a reality we can look forward to with a real and steady hope.

What we have here is a three-part moral picture built on God's grace. By God's grace we can find the forgiveness we desperately need for having fallen short of the moral standard. By God's grace we can be set free from both our subjective feelings and objective condition of guilt. By God's grace we can be gradually changed and made more like Christ, with less and less of a taste for sin, and more and more of a hunger for righteousness. And by God's grace we will be eventually conformed to the image of Christ and delivered completely from sin's hold and consequences.

From first to last, what answers our deepest moral needs—for forgiveness, for change, and for perfection—is the astounding grace of a good God perfect in holiness and perfect in love, mediated by the Holy Spirit. And once more, this is a delightful example of how following the moral evidence where it leads points not just to God's existence but to his goodness and love and grace—and not just to theism but to Christianity in particular.

The Maligned Sibling of Shame

Fixing the guilt issue is one thing, but now we need to address guilt's often maligned sibling: shame. Shame can pose a serious threat to the beliefs that God is good, God loves each one of us, we can be reconciled with God and others, and we are valuable and worthwhile.

Whereas guilt reveals that we have morally transgressed, shame has more to do with who we are, not just what we have done. And so it can be particularly damaging if we allow shame to detract from recognizing the value we have in God, which it can all too easily do. If we become convinced that we are useless, that our lives are pointless, that we lack value, it becomes exponentially harder to see ourselves as creations of God with infinite dignity, value, and worth. It is for just such reasons that, for many believers and unbelievers alike, the temptation is to think that all shame is nothing but a toxic emotion. Guilt might be fine; we can ask forgiveness and such and get past it. But shame is thought to saddle us with negative emotional baggage.

In some cases, this is obviously true. Victims of abuse may feel great shame over what happened to them, even though they did nothing wrong. That is *undeserved* shame, and the problem is not theirs. It is all of ours; we need to listen to such victims, not sideline them, nor silence them, but give them a voice and really hear them. We will give another example of undeserved shame in just a moment.

There is also *deserved* shame. If we do something shameful, we should feel shame—if we had abused that victim just discussed, for example. We don't mean to suggest that anyone should let shame decimate their sense of self or think of themselves as unredeemable, nor that we should engage in the practice of shaming. That is different and compatible with loving our neighbors as ourselves. But if we don't feel at least some shame for doing something genuinely shameful, then we are being shame*less*.

From Aristotle to Aquinas to so many others in the history of philosophy and theology, the capacity to feel shame has been thought to be a virtue and the loss of the ability a vice. It is only more recently that as a society we have started to think otherwise, casting shame as categorically toxic and attempting to be rid of it altogether. Again, if the shame is undeserved, that is a problem we all need to address; but when shame is deserved, feeling the shame can be a step to healing. So let's consider each form of shame in turn.

Let's start with another example of undeserved shame. If you have never seen it before, there is a 1981 YouTube clip of Mister Rogers hosting a ten-year-old wheelchair-bound Jeffrey Erlanger.[21] They had originally met five years before, and Rogers remembered him and invited him to his *Neighborhood*. Mister Rogers would later say that these unscripted ten minutes were his most memorable moment on television.

It is deeply moving, and if there is any doubt as to why, we might suggest it has to do, at least in part, with this matter of shame. Ours is sadly a society in which certain people—those who have been sexually abused, those with visible disabilities—carry a stigma and are often, for no fault of their own, riddled with a sense of shame—a loss of social standing, and a resultant tendency to shrink and hide. It threatens their sense of humanity. The solution has to be communal, usually involving someone with social capital to spare conferring honor upon them.[22]

Arguably that is exactly what makes those ten minutes of television so undeniably magical. It is a simply profound microcosm of the divine love

---

[21] WPBS-TV, "MRN Clip Jeff Erlanger," WPBS-TV, streamed live on August 26, 2023, YouTube video, 1:58, https://youtube.com/watch?v=UNUficgWE3U.

[22] An excellent book on the topic is Gregg A. Ten Elshof's *For Shame: Rediscovering the Virtues of a Maligned Emotion* (Grand Rapids: Eerdmans, 2021).

that deigns and condescends to broken and marginalized people and, in the process, exalts them, replacing shame with honor, beauty for ashes. Like Mister Rogers did for Jeffrey—who was on the stage years later to confer on Rogers his Lifetime Achievement Award—this is a means by which to make goodness attractive, which is part of our job description as Christians. It is a vitally important way to love God and our neighbor.

Now an example of deserved shame. The pages of Scripture are replete with narratives of honor and shame, from Adam and Eve to the story of the prodigal son. Readers are likely familiar with the story of the prodigal son in Luke 15. He insists on his inheritance ahead of time and engages in profligate spending and living, bringing shame on himself and an almost complete loss of social standing as a result. Finally, he repents and comes home, and the father, seeing him far off, comes running to him with a kiss and embrace. Here is a young man who did shame-worthy things. He felt shame, and he deserved to and couldn't fix it on his own. He needed someone to confer on him the honor he had lost. His loving father did.

This gives us as believers a simply wonderful opportunity. All of us, whether we have social capital to spare or not, are in a position to remind those around us that each and every person is loved and pursued by the God of the universe. The maker of heaven and earth is in a full sprint—robes and all—to embrace you, kiss you, put a ring on your finger, and throw a feast in your honor. Whatever the opinion of the company you keep, you are of immeasurable value to the One who matters most. You are so valuable that the God of the universe suffered the indignity of limited human form, betrayal, public humiliation, and naked crucifixion to rescue you not just from guilt but also from the shame of your condition, all to enjoy an eternal life of friendship and communion with you.[23]

If there is any doubt that this is what the life and work of Jesus was all about, recall the Old Testament passage that inaugurated his public ministry

---

[23] Ten Elshof, 142. All the credit to Ten Elshof for the language of this beautiful imagery.

in Luke 4, from Isa 61:1–3: "The Spirit of the Lord GOD is on me because the LORD has anointed me to bring good news to the poor. He has sent me to heal the brokenhearted, to proclaim liberty to the captives and freedom to the prisoners; to proclaim the year of the LORD's favor, and the day of our God's vengeance, to comfort all who mourn, to provide for all who mourn in Zion; to give them a crown of beauty instead of ashes, festive oil instead of mourning, and a splendid clothes instead of despair."

8

Evil, Hell, and Suffering

In this volume, we have been examining Christian theology through the lens of the goodness and love of God. The distinctiveness of this approach is based on the conviction that God is perfectly good, an inference warranted by, among other things, the claim that God provides the most robust and compelling explanation of a range of moral phenomena—from objective moral values to duties, moral freedom and knowledge, moral transformation and rationality. There is, however, another moral data point that far less obviously points to the existence of a good God, and arguably points away from it. This is the notorious challenge posed by the pain and evil that we experience in this world.

Such obstinate realities as intense suffering, heart-wrenching injustice, and excruciating loss are among the moral evidence that we must strive to come to terms with, and they make it pressing to face a question head on: Are the horrific pain, abject degradation, and unspeakable cruelty of this world able to be reconciled with an all-good God? Recall from chapter 1 that Yoram Hazony considered the problem of evil and the resulting incoherence of trying in vain to fit the divine perfections together as evidence against an Anselmian God.

More challenging still, perhaps, is the specific doctrine of hell and eternal damnation. Is not this terrifying aspect of Christian theology implicated in the most intractable variant of the problem of evil of all? These are the challenging questions that will occupy our attention in this chapter, and we will delimit the discussion by, once more, approaching this important investigation with the tools and resources of moral apologetics.

A Brief History of the Problem of Evil

The problem of evil has a rich history, of which the following are just a few highlights. David Hume's 1779 *Dialogues Concerning Natural Religion*, after demonstrating the failure of the teleological argument as presented by Cleanthes, features Philo foreshadowing the development of another formulation of the problem of evil. Philo argued that an evidential theology must infer the qualities of God from the characteristics of the world. How, though, can one on this basis reason to God's infinite goodness since the world as we experience it appears morally neutral at best? Hume also famously employed some hyperbole to capture the problem of evil succinctly: "Is [God] willing to prevent evil but not able? Then he is impotent. Is he able, but not willing? Then he is malevolent. Is he both able and willing? Whence then is evil?"[1] Paul Draper, incidentally, is a contemporary proponent of a view in the vicinity of Hume's, arguing with a confirmation-theoretic approach that certain facts appear more probable on naturalism than theism.

In the twentieth century, J. L. Mackie's notable version attempted to demonstrate that the Anselmian qualities of God are logically inconsistent with the existence of evil. If God is omnipotent, if God is omnibenevolent,

---

[1] David Hume, *Dialogues Concerning Natural Religion and Other Writings*, ed. Dorothy Coleman (Cambridge, UK: Cambridge University Press, 2007), 74.

and there is evil, this leads to an inconsistency on the basis of a few noncontroversial assumptions with respect to the expected actions of an omnipotent and good God. If omniscience is not subsumed under omnipotence, that can be added to the set of propositions under investigation.

More recently, William Rowe's 1979 version claimed that the existence of a good and omnipotent God is incompatible with the existence of what he termed "pointless evils." As Rowe defines it, a pointless evil is an evil that God (if he exists) could have prevented without thereby losing an outweighing good or having to permit an evil equally bad or worse.[2] Sometimes this sort of evil is called "gratuitous." Bruce Russell, for example, tends to use this phrase. Since the existence of God is inconsistent with the existence of pointless evils, and assuming the existence of pointless evils is probable, Rowe concluded that God probably does not exist.

This is an example of what Swinburne calls a C-inductive argument, according to which God's existence is less likely than not.[3] Rowe also offers a P-inductive version according to which certain instances of evil result in the probability of the existence of God being less than it would otherwise be. The latter is less ambitious and the arguably stronger argument, though of course it remains potentially consistent with an ultima facie judgment that an Anselmian God exists after all.

Goodness, Badness, and Evil

When C. S. Lewis wrote a book on the problem of evil, he called it *The Problem of Pain*. Now, it might be thought that pain and evil are largely interchangeable, but Immanuel Kant was careful to distinguish them. The way he did it was by contrasting badness with evil. Badness, for Kant,

---

[2] William Rowe, "The Problem of Evil and Some Varieties of Atheism," *American Philosophical Quarterly* 16, no. 4 (October 1979), 335–41, https://rintintin .colorado.edu/~vancecd/phil201/Rowe.pdf.

[3] See Richard Swinburne, *The Existence of God* (Oxford: Clarendon, 2004).

pertained to the production of painful consequences, whereas evil was a distinctively moral category, a feature of the human heart. Especially among contemporary secular ethicists, pain is often cast as "bad," and its elimination "good," and by a sort of sleight-of-hand the line from *nonmoral* goodness and badness is crossed to categories of *moral* goodness and badness. This is a mistake. To understand why, let's start with goodness.

The topic of goodness, like that of truth and beauty, is of infinite richness, particularly if the good and God himself are as intimately tied together as one like Augustine thought. If God himself is the ultimate good, then it makes perfect sense that it is no easy matter to say just what goodness is, for the ultimate good would be nothing less than God himself, who defies our finite understandings and escapes our ability fully to define or comprehend. This is why Robert Adams suggests that, if such a picture is remotely accurate, we should retain a "critical stance" toward various and sundry accounts of goodness, because they are unlikely to capture the whole picture.[4]

Nowadays goodness tends to be treated in domesticated and deflationary ways. Goodness is that which conduces to our flourishing, we hear it said, or goodness is what promotes social harmony. Or, following Aristotle, goodness is said to pertain to the function of something. A good car provides reliable transportation, for example. But arguably such an Aristotelian depiction of the good is inseparable from a more Platonic conception— what is *good for us as human beings*, for example, seems impossible, or at least unwise, to divorce from *what is good in and of itself.*

Although it makes sense to say that something is good to the extent it performs its function, a further question then always should be asked: Is that function a good thing? This is an especially important question to ask if we wish to think about moral goodness in particular. Of course, goodness is broader than moral goodness, but moral goodness is a quite important part

---

[4] Robert Merrihew Adams, *Finite and Infinite Goods: A Framework for Ethics* (New York: Oxford University Press, 1999).

of goodness. And in fact, in many contemporary discussions, quite a bit of confusion reigns when it comes to moral and nonmoral goodness.

For example, we often hear that pain is bad, and surely it is. But it is not morally bad per se. It is nonmorally bad. What is morally bad is the needless infliction of pain. It tends to be *people* who are morally good or morally bad. This was Kant's point. In plenty of contexts badness and evil (moral badness) are used interchangeably, but he used the distinction to highlight the difference between something that produces painful consequences and something distinctively and robustly, even perniciously, immoral. Inadvertently missing the nail with the hammer and hitting my thumb instead is surely the former, but hardly the latter. My intentionally hitting someone else's thumb with my hammer, however—at least without some morally overriding justification—would be evil.

So the problem of evil is not simply about the existence of pain and suffering, but why God allows it—or worse, causes it. The pain itself is not what is evil, but arguably God's allowing it or causing it is evil, and, so the argument goes, inconsistent with God's perfect goodness and love. This is why it would be a mistake to say that the problem of evil is just as much a problem for secularists as it is for theists. As a term of art, the "problem of evil" has to do specifically with reconciling a God who is all-powerful, all-good, and all-knowing with the evil and suffering we find in this world, and that is a challenge for theists, not atheists. Still, the evils of this world do pose a significant challenge for our secular and atheist interlocutors, as we will see.

The Intellectual Problem of Evil

The problem of evil is usually cast as coming in two variations: the intellectual problem of evil and the existential (or psychological or pastoral) problem of evil. The intellectual problem then can be subdivided into the logical and probabilistic versions. Let's discuss these two in turn, and then the psychological variant in the next section. The first intellectual variant is the version of the problem of evil that suggests, as Hazony seems to believe, that there is an incoherence in affirming all of the divine omni-qualities in the face of the suffering of this world. Any two of God's qualities are consistent with evil, but not all three together. As we saw above, Mackie was known for advancing this sort of deductive or logical variant of the problem of evil, and Alvin Plantinga is best known for addressing this version of the problem and is thought by many to have provided a definitive refutation of it.[5]

What Plantinga did was construct a defense. His defense had for its aim to show that Mackie had failed to make his case by identifying possible ways in which to account for the *moral evils* of this world—the evils perpetrated by people—and the so-called *natural evils*—cancers, devastating tornadoes, tsunamis, and the like. He was under no obligation to argue that these possibilities were actually the case. Their mere genuine possibility was enough to show that the alleged airtight case against Anselmianism did not work.

The salient possibility he adduced for moral evils was libertarian free will, with which people can choose to do awful things to other people, animals, the environment, and themselves. Again, he didn't have to argue that in fact we have such free will; the mere possibility of such an account was enough to do the trick. The possibility he cited to account for natural evils was the activity of dark spiritual forces at work in the world. That such forces exist is a longstanding Christian view and a thoroughly biblical one, but once more, the mere possibility of such an explanatory account was all he needed to show that the logical argument from evil failed to make its case.

Subsequent to Plantinga's groundbreaking work, much of the discussion of the problem of evil shifted from the logical version of the problem to the evidential version. The latter variant of the problem suggests that the quality and quantity of the sufferings we find in the world may not logically entail that an Anselmian God does not exist, but nevertheless effectively renders God's existence improbable. After all, we find ourselves thinking, if

---

[5] See Plantinga's *God, Freedom, and Evil* (Grand Rapids: Eerdmans, 1989).

we had the chance to put an end to the suffering of the world, most of us would choose to do so, despite our moral fallibility. Intuitively this world is far from what we would envision a world to be that is created by a perfect and all-loving, omniscient, and all-powerful God.

This version of the argument allows that some sufferings may be consistent with an Anselmian God, but it insists that what is not allowed are "gratuitous sufferings" beyond the pale and pointless, sufferings neither counterbalanced by valuable goods nor needed to avoid even worse sufferings. Putting it this way raises a question about sufferings produced by the operation of free will. If people have libertarian freedom, that will invariably introduce the possibility of grievous sufferings when the freedom is abused to inflict needless harm. So is this a case where the preservation of free will is a good sufficient to allow such sufferings, or a case of gratuitous sufferings since those sufferings themselves, in a real way, make the world worse rather than better?

In the former case the sufferings would not be gratuitous, and in the latter they would be gratuitous. Allowing things to happen that make the world worse does not seem inconsistent with an Anselmian God, because his choice to confer meaningful freedom introduced the possibility of such sufferings, and it is not immediately clear that a world without meaningful agency would be better than one with it. Likewise with sufferings produced by the existence of, say, stable natural laws. Although it is not the case that the actualization of every instance of suffering that comes about as a result of libertarian free will or stable natural laws makes the world better, such sufferings, even if gratuitous in that sense, are arguably consistent with an Anselmian God.

Perhaps this seems more like assertion than argument, but efforts are many and various to construct various theodicies to help answer probabilistic versions of the problem of evil. A theodicy is more ambitious than a defense. A theodicy aims to account for why God actually permits the evils in the world, which is a challenging exercise. We cannot hope to discuss the range of such efforts here, but in keeping with our moral apologetic focus, let's consider and subject to scrutiny an important thought experiment that might lead people to suggest that sufferings that make the world worse are problematic for the Anselmian. It goes like this: If God is what Anselmians suggest, then God is relevantly analogous to a loving parent, and no loving parents would allow one of their children to take a hammer to a sibling, even if preventing it violated the child's free will. So, the argument goes, a loving God would similarly intervene.

There is something initially intuitive about this argument, but a bit of reflection considerably detracts from its appeal. Suppose that God were to make a habit of intervening to prevent people from harming others. This would result in the vitiation of a huge swath of meaningful human choice in this world. Such interventions could not help but become objectionably ubiquitous. How could the suggestion of the argument be anything but the insistence that God is supposed to intervene every time any child is about to do considerable harm to another? Among other things, such ubiquitous intervention would actually liberate parents from having to prevent such harms. If they don't stop it, God will! If a parent doesn't feed his child, God will. Parents could bat their babies off the Empire State building for fun and God would intervene to prevent the children from being harmed. Presuming that any of this is somehow dutiful for an Anselmian God is problematically presumptuous in the extreme. The disanalogies between earthly parents and God, for one thing, are large and numerous, including that God, as we will argue later on, has the capacity to effect a redemption of sufferings that earthly parents simply do not.

Probabilistic variants of the problem of evil are often predicated on the notion that if we encounter unanswered questions about why God might allow certain sufferings, then the best explanation of our inability is that there is no explanation to be found. This remains one possibility among many others, but it is far from the obviously right inference to make. Arguing to a "best explanation" requires taking on all comers, and a full consideration of the entire range of relevant facts in need of explanation. This is where cognitive limitation defenders and skeptical theists often start to make their voices heard, reminding us that we likely are in no position to understand all of God's reasons for his actions.

C. S. Lewis, for example, once wrote the following: "If human life is in fact ordered by a beneficent being whose knowledge of our real needs and of the way in which they can be satisfied infinitely exceeds our own, we must expect a priori that his operations will often appear to us far from beneficent and far from wise, and that it will be our highest prudence to give him our confidence in spite of this."[6] The idea here is that, even if our best efforts at theodicy fall short, individually and collectively, this is actually not surprising and potentially not problematic for the thoughtful theist.

To which some atheists might wish to retort by suggesting that such a response cuts both ways, and if we are thus saddled with such epistemic limitations, there is not much hope of principled confidence in God's goodness and reality. There is a distinction to be drawn, however, between facing a difficult challenge into which we have only some measure of insight and retaining grounds for a hopeful resolution, on the one hand, and facing certain intractable challenges to rationality that we ignore on pain of sacrificing intellectual integrity. So while we do wish to acknowledge that there are limitations in what we can understand about God, we consider ourselves to have solid reasons to believe in God's perfect goodness and that this conviction does in fact rule out approaching the problem of evil with too credulous or fideistic a mentality, an issue we will touch on in the final sections of this chapter. As to whether morality overall points toward or away from God remains the question this chapter is considering.

Before moving on to the next version of the problem of evil, let's take a brief detour into the history of the moral argument. When Cambridge philosopher William Sorley was working on his Gifford Lectures on the moral argument during World War I, he sent early chapters to his gifted son Charles, who was in the throes of the fight. Sorley was writing about the

---

[6] C. S. Lewis, "On Obstinacy of Belief," in *Philosophy of Religion: An Anthology*, ed. Louis P. Pojman (Belmont, CA: Wadsworth, 1987), 377.

goodness of God in these lectures when something happened that brought the problem of evil home in the most personal way possible. The devastating news arrived that his beloved Charles had been killed in action.[7] His resultant grief and abiding faith despite his son's tragic loss resonates on every page of the lectures, later published as *Moral Values and the Idea of God*. The moral law is real, Sorley was convinced, but he could hardly deny the existence of evil, facing it as he did in a personally excruciating way.

Sorley saw in a new way the dispute between Kant and Hume on this score. Kant's formulation of the moral argument suggested that the moral law requires God as a practical postulate necessitated by moral reason. Hume in contrast used the facts of morality to argue against an Anselmian God. Sorley saw that the most serious objection to theism is the problem of evil, for it raises the dreadful possibility that the natural order and the moral order are working at cross-purposes with each other, locked in an intractable, irremediable conflict. Sorley saw that Kant and Hume were approaching the question from different points of view. Hume directed his attention to the struggle of mankind, what men suffered, the cruelty of the world, the havoc of life. Kant, though, contemplated the inward law of goodness; rather than looking at the extent of its actualization, he assigned primacy to the idea of goodness, which consciousness revealed to him, and recognition of which secured him a position above the play of merely natural forces.[8]

How, then, might nature after all be regarded as a fitting context for the realization of goodness? The answer depends not on what a perfect world looks like but what a world might need to look like in order to make growth in goodness possible and likely. Real agents, rather than marionettes and automatons, require the possibility of missing the mark. Only by this means might they come to have goodness and consciousness of the good, not to mention communion with God himself. Sorley argued that suffering and

---

[7] Charles Sorley is known as one of the four great War Poets from World War I.

[8] For a summary of Sorley's work, see chap. 6 of David Baggett and Jerry L. Walls, *The Moral Argument: A History* (New York: Oxford University Press, 2019).

evil are possible in a theistic worldview if finite minds are gradually recognizing moral ends that they are free to accept or reject. Both the moral order and the order of nature belong to the essence of reality, and if it is synthesis and integration we seek, they can be harmoniously united in one universe only when nature is understood not merely in its present appearance but as working out the purpose of making moral beings.

The Existential Problem of Evil

When I (Dave) used to teach a lot of introductory philosophy courses, I usually saved for my last lecture the least philosophical lecture of all: a treatment of the personal or psychological, existential, or pastoral version of the problem of evil. It was my conviction that this, more than any other challenge to faith, was the hardest one of all, not for philosophical reasons but for psychological ones.

Believers who have a grasp of a number of compelling reasons not to be surprised at horrific sufferings in this world may nevertheless be emotionally ill-equipped to handle instances of suffering on a personal level. We see this to some measure even in the great C. S. Lewis, whose book on the problem of evil is something of a classic, but then, tragically, he lost his wife, seventeen years his junior, to cancer. In the notebook he wrote in the aftermath of that devastating loss, we find some sentences and sentiments that amaze us they were written and entertained by the same man who had written *Mere Christianity* or *The Problem of Pain*. For example, "What reason have we, except our own desperate wishes, to believe that God is, by any standard we can conceive, 'good'? Doesn't all the prima facie evidence suggest exactly the opposite? What have we to set against it?"[9]

---

[9] C. S. Lewis, *A Grief Observed* (New York: Bantam Books, 1976), 33–34. For further reflections on this part of Lewis's life, see David Baggett, "Is Divine Iconoclast as Bad as Cosmic Sadist?" in *C. S. Lewis as Philosopher: Truth, Goodness,*

Obviously enough, *A Grief Observed* is a remarkably raw book and perhaps one of Lewis's most brutally honest. It is a very good set of reflections primarily, we think, because of the light it sheds on the personal variant of the problem of evil. Lewis was quite adept at thinking about issues of suffering theologically, but his personal loss was the real thing—not a dissertation or lecture, but grim reality. And though his faith didn't tumble, it at least momentarily wobbled. Pain and loss hurt, and the goodness and love of God do not tend to be the first things that leap to our minds when we are in their throes.

Earlier in Lewis's life, when he was just a boy, he had lost his mother, and the movie *Shadowlands* touches on that topic a bit. There is a scene in the dark attic where Lewis's stepson is alone in his grief after losing his mom, sitting in front of the wardrobe that had already proven a disappointment. Lewis goes to talk to him. The boy claims not to believe in heaven, to which Lewis says, "That's okay," discerning the wisdom of saving that conversation for another day. The boy says he does not understand why she had to die, and Lewis admits the same; but it's when the boy finally cries and admits he hopes to see her again that Lewis breaks down, hugs the boy, and says through his tears, "Me too." Then they simply weep and hold one another. Sometimes that is simply the best we can do in the face of our pain and suffering, weeping with those who weep, saving substantive theological conversations for later. Lewis himself came to admit in *A Grief Observed* that none of us see clearest when our eyes are full of tears.

Jerry Walls has described how some live in hope only because they bury their heads in the sand and do not honestly face the brutal reality of how horrifying evil and suffering can be. They make glib and simplistic statements that suggest they have filtered all real suffering out of their worldview. But Christianity's counsel is far different from this approach. As Marilyn Adams once put it, "God is not content . . . to watch his writhing creatures with the

---

and Beauty, ed. David Baggett, Gary R. Habermas, and Jerry L. Walls (Downers Grove: IVP Academic, 2008).

cool eye of reason. . . . He knows from experience what it is like for pain to drive everything else from a finite consciousness and to press it to the limits of its endurance. . . . Christ crucified [provides] the company that misery loves."[10]

Christianity does not shy away from the pain of pain and evil of evil. Christ himself drank of unspeakable sufferings to their dregs, even to the point of death, and in the process overcame it. There is nothing plastic or sanitized or artificial about Jesus, suffering, or the cross in the Christian worldview. God is not at all isolated from the harsh realities of the sufferings of this world, but is in the process of redeeming them somehow, enabling us not merely to endure them but to be transformed by them. There remains quite a bit of mystery about the role that suffering plays in our lives, but the Bible says that even Jesus learned obedience through suffering (Heb 5:8–9); and if Jesus did, can his followers realistically expect anything less?

The topic of the resurrection will occupy the last chapter, but it is powerful to remember the comfort it can provide us as we struggle with pain that seems too much to bear, beyond the scope of redemption, tempting us to despair. These words from Nicholas Wolterstorff, written while reeling from the tragic loss of his graduate school-aged son, have provided great consolation to many:

> To believe in Christ's rising from the grave is to accept it as a sign of our own rising from our graves. If for each of us it was our destiny to be obliterated and for all of us together it was our destiny to fade away without a trace, then not Christ's rising but my dear son's early dying would be the logo of our fate.
>
> God is love. That is why he suffers. To love our suffering, sinful world is to suffer. God so suffered for the world that he gave his only Son to suffering. The one who does not see God's suffering does not see his suffering love.

---

[10] Marilyn Adams, "Redemptive Suffering: A Christian Solution to the Problem of Evil," in *The Problem of Evil: Selected Readings*, ed. Michael L. Peterson (Notre Dame: University of Notre Dame Press, 1992), 180–81.

So suffering is down at the center of things, deep down where the meaning is. Suffering is the meaning of our world. For Love is the meaning. And Love suffers. The tears of God are the meaning of history.[11]

Wolterstorff's words here, even if we bear in mind some rhetorical flourish, may go a bit too far. If to love is (necessarily) to suffer and if "suffering is the meaning of our world," then it is very difficult to see how God's redeeming love serves the purpose of ultimately, finally, and victoriously delivering us from sin, and from suffering. It is almost written as if suffering is not only necessary to the world but to the identity of God. And if that were true, there would be no hope of deliverance from suffering. So bearing in mind that crucial caveat, we can certainly appreciate the suggestion that, in ways we can only begin to imagine, God can use and redeem suffering in powerfully transformative ways.

Where Does Morality Point?

Probability assessments about the likelihood of God's existence in the face of the sufferings of this world should not be considered in isolation. They invariably involve consideration of a range of background assumptions. This is one of those junctures where it becomes clear that the problem of evil and the enterprise of moral apologetics are locked in a zero-sum game in which one will win and the other lose. Appeals to the prescriptive nature of judgments about the entailments of justice, binding moral obligations, basic human rights, or intrinsic human dignity presuppose a strong form of moral realism. To the extent that variants of the moral argument prove efficacious, there is principled reason to think that the better account of such moral verities can be found in theism than atheism.

---

[11] Nicholas Wolterstorff, *Lament for a Son* (Grand Rapids: Eerdmans, 1987), 92.

Thus, what the atheist needs to do, in our estimation, is illegitimately borrow from a worldview they have roundly rejected while acting like they can retain their deep moral convictions on the basis of far weaker metaphysical foundations. Taking seriously categories of injustice and tragic suffering, not to mention our binding and authoritative duties to reduce such evils in this world, provides evidence *in favor* of theism, not *against* it. Confining one's attention to the worst of this world's sufferings alone, while affixing blinders to consider the broader context, might naturally raise suspicions that God does not exist; but taking such evils seriously provides evidence that the world is not what it ought to be and is in serious need of getting remedied and rectified. This analysis makes good sense on a Christian understanding that this is a fallen world in the process of getting redeemed, and precious little sense on a naturalistic picture of a world and its inhabitants playing out their programming according to which there is no reason at all to think it or they should be any different from what they are.

The insistence that God immediately wipe out the evil in this world sounds good in theory, but, as any actually good parent knows, the process of moral maturation requires patience and cannot be rushed. Children have to be able to make mistakes, learn from them, see there are consequences for their choices, and gradually come to care for what is of value. Striking the right, changing, and delicate balances between their growing autonomy and needed strictures and constraints to help them mature is a perennial challenge. If God were to short-circuit the process of moral maturation among persons by wiping out evil, that would likely result in his removing each of us from the picture, for evil resides within each of us.

On a Christian understanding of things, each of us is afflicted with what Kant called a "dear self." As Anselm and Scotus put it, we each tend by nature to privilege an affection for advantage over an affection for justice; again as Kant put it, our proclivity is to privilege the bad maxim over the good maxim, subordinating duties to preference rather than vice versa. As Luther famously put it, we are all of us curved inward on ourselves. All of us are implicated in a broken, sinful condition from which we need deliverance. It is a mercy that God in his holiness not simply wipe us from the planet to eliminate the gratuitous sufferings of this world. His is fortunately an agenda motivated by perfect love that aims to save and redeem, heal and transform, and ultimately perfect and glorify. Pascal similarly argued it was a mercy that there is a large measure of divine hiddenness in our currently sinful state; for us to see God in all his resplendent mercy in our present state would destroy us; how can we see God's face until we have faces?[12]

So let's consider a broader range of moral realities and background assumptions. There is evil—not just intense suffering, but soul-crushing morally hideous evil that calls for a reckoning. Recall that Paul and Socrates agreed on a judgment to come and balancing of the moral scales. There is the evil within the heart of men; as Clay Jones argues, all of us are Auschwitz-enabled; under the right circumstances, each of us is capable of doing hideous things.[13] Our moral improprieties and foibles are not just trivial inconveniences easily fixed; we all seem riddled with a deep moral malady in need of radical fixing. We experience deep moral regrets for not doing actions we should and for performing actions we shouldn't. The category of moral regret, however, makes little sense in a world in which there is not adequate moral freedom. If this is a wholly determined world, libertarian freedom and meaningful agency seem eminently unlikely, carving out no space for the category of moral regret at all. Like William James once said, it's a good fit with a mechanical universe but a bad moral fit.[14] We have a nonnegotiable sense that this is

---

[12] Divine hiddenness is a recurring theme in Blaise Pascal's *Pensées and Other Writings* (Oxford: Oxford University Press, 1995). Here is one example: "There is enough light for those whose only desire is to see, and enough darkness for those of the opposite disposition" (81; section 274).

[13] Clay Jones, *Why Does God Allow Evil? Compelling Answers for Life's Toughest Questions* (Eugene, OR: Harvest House, 2017).

[14] See William James, *The Dilemma of Determinism* (Whitefish, MT: Kessinger, 2010).

not the way the world ought to be. We have binding authoritative moral obligations to decrease the suffering in this world, to fight for the objective deliverances of justice, to protect the basic human rights of people, to value the intrinsic dignity of persons, to promote values of goodness and beauty and truth.

What percentage of this more robust list of relevant moral background assumptions can a naturalistic worldview realistically make good sense of? Next to none of them, we have argued at length elsewhere. Why, on such a worldview, even expect the world to be different from what it is? What room is there for the category of moral regret when, at the macroscopic level, determinism rules out other outcomes? Rather than explaining evil, it explains it away, which is far worse than the challenge posed to theists. And rather than retaining hope that the worst evils will eventually be somehow overcome, it instead insists that the worst this world has to offer will forever remain unresolved.

In diametric opposition and patent contrast, theism generally and Christianity particularly can explain all of the moral facts quite well, even if the theist admits there remain certain ongoing challenges to fully understand the quality and quantity of the sufferings of this world. Despite such unanswered questions—owing to the size of the questions, the limitations with which we are confronted, etc.—believers can retain principled hope in the fact that one day we will no longer see through a glass darkly, all our tears will be wiped away, and all our curiosities satisfied when we see the face of God.

Perhaps suffering is not the best place to start to lay out the theistic case, but having explained the other central moral facts, it can then turn to the matter of this world's brokenness. It can explain why the world is broken and what God is doing to fix it; it can inspire principled hope for an ultimate solution to the problem. It can remind us that our temporal happiness is not the chief purpose in life. The world is to be a place in which we grow morally and spiritually, which requires a context in which there are challenges to endure. That human beings have rebelled in this fallen world in need of redemption helps explain its dysteleological aspects, and that this life is not the only life there is inspires us to look for goods that are more than merely immanent. The promise of intimacy with the ultimate good provides grounds for believing that even the most hideous of evils in this life can ultimately be defeated.

Christianity provides principled reasons to hope for a world redeemed, for gratuitous evils to be defeated, for the loveless to be embraced, for injustices to be rectified. Here is how Richard Creel makes such a case:

> As long as it is logically possible that evil is defeated, that innocent suffering is not meaningless and final, it seems to me that we have a moral obligation to hope that that possibility is actual. Therefore we have a moral obligation to hope that there is a God because, if there is a God, then innocent suffering is not meaningless or final. . . . To be sure, the Holocaust was enormously tragic—but without God it is even more tragic. Indeed, a far greater evil than the evils of history would be that the evils of history will not be defeated because there is no God. This seems to me a terribly important point that Dostoyevsky's Ivan failed to consider.[15]

The Problem of Hell

The thorniest aspect of the problem of evil is usually identified to be hell, especially if hell is thought to persist forever. What good is accomplished by that? Annihilationists and universalists deny that any human being will be relegated to hell forever, so hell is less a problem for them than those who hold to a traditional view of hell as unending and consciously experienced. Some even gravitate toward a literal understanding of hellfire, so that hell gets cast as the ultimate torture chamber that never ends. Understandably this raises questions about the love and goodness of God,

---

[15] Richard E. Creel, *Divine Impassibility: An Essay in Philosophical Theology* (Eugene, OR: Wipf & Stock), 149–50.

so no discussion of the problem of evil can ignore the challenge posed by the doctrine of damnation.

One fairly standard way to try to reconcile the perfect love of God with the relegation of some to an eternal hell is by remembering that, though God is loving, he is also just and holy. We are to fear God, after all, who can throw us, body and soul, into hell (Matt 10:28). The wrath of God is a fearful thing, and hell is what we all deserve, after all. It is nothing but a mercy that any of us is spared of it. We are inclined to affirm certain truths at least adjacent to this sort of answer, but this approach is not the one we will take here. Starting with the problematic conjunction "but" that contrasts, explicitly or implicitly, God's love and justice, or God's love and holiness, this contrast strikes us as fundamentally misguided, as if there is something of a tension between them.

We would rather affirm that God is loving *and* just and holy, no "but" required. These exist in perfect harmony, not tension or dissonance. On our view, if any human being ends up in hell, it is a tragedy. It did not have to happen. If anyone goes to hell, it is because of their stubborn resistance of God's overtures of love to the bitter end until their choices—hardened into habits and character—finally becomes determinative of who they are and of their destiny. Having turned from light, their choice is for darkness instead; having spurned life, the result is death; having renounced joy, their ultimate destination is misery.

An important question here, then, is what the cause is of the misery of hell. As long as it is understood as largely an externally imposed threat— like fire—the doctrine of hell gets easily mistaken as nothing but an elaborate prudential threat of a horrible state of affairs to avoid. Repent or burn seems to be the prevailing idea. But such literalism is no more required than believing that heaven is paved with literal streets of gold rather than such an image conveying something of symbolic significance. A more substantively ethical view of hell understands its import rather differently, where the sufferings of hell—as Dante conceived it in his fiction—are not an arbitrary external threat, but more intrinsically connected to sins the damned stubbornly cling to until the bitter end. Rather than responding to God's overtures of love and invitations to eternal joy, they reject God— by turns depicted in Scripture as light, life, and love. Such a rejection is tantamount to a choice for darkness, death, and hatred; it's a choice to live against the grain of reality, an attempt to derive happiness from a source that cannot possibly offer it. It is a willful forfeiture of the only real joy there is in the universe; it is, nevertheless, a real place of divine judgment. It's a terrifying prospect to be given what tenacious depravity and denial of love demands.

This depiction of hell stands in obvious dependence on a robust measure of meaningful agency on the part of human beings. Such an assumption might be thought to be a dubious one in light of a doctrine like total depravity, according to which human beings are utterly implicated in sin and rebellion. To affirm the requisite freedom to repent of one's sins might be thought to be a Pelagian or semi-Pelagian theology. How might we attempt to reconcile original sin and a deep sense of human depravity with the sort of moral freedom on which our approach is predicated? One way is to affirm something like a doctrine of prevenient grace, the grace of God that is operative even among unbelievers drawing them to himself, restoring to them a measure of meaningful agency, and giving them the opportunity to recognize their sin and need for repentance.[16] On our view, though, such grace, though universal, is resistible, in contrast to its being offered only to some and being irresistible.

Those who would affirm the latter would encounter challenges in making sense of hell that we do not—including what seems the obvious entailment that hell itself is not even a tragic thing—since on our view the offer of salvation and the grace by which to accept salvation is universal, though

---

[16] Prevenient grace, classically construed, is the light by which the Son of God enlightens everyone who comes into the world (John 1:9), showing each one "to act justly, to love faithfulness, and to walk humbly with your God" (Mic 6:8).

resistible. Those who reject the offer do so in a culpably free fashion, possessing the capacity to do otherwise but not availing themselves of it. In a real sense, on our view, anyone who goes to hell chooses hell, at least indirectly. By rejecting God, refusing to repent, and seeking their ultimate happiness in sources outside of God, they relegate themselves to the misery that results from such a defiant rejection of reality. As C. S. Lewis once put it:

> God made us: invented us as a man invents an engine. A car is made to run on petrol, and it would not run properly on anything else. Now God designed the human machine to run on Himself. He Himself is the fuel our spirits were designed to burn, or the food our spirits were designed to feed on. There is no other. That is why it is just no good asking God to make us happy in our own way without bothering about religion. God cannot give us a happiness and peace apart from Himself, because it is not there. There is no such thing.[17]

What we can realistically expect and gloriously hope from a God whose character is perfect love is that he will not primarily look for reasons to *damn* us but for reasons to *save* us. The Bible clearly teaches that God did not send his Son into the world to condemn the world but that the world through him might be saved (John 3:17). It is not God's desire that any should perish (2 Pet 3:9). If some end up in hell, then, has God been defeated? Is the notion that love conquers all a lie? Perhaps it depends on what one means by "conquer." If it is taken to mean that love can ensure particular results despite people's free will, then it is pretty clear it does not conquer all. Unrequited love exists, after all. And loved ones suffer from horrible and deleterious addictions contrary to the earnest wishes of family and friends. So that is a fairly naive construal of what conquering amounts to; it would require that love vitiate meaningful agency.

---

[17] C. S. Lewis, *Mere Christianity* (New York: Macmillan, 1952), 53–54.

Might there be some other ultimate sense in which love wins? We suspect so. God's love conquered death, for example, in the resurrection. There is a richer and more nuanced way in which something can be affirmed about love's ultimate victory, though it leaves open the possibility, if we are meaningfully free, that some might choose to turn their back on light and life and love, with tragic results. God loves everyone, yet are some sent to hell? The traditional view in the Christian tradition is that universalism is false and some do sadly and tragically end up experiencing damnation (Matt 25:41–46). Is this a "defeat" of love? Much depends on what we mean by the relevant terms. If love is offered and obstinately rejected, and, with the love, joy and peace and fulfillment, the loss of all those things is the result. That seems less like the defeat of love, though, than the intentional and deliberate, repeated and ultimate rejection of love. The choice of darkness over light and death over life, does not veto love but rather sadly closes its heart to love. But love does not give up, even when it can seem hopeless. Like faith and hope, love endures.

Although not explicitly about hell, sometimes the narrative about the hardening of Pharaoh's heart in the Old Testament is cited as a particular form of predestination that denies the sort of requisite freedom we have been discussing. Eleonore Stump, in her magisterial *Wandering in Darkness: Narrative and the Problem of Suffering*, offers some very useful insights that may shed some light on this topic. As human beings we are internally fragmented and double-minded. Our deepest freedom is compromised when there is a fundamental disconnect between our (first order) *desires* and our (second order) *desires about our desires*.[18] So if I have an overwhelming desire to gamble but a desire not to have that desire, I am in a dissonant state and my deepest agency is somewhat compromised. Suppose I ask God for help and to take away my desire to gamble, and in an act of miraculous deliverance he does. He has not thereby vitiated my freedom by this gift of sanctification; to the contrary, he has enhanced it, by enabling my first order

---

[18] Eleonore Stump, *Wandering in Darkness: Narrative and the Problem of Suffering* (Oxford: Oxford University Press, 2012).

and second order desires to move into alignment and for me to live more effectively as the person I want to be.

An inverted example is a case like Joseph Goebbels, Hitler's Nazi propagandist, who wanted his own heart to harden so he wouldn't feel compassion for the suffering Poles when he saw a graphic account of the hideous atrocities they were suffering at the hands of German soldiers. "Be hard, my heart, be hard," he told himself. On reflection his choice was to be that kind of cruel and uncompassionate person. His first order desire, at least fleetingly, was one of compassion, but his second order desire, which more accurately reflected who he wanted and deliberatively chose to be, was not to have those compassionate desires. If God, suppose, were to intervene and harden Goebbels's heart, taking away some of that compassion, he would be bringing Goebbels's lower and higher order desires into alignment, making him a more internally integrated person. Rather than detracting from his volition, he would be enhancing it a bit, even though it would put Goebbels more in the grip of sin. God would be giving Goebbels what he really wanted down deep, what he chose when, presumably, he could and should have done otherwise.

So when Pharaoh hardened his own heart and God hardened it even more, God was actually honoring Pharaoh's choice.[19] God loves us, and desires that none would perish; love is not just what God *does*, it's who he *is*. But God will also honor our choices if we decide to hold on to sin tighter than we hold on to him; if we renounce the only ultimate source of Joy there is, we may just get what we want. Of course, the clearest picture we have of the immeasurable love of God is the cross; the Pharaoh passage is one of

---

[19] Sometimes Pharaoh hardens his own heart: "But when Pharaoh saw there was relief, he hardened his heart" (Exod 8:15). "But Pharaoh hardened his heart this time also" (Exod 8:32). Other times God hardens his heart: Exod 7:3–4 (NIV) says, "But I will harden Pharaoh's heart, and though I multiply my miraculous signs and wonders in Egypt, he will not listen to you. Then I will lay my hand on Egypt and with mighty acts of judgment I will bring out . . . my people the Israelites."

those challenging ones we have to think about a bit more to understand—in light of the cross.

The choice of hell results in sufferings best understood as intrinsically connected to those sins the damned refuse to repent of. The condemned choose to forego the identity they could have experienced in relationship with God and choose instead to forge an identity stamped forever by their rebellion against light and life and love. Those relegated to hell provide a sort of left-handed testimony to the fact that our ultimate fulfillment and joy come only from loving God and others as we ought. To make something else one's "god" is to treat it as worship-worthy rather than God himself, who is the one truly worthy of worship. To worship at the altar of false gods, entrusting ourselves to gods incapable of offering us the blessed life for which we yearn, is to consign ourselves to perpetual dissatisfaction and ultimately misery. In fact, sin and idolatry result in the ultimate sort of bondage; in contrast, serving God and seeking the true good ultimately make us maximally free in the deepest sense of all—freed entirely from the shackles of sin and freed to become the people we were meant to be and best versions of ourselves by the operation of God's grace. And this brings us to the final chapter.

9

Heaven, Resurrection, and Future Hope

The previous chapter was about evil, and this chapter will take up the resurrection and the doctrine of heaven. In some ways these topics could not be more different, but in other ways this chapter is an organic continuation of the discussion. No treatment of God's solution to the problem of evil is complete without consideration of the doctrine of heaven. Another parallel with the previous chapter is that a discussion of heaven needs to be infused with moral seriousness. What is most important about heaven are not literal streets of gold, but experience and enjoyment of the ultimate goods for which we were designed—fellowship with God most of all. To understand heaven requires we see that this world is not enough and that our perceived good is, too often, far too small.

The needed corrective gives us an opportunity once more to emphasize the centrality of the goodness and love of God, which we are privileged to enter into and enjoy forever in the life to come for which we were made. The new heaven and earth is where love of God and love of neighbor will take center stage. The Bible speaks of a glory to come that will make all the present sufferings pale into insignificance by comparison (2 Cor 4:16–18).

Paul spoke in such terms and knew of what he spoke. He endured beatings, starvation, shipwrecks, and more.

> Five times I received from the Jews the forty lashes minus one. Three times I was beaten with rods, once I was pelted with stones, three times I was shipwrecked, I spent a night and a day in the open sea, I have been constantly on the move. I have been in danger from rivers, in danger from bandits, in danger from my fellow Jews, in danger from Gentiles; in danger in the city, in danger in the country, in danger at sea; and in danger from false believers. I have labored and toiled and have often gone without sleep; I have known hunger and thirst and have often gone without food; I have been cold and naked (2 Cor 11:24–27 NIV).

Yet he remained confident that none of this was even worth mentioning because of the glory to come.

Interestingly enough, however, the doctrine of heaven does not play a prominent role in the Old Testament. Lewis once conjectured as to why, and what he has is an important reminder:

> It is surely . . . very possible that when God began to reveal himself to men, to show them that He and nothing else is their true goal and the satisfaction of their needs, and that He has a claim upon them simply by being what He is, quite apart from anything He can bestow or deny, it may have been absolutely necessary that his revelation should not begin with any hint of future Beatitude or Perdition. Those are not the right point to begin at. An effective belief in them, coming too soon, may even render almost impossible the development of (so to call it) the appetite

for God; personal hopes and fears, too obviously exciting, have got in first.[1]

Lewis considered such doctrines as hell and heaven vitally important, but better to *end* with than *start* with. Holiness and loving God are even more important than issues of happiness. This is in no way to drive a wedge between them, but to stress that the former has spiritual priority. We are told to seek first the kingdom of God and his righteousness—and the distinguishing feature of God's kingdom is God's lordship and kingship in our lives, not the destination of heaven.

Of course, amazingly enough, the story does not end there. After seeking first God and his kingdom, we are promised that "all these things" shall be added unto us (Matt 6:33). God knows our needs and desires and fondest wishes, and he wants to grant us the deepest fulfillment and joy of which we are capable. Paradoxically, the way to our deepest happiness is not by seeking happiness, but by seeking intimacy with God, his lordship, and love of God and neighbor. But let's back up a bit and spell all this out a bit more systematically, starting with the resurrection of Jesus.

The Resurrection of Jesus

The resurrection of Jesus is both a powerful piece of apologetics for the truth of Christianity and, according to biblical teaching, an utterly pivotal game-changing moment in history. It would make perfect sense, incidentally, that something so centrally important would also be so powerfully evidenced. Elsewhere we have written about the evidence for the resurrection, and the resultant rationality of a resurrection inference based on it. There we also explored various skeptical challenges and a range of underlying philosophical questions that arise when discussing the case for the historicity of

---

[1] C. S. Lewis, *Reflections on the Psalms* (New York: Houghton Mifflin Harcourt, 1964), 40.

the resurrection.[2] We won't reiterate that material here, but rather explore a few of the powerful theological implications of the reality of the resurrection.[3]

Rather than resurrection coming only at the eschaton as a widespread event, like many Jews believed, it happened to Jesus alone first, while still in the midst of the unfolding events of history. This unexpected turn of events leads to the operative notion of the "already/not yet" in Christian theology. In one sense the kingdom of God has already come in the life, death, resurrection, and ascension of Jesus, and in another sense it has yet to come in all of its resplendent glory.

In the meantime, believers are to continue to labor in this world to proclaim and showcase God's kingdom life but do so in confidence and with soaring hope because the battle has already been won and the outcome secured. Death has already been defeated and no longer needs to be a source of fear. The same power that raised Jesus from the dead is at work among believers, anointing them for the work to which they are called and enabling them to live in victory over sin.

In his *Resurrection and the Moral Order*, Oliver O'Donovan places resurrection at the center of his understanding of ethics. For him the Christian needs to put the resurrection of Christ and the hope it engenders at the heart of our understanding of the moral order. He doesn't approach this matter as an apologist, in either sense of the word, but as a confident theologian desirous of exploring the rich implications of the resurrection for how it is we ought to live as people animated by the power of the Holy Spirit. In this way his words are reminiscent of C. S. Lewis's sentiment that Christians don't walk uprightly in order to earn heaven but because the spark of heaven is already within them.

---

[2] *Did the Resurrection Happen? A Conversation with Gary Habermas and Antony Flew*, ed. David Baggett (Downers Grove: IVP, 2009).

[3] As mentioned, one of the implications speaks once more to the problem of evil. If the resurrected one is also the crucified one who knows firsthand the power of temptation, the agony of real nails, and the pain of betrayal, then indeed, we can understand evil in a way that is both *honest* and *hopeful*.

Death, darkness, and hatred are bound together as the perversion and privation of life, light, and love. The resurrection is arguably the central piece of God's plan to fix this world's brokenness, to defeat evil, to promote abundant life, to dispel darkness, and to replace hatred with love. There is both a qualitative and quantitative aspect to the life that the defeat of death makes possible. Even now believers can enter into the life for which we were intended, marked by love of God and neighbor and doing good works prepared beforehand for us to do. We can be filled with the astounding hope that death is not the end but just a doorway into a never-ending experience of love of God and neighbor and meaningful work in a context liberated completely from the deleterious and acidulous taint of sin.

Before moving on, it bears repeating what happened in Acts 17. The setting was Athens, where Socrates had proclaimed his ignorance (though not of objective morality or a coming judgment). In a move sure not to be missed in that context, the apostle Paul proclaimed a judgment to come. The hour of ignorance was over, he said, and why? Because of the resurrection of Jesus. That event was proclaimed right there at the epicenter of philosophy's origin. Verses 30 and 31 read like this: "In the past God overlooked such ignorance, but now he commands all people everywhere to repent. For he has set a day when he will judge the world with justice by the man he has appointed. He has given proof of this to everyone by raising him from the dead" (NIV).

An Argument for Immortality

The reality of resurrection introduces the possibility of an afterlife, perhaps even something like immortality. Mortality and morality are related in a number of interesting ways. For example, Pascal once said, "The immortality of the soul is something of such vital importance to us, affecting us so deeply, that one must have lost all feeling not to care about knowing the facts of the matter. All our actions and thoughts must follow such different paths, according to whether there is hope of eternal blessing or not, that the only possible way of acting with sense and judgment is to decide our course in the light of this point, which ought to be our ultimate objective."[4]

Immanuel Kant actually gave an argument for immortality based on ethics. The gist of his argument was this: since we will never be able to achieve God's holy will, it will take all of eternity for us to approach it closer and closer, but such a process will never be completed. Thus, if the binding dictates of morality are to be taken seriously, we must postulate the existence of an afterlife to enable us forever to approach God's holy will, which is to say a process that will never be completed.

Part of what analyzing this argument requires is consideration of what exactly God's "holy will" consists of. Even if we are fully delivered from the power of sin, we will never presumably bear the same relation to moral perfection as God does. Our perfection is contingent; God's is necessary, for example. Still, Christian theology teaches that the process of salvation will be completed at the day of Christ Jesus. Typically, Christian theologians teach that at "glorification" full deliverance from the power and consequences of sin will take place. At that point believers will be saved to the uttermost, conformed entirely to the image of Christ. If this is what is meant by a "holy will," then it is something that will be achieved after all, contra Kant.

Still, however, there seems something right about Kant's suggestion. Complete deliverance from sin is achievable, according to a Christian view of things, but even subsequent to experiencing the beatific vision, believers will still presumably be able to continue growing ever closer to God and one another, and growing in love. That indeed seems to be a process that can continue indefinitely. Since the arguably most central experience of heaven will involve intimacy with God himself, and God's goodness is literally infinite, that provides us reason, too, to think that the pursuit of such intimacy is a process that will never be completed. This suggests a

---

[4] Blaise Pascal, *Pensées*, trans. Honor Levi (Oxford: Oxford University Press, 1995), 143.

quantitative component to eternal life, in addition to the qualitative sense of eternal life that we can partake of in some measure even during our earthly lives.

That the possibility of continued growth remains possible even after experiencing the beatific vision would suggest that Kant was indeed on to something. The picture is not a static one but a dynamic one, a reality to which a luminary from the history of the moral argument, A. E. Taylor, pointed and explicated in his *Faith of a Moralist*. As Taylor put it, complete deliverance from sin's power is not the end of life but rather marks the beginning of the richest, deepest life for which we were created. Here is just one example of Taylor's reflections:

> The moral life does not consist merely in getting into right relations with our fellows or our Maker. That's only preliminary to the real business: to live in them. Even in this life we have to do more than unlearn unloving. We have to practice giving love actual embodiment. This is continuous with what is morally of highest importance and value in our present life. . . . Heaven must be a land of delightful surprises. We should have learned to love every neighbor who crosses our path, to hate nothing that God has made, to be indifferent to none of the mirrors of His light. But even where there is no ill-will or indifference to interfere with love, it is still possible for love to grow as understanding grows.[5]

Complete deliverance from sin, according to a Christian perspective, marks both the highest form of freedom of which we are capable and also entrance into our deepest sense of personal identity. Questions of identity occupy the attention of plenty of contemporary writers preoccupied with the matter. From a Christian perspective, there is a uniqueness to persons (that philosophers might like to refer to as a person's haecceity), a specificity with respect to vocations (a strong teaching in the Reformed tradition), and

---

[5] A. E. Taylor, *Faith of a Moralist* (New York: Macmillan, 1930), 412.

a passage from the book of Revelation that might suggest another feature of each person's distinctive identity. We are told that on a white stone there will be a name written for each believer, a secret between that person and God (Rev 2:17). This is their "real name." John Hare speculates that this intimates at something of their core identity.[6] If such a view is even approximately right, then Sartre was right to think that the Christian view (unlike his own) features essence preceding existence. God had in mind when he created each of us what we are meant to become and, by partaking of God's nature, *will* become: a unique, *sui generis* reflection of God's glory.

The Coincidence Thesis

Let's continue our Kantian theme by highlighting another aspect of his work germane to the blessed life. Kant is notorious for an ethical system that put its emphasis not on the consequences of our actions but on their intrinsic features. An action's unfortunate consequences may be bad, but what is the distinctively moral category would be the intention to effect such (nonmorally) bad consequences. Will and motivation for Kant were central to our moral judgments. Only those actions motivated by respect for the moral law, he thought, possess moral significance.

It is fascinating that Kant, of all philosophers, also recognized that human beings cannot help but care about issues of happiness. We are not just spiritual creatures who care about virtue; we are hardwired such that we cannot help but also care about our happiness. Ultimately, then, he realized that greatest good *for human beings* cannot be virtue alone but the conjunction of virtue and happiness.[7] Kant's recognition was something like this: the very enterprise of morality, to make full rational sense, or to be fully rationally

---

[6] John Hare, *God's Command* (Oxford: Oxford University Press, 2015), 288–89.

[7] To understand Kant rightly, we have to construe of it in quite robust terms—thinking in the vicinity of the Judaic conception of *shalom* or the Greek notion of *eudaimonia* may help.

stable, must feature an ultimate connection between human joy and flourish-ing, on the one hand, and moral virtue and character, on the other.

Kant was not the first philosopher to recognize this, but he was the first to construct an elaborate moral argument on its basis. Before him, though, Berkeley and Butler, Locke and Reid, Pascal and Descartes, all rec-ognized something in the vicinity of this coincidence principle that insists on a connection between happiness and virtue. Reid is particularly notable, insisting that what would best account for such coincidence is benevolent administration—a good God who sovereignly ensures that, ultimately, the vir-tuous are happy. Reid thought a commitment to such a principle was natural, virtuous, and intuitive, but he thought its truth not altogether established.[8]

Kant, however, who came along soon afterwards, pushed it a step fur-ther, insisting that a rational moral being must will the "highest good," a world in which happiness and virtue correspond. For Kant, too, moral virtue must be the condition of happiness; he cared more that the happy deserve to be happy than that people are happy, accounting for his resis-tance to utilitarianism. Kant next realized that if this willing of the highest good is to be rational, the world must be ordered in a certain way, operating under what Reid had called benevolent administration. By such means Kant constructed one of his famous arguments for God's existence, an argument from providence, according to which God exists as the providential orderer of the world who ensures that ultimate airtight connection between hap-piness and virtue and that the virtuous are happy because of their virtue.[9]

---

[8] See Thomas Reid, *Essays on the Active Powers of the Human Mind*, intro by B. Brody (Cambridge, MA: MIT Press, 1969 [1788]), 256; Thomas Reid, *Practical Ethics: Being Lectures and Papers on Natural Religion, Self-Government, Natural Jurisprudence, and the Law of Nations*, ed. K. Haakonssen (Princeton: Princeton University Press, 1990), 120; and Terence Cuneo, "Duty, Goodness, and God in Reid's Moral Philosophy," in *Reid on Ethics*, ed. Sabine Roeser (New York: Palgrave Macmillan, 2010), 256.

[9] Kant gave the argument in the Dialectic in the *Critique of Practical Reason*, at the beginning of *Religion within the Bounds of Reason* alone, and at the end of the first and third *Critique*. *Critique of Practical Religion*, trans. Lewis White Beck,

Now, all of this might sound problematically close to something like works righteousness, but even in Kant there are at least hints of a radical departure from such a paradigm. Owing to his Lutheran upbringing, Kant was well aware of Luther's idea that we are all sinfully curved inward, and Kant spoke disparagingly of our "dear self" that needs to be overcome. This is actually the basis for a second moral argument of his that appeals to God's grace to close the moral gap we cannot close on our own. We examined that argument in an earlier chapter.

For now, the emphasis is on the necessity of something like a blessed afterlife to make full rational sense of morality. This is the present connection between the topic of this chapter and our moral apologetic motif. On a Christian view, of course, none of us are righteous in ourselves; we are sinners all, deserving of God's wrath. We need to be made into new men, not just better men, but our sinfulness is only a contingent feature of us. More central to our identity is that we have been created by God and we are, each of us, loved immeasurably by God. And part of what God's love for us implies is that he wants us to be satisfied and fulfilled completely, and offers us just such an opportunity. Moreover, the happiness, consistent with Kant's picture, is a result of intimacy with God and deliverance from sin, so it is infused with moral significance. By God's grace we can be forgiven, changed, and ultimately perfected, made able to experience perfect intimacy and fellowship with God and neighbor for all eternity. Christian theology thus impeccably satisfies the coincidence requirement, providing another moral reason to take its truth claims seriously.

Before the next section, one more word is in order about connections between our earthly lives and the afterlife. Contrary to the claims that we can be so heavenly minded that we are of no earthly good, it is a useful

---

3rd ed. (Upper Saddle River, NJ, 1993); *Critique of Pure Reason*, trans. J. M. D. Meiklejohn, rev. ed. (New York: Willey Book, 1900); *Religion within the Boundaries of Reason Alone*, trans. Theodore M. Greene and Hoyt H. Hudson (New York: Harper & Row, 1960).

reminder that history is replete with stories of those who made a tremendous positive difference in this life. Paul Copan has usefully delineated a number of such examples, adding an historical twist to the moral argument. He cites specific cultural developments that can be shown to have flowed from the Jewish-Christian worldview, leading to societies that are "progress-prone rather than progress-resistant," including such signs of progress as the founding of modern science, poverty-diminishing free markets, equal rights for all before the law, religious liberty, women's suffrage, human rights initiatives, and the abolition of slavery, widow burning, and foot binding.[10]

This actually makes good intuitive sense, because what the resurrection, Christian theology, and a robust doctrine of heaven does is expand our understanding of the ultimate good. It can enable us to understand that there are goods higher than merely earthly and temporal ones. The juxtaposition and integration of happiness and holiness may have been for Kant the highest good for human beings, but in Platonic fashion we probably need to supplement his point by saying that our highest happiness and joy are impossible apart from what is the highest good in and of itself. On the Christian view this is no mere form or archetype, impersonal principle or abstract truth, but a personal and perfectly loving God. In yet another paradox, setting our sights on the ultimate and infinite good makes possible the achievement of all sorts of finite and lesser goods along the way. Lowering our sights to the imminent and transitory goods of this world alone often robs us of the capacity to achieve and enjoy even those as we ought.

Charles Taylor speaks of exclusive humanism and the way in which our secular age privileges the "immanent frame," inclining the modern mind

---

[10] Paul Copan, "Reinforcing the Moral Argument: Appealing to the Historical Impact of the Christian Faith" (Conference paper, Evangelical Theological Society, San Diego, November 20, 2014). See also Paul Copan and Thom Wolf, "Another Dimension of the Moral Argument: The Voice of Jesus and the Historical Fruits of the Christian Faith," in *A New Theist Response to the New Atheists*, eds. Kevin Vallier and Joshua Rasmussen, Routledge New Critical Thinking in Religion, Theology, and Biblical Studies (London: CLC/Routledge, 2020), 131–52.

to find fulfillment without recourse to any transcendent source, settling for merely temporal and earthly ones.[11] A recent television show, *The Good Place*, provides a telling example of this widespread phenomenon. The show depicts something of a secular vision of heaven. Ultimately the gang makes its way there, not to experience anything like communion with God. In fact, God is never mentioned in the show. Those in charge are generally incompetent and feckless. Heaven is just the "good place," a world of satisfaction of various wants and desires, all quite garden-variety goods—nice dinners, beautiful sunsets, even love relationships with other people. But ultimately the people grow bored, and, faced with an eternity of more of the same, each participant eventually gladly chooses dissolution over such a heaven.

The doctrine of heaven and what it represents is profoundly countercultural. The modern romantic relationship is all that many have left after the "death of God," but even human loves fall short. They admit of boredom and fail to satisfy after a certain point. Understandably so since, as Ernest Becker puts it, "No human relationship can bear the burden of godhood."[12] But what if that is all there is, as *The Good Place* suggests? What if all we have to look forward to is monotony-induced enervating ennui, relieved only by the dissolution of the self? What else is to be said but that this would be a tragic state of affairs? Such a picture is one in which the highest possible good isn't large or transcendent enough to satisfy forever.

David Bentley Hart has written, "Among the mind's transcendental aspirations, it is the longing for moral goodness that is probably the most difficult to contain within the confines of a naturalist metaphysics."[13] It would be profoundly sad if eternal joy were an oxymoron, a contradiction

---

[11] Charles Taylor, *A Secular Age* (Cambridge, MA: Harvard University Press, 2007), 18.

[12] Ernest Becker, *The Denial of Death* (New York: Free Press Paperbacks, 1997), 166. For further discussion on this, see Alan Noble's *Disruptive Witness* (Downers Grove: IVP, 2018), chap. 3.

[13] David Bentley Hart, *The Experience of God: Being, Consciousness, Bliss* (New Haven, CT: Yale University Press, 2013), 251.

in terms. Only an infinite good could liberate us from such a fate. *The Good Place* either can't or won't imagine for its characters a source of unending bliss and eternal satisfaction. That is tragic. Although the show is second to none as a brilliant sitcom, we have principled reason to hope for an even more divine comedy.[14] If heaven is real, life is a comedy indeed.

Defeating Evil Once More

Understanding and partaking in the ultimate goodness of God is what heaven is most fully about. This is a process that has already begun among believers in this life, and it is a process that will continue forever in heaven. It is not a process that will ever be completed; we will never get to the bottom of God's goodness. God is literally the infinite source of all goodness and truth and beauty, and ours will be the unspeakably great and blessed privilege to enjoy him forever.

The intentional, integrating subtext of this introduction to philosophical theology is that objective moral truth provides a powerful way to think about who God is and the sort of relationship with him to which we are called. John Henry Newman was convinced that a variety of arguments could be adduced as evidence that God exists but that morality could be used not just to know that God exists but to know God himself.[15] This was the difference between what he called merely *notional* assents and apprehensions, and *real knowing*. It is in the neighborhood of what philosophers call knowledge *de dicto*—knowing things about God—and knowledge *de re*—knowing God himself. We are called to know God experientially and to be transformed and empowered by that relationship of intimacy. Christianity

---

[14] See Marybeth and David Baggett, "How Do You Like Them Ethics?" in *Telling Tales: Intimations of the Sacred in Popular Culture* (Houston: Moral Apologetics, 2021).

[15] John Henry Newman, *An Essay in Aid of a Grammar of Assent* (Notre Dame: University of Notre Dame Press, 1979 [1870]), chap. 4.

teaches that this is what we were made for, and ultimately nothing else will satisfy us completely. Nowhere else can our deepest joy and truest identity be found.

Scripture teaches that, at the day of Christ Jesus, the good work that has been begun within us will be completed. The beatific state represents the culmination of the process of salvation, when we are entirely conformed to the image of Jesus and delivered from the power and effects of sin. Recall that this was the third major existential moral need all of us as human beings have, after the need to be forgiven and transformed. We need to be changed to the uttermost, transformed completely, perfected. Heaven makes such a hope realistic and principled, not a Pollyannaish pipe dream.

It is intimacy with God, partaking of his nature, and beholding his glory that will both transform us completely and fill us with the deepest joy for which we were made. Scripture speaks of a glory to come that is practically beyond our imagination to conceive. We have but furtive glances and inchoate hints of how glorious it will be. And once more, the greatness of such goodness will be enough to defeat the worst of evils endured in this life. This is no merely intellectual defense against the problem of evil that leaves the heart cold. This is the most glorious, resplendent solution imaginable. As bad as the worst that this world can be, God's goodness is infinitely greater.

This is why Marilyn Adams, in her powerful book on the problem of evil, put it this way: "If Divine Goodness is infinite, if intimate relation to It is thus incommensurably good for created persons, then we have identified a good big enough to defeat horrors in every case."[16] Adams, by the way, makes for an interesting study in contrasts with Eleonore Stump. Both are tremendous Christian philosophers who wrote powerful books on the problem of evil. Where Stump wishes to focus on the nature of the suffering endured, which is good to do, Adams tends to focus on the

---

[16] Marilyn McCord Adams, *Horrendous Evils and the Goodness of God* (Ithaca, NY: Cornell University Press, 1999), 82–83.

beatific vision, which is also powerfully useful. Here is a way to incorporate their approaches.

Perhaps the nature of the beatific vision varies from one person to the next, depending, among other things, on the nature of the sufferings endured in this life. Certain particularly horrific sufferings might enable a different, perhaps deeper, insight into who God is—at least for those open to God's grace to transform the suffering into something blessed. Having lost a child, for example, might give the grieving parent a deeper way into that aspect of the Trinity involving the Father watching his Son die. Perhaps a horribly scarred person in this life can somehow in the beatific vision experience the glory of the scars Jesus endured for us more deeply. Perhaps the teenage girl who gets her limbs cut off before being killed can, for having gone through so excruciating and terrifying an ordeal, identify more deeply with the sufferings of Christ, altering the quality (and perhaps quantity) of her experience of the beatific vision.

We do not entirely know that it means that the glory to come will make present sufferings pale into insignificance, but if such glory is infinitely more than enough to definitively defeat the worst of the evils of this world, we can think of few prospects more splendidly exciting than that, even if the details reside beyond our ken or pay grade. And if it is true, as we have principled reasons to believe it is, what *makes* it true, most ultimately, is nothing less than the amazing grace and unspeakable love of God. The resurrection and the promise of glory to those who believe came about because of God's love—by means of a series of steps undertaken while we were yet sinners. Even in our utterly sinful and vile states God loved us enough to make provision for our salvation and offer us an eternity of communion with him and one another. What the resurrection shows is that love is more powerful than death, and it provides a reminder that many need to hear: God really does love each and every person, death is not the end of the story, pain does not have the final say, and the gospel truly is good news.

It bears repeating too, when people insist that a good God would immediately eliminate all evil, that this would entail the destruction of us all. We should be exceedingly thankful that God did not deal with evil in so summary and categorical a fashion, because it would have rendered us all utterly without hope. A. E. Taylor admitted that the biggest weakness of ethical treatises tends to be their treatment of evil, but he meant the evil not just out there in the world, but within ourselves. He noted, for example, that it's barely mentioned in G. E. Moore's *Principia Ethica*. Taylor thought only Kant and Plato showed a keen interest in human sinfulness. The contrition that makes itself heard in the penitential psalms seems almost unknown to philosophical ethics.[17]

Good philosophy and honest theology matter. A deficient understanding of God or of the goods for which we were designed cannot help but lead to a deficient view of others and of ourselves. This is why the first two commandments, solidly reflecting God's essential nature of love, are inextricably tied to one another: to love God with all of our hearts and souls, minds and strength; and to love our neighbors as ourselves. A warped understanding of who God is will invariably diminish one's conception of ultimate goodness. So to insist that we provide a quick and easy answer to what goodness is without realizing that the right answer depends on both an accurate picture of who we are and who God is will relegate one's answers to superficiality. Few topics are handled so poorly without due consideration of issues of transcendence and the sacred.

The topic of goodness is, frankly, endlessly fascinating, and for a number of reasons, one of which is that, like beauty, there is something ineliminably experiential about it. Those without the requisite taste of goodness in their lives are less likely to be moved by something like a moral argument for God's existence, just as those without the requisite experience of beauty are less likely to be persuaded by an aesthetic argument. This is also why it is a powerful reminder to prospective theologians and apologists, as they strive to be salt and light in this world, to offer not just arguments but their very

---

[17] A. E. Taylor, *Faith of a Moralist* (New York: Macmillan, 1930), 163.

lives as evidence of the truth of the gospel. Like Fred Rogers would often say, our job is to make goodness attractive. And here again we see the truth that goodness and beauty are, as Plato could see, flip sides of the same coin. For goodness is, by its very nature, beautiful, which is why we find ourselves so drawn to it.

We recently heard it said that God does not want us happy, but holy. We think such a sentiment to be deeply misguided. Surely God wants us holy—as he is holy. He is in the process of sanctifying us through and through, making us good, the people we were meant to be, the distinctive reflections of Jesus that God had in mind when he created us. But in that sanctified life, the joy of the Lord is our strength; there is the deepest fulfillment of which we are capable, the richest joy we can experience as we allow the divine life to take hold within us. We are made for fellowship, and we are told that the glory to come will render all the present sufferings insignificant by comparison. We are meant for goodness and holiness, it is true, and these do have a sort of primacy over happiness, but ultimately there is not the slightest tension between them. Rather than mutually exclusive, they are ultimately of a piece. We were meant for both goodness *and* eternal joy. The beatific vision for Christ-followers could produce nothing less.

More Than Mere Morality

Having used a constellation of moral truths as the template or lens through which to consider philosophical theology, it should be emphasized that morality is penultimate. Its function is penultimate and importantly semiotic, pointing beyond itself to something yet more ultimate.

C. S. Lewis was famous for writing *Mere Christianity*, but on a few occasions he used the description "mere" to qualify morality. As the writer who gave the world the most popular version of the moral argument in Book 1 of *Mere Christianity*, he was clearly someone who took morality seriously.

He talked about the difference between the moral argument and other arguments for God's existence as the difference between finding out about a person himself versus finding out about something the person created. He apprehended the deeply personalist and existentially vital dimensions of moral apologetics, and nearly everything he wrote about God was conditioned by his convictions of the goodness of the good news of the gospel and the greatness of God's infinite love for all. Still, though, he recognized that morality ran into its limitations.

One of the references can be found in *God in the Dock*. Lewis was fond of this image of God being in the dock—it came from his recognition that modern men often think themselves able to subject God to scrutiny, as if the reckoning is to hold God's feet to the fire rather than his holding ours. Needless to say, Lewis considered this mentality to be just about as confused as possible.

Such an image was at the heart of his greatest novel *Till We Have Faces*, in which the character of Orual had thought she would put God on trial, but found herself to be on trial instead. Fortunately, she died before she died, realizing the darkness within herself; she had acquired her face before seeing God's face. She realized the ravenous darkness within herself, the clamor and rancor of selfishness, that what she had thought was her best was actually her worst. Before it was too late she also came to see the grace available to be transformed, the divine surgery that can excise malady within. She stopped fighting joy, the antidote to her guilt and shame, deliverance from her dear self, a transformation that made the imminent reckoning not something dreadful but something beyond wonderful.

Lewis says, "*Mere morality* is not the end of life. You were made for something quite different from that. . . . The people who keep on asking if they can't lead a decent life without Christ, don't know what life is about; if they did they would know that 'a decent life' is mere machinery compared with the thing we men are really made for. Morality is indispensable: but the

Divine Life, which gives itself to us and which calls us to be gods, intends for us something in which morality will be swallowed up."[18]

George Mavrodes wrote that a day will come in the distant beatific future when words like "rights" and "duties" will have largely been forgotten, replaced by "gift" and "sacrifice":

> I come more and more to think that morality, while a fact, is a twisted and distorted fact. Or perhaps better, that it is a barely recognizable version of another fact, a version adapted to a twisted and distorted world. It is something like, I suppose, the way in which the pine that grows at timberline, wind blasted and twisted against the rock, is a version of the tall and symmetrical tree that grows lower on the slopes. I think it may be that the related notions of sacrifice and gift represent (or come close to representing) the fact, that is, the pattern of life, whose distorted version we know here as morality. Imagine a situation, an "economy" if you will, in which no one ever buys or trades for or seizes any good thing. But whatever good he enjoys it is either one which he himself has created or else one which he received as a free and unconditional gift. And as soon as he has tasted it and seen that it is good he stands ready to give it away in his turn as soon as the opportunity arises. In such a place, if one were to speak either of his rights or his duties, his remarks might be met with puzzled laughter as his hearers struggled to recall an ancient world in which these terms referred to something important.[19]

---

[18] C. S. Lewis, "Man or Rabbit," in *God in the Dock* (Grand Rapids: Eerdmans, 1970), 112.

[19] George Mavrodes, "Religion and the Queerness of Morality," in *Ethical Theory: Classical and Contemporary Readings*, 2nd ed., ed. Louis P. Pojman (New York: Wadsworth, 1995), 588.

Although morality is penultimate, it remains important. Though fragmentary, it's illuminating and revelatory. As Lewis himself once said, the road to the promised land runs past Sinai. It is only when we try and fail to be good that we recognize our need for a Savior. Allowing God's grace not just to pronounce us forgiven but to transform us, making us holy as God is holy, is the process of learning the trinitarian dance steps.

That we will be ultimately delivered from sin entirely is wonderful, yet even here and now we can catch glimpses of it, for the seeds of it have been planted within us. Every now and then—in the face of a baby, in fellowship over a meal, in a laugh with a Christian brother or sister, in a hymn at church that takes our breath away, when beholding the starry heavens above or moral law within—we catch an enchanting glimpse of the sacred and haunting presence of the eternal.

In light of both the rich history of the moral argument and theological reflections about right and wrong, good and evil, virtue and vice, and because of the recent resurgence of interest in moral arguments for God, we thought it would be worth our while in a volume on philosophical theology to be intentional to approach this impossibly vast topic along the particular dimension of moral apologetics.

What goes by morality is just the first step in an infinite journey culminating in the divine life. At a time when many devalue and depreciate morality, subjectivizing it, perverting it, inverting it, demonizing it, our approach has been predicated on something quite different. In morality we are inclined to think we catch a glimpse of the eternal. Living with the truths of morality, allowing them to sink in, being attentive to their counsels and commands, takes us beyond discursive analysis and abstract reasoning. It speaks and tugs inwardly, implicitly, gently, wooing both the heart and mind. The voice of conscience speaks to us from the inside out.

If God is the source and root of morality, as we have reason to believe, then the pull of morality within is less like a cold deliverance of reason and more like a warm and personal invitation to come and partake, to drink from a brook whose water quenches our thirst in the most satisfying way we can imagine. The voice of morality is the call of God to return to our only true and ultimate source of happiness. It is not an overactive superego or societally imposed joy-killing curfew but an intimation of the eternal, a personal overture to run with rather than against the grain of the universe. It is confirmation of our suspicions that love and relationship have not just happened to bubble to the top of the evolutionary chain, reflecting nothing, but rather that they penetrate to the foundation of all that is real. Reason and relationship, rationality and relationality, go hand in hand, and they were not merely the culmination of the elaborate process that enabled us to reflect about it all and inquire into the meaning of life and the nature of God and the human condition. No, they were what began it all and imbued the process with meaning right from the start.[20]

Conclusion

In this book we set our sights on bringing together a powerful picture of the Christian God—a view of God deeply rooted in Scripture and fortified through reason—and how this God makes good sense of a range of important realities, especially moral ones. The God we have argued for is Anselmian in nature, yet a God who is deeply personal, relational, and religiously available to his creatures through providential action, care, and concern. So much so that, in the person of the Son, this God took on our humanity and dwelt among us, died for our sins, and rose again so that we may be reconciled and enter into a renewed relationship with him.

Throughout we have explored a wide range of beliefs, such as the incarnation, *imago Dei* and human worth, salvation, heaven, hell, and resurrection, and sought to forge a connection between a good and loving God and those important Christian doctrines. Our understanding of God shapes

---

[20] David Baggett and Jerry L. Walls, *Good God: The Theistic Foundations of Morality* (New York: Oxford University Press, 2010) 185.

each one of these doctrines. And as we argued, the Trinity provides grounding for nothing less than ethics itself.[21]

One of the takeaways from the analysis is how interconnected are issues of biblical exegesis, systematic theology, and philosophical reflection. Another is the utter centrality of God's character and identity. A recurring, if relatively minor theme of the book has been an apologetic one: evidential considerations to take belief in God's reality seriously. An equally important matter, though, is who God is. A proper understanding of God's reality and nature is what's needed to inform our understanding of the human condition and the world, of meaning and morality. This was why we intentionally wove together in this book theological and apologetic concerns, biblical and philosophical resources. By turns we put on different hats: the biblical theologian, the philosophical theologian, the philosophical apologist. But it was one head wearing the different hats. It is our hope that the result will be of benefit and blessing to committed believers, fledgling believers, almost believers, and unbelievers alike.

Upon deeper reflection of the Christian God, we find ourselves in a place of awe and wonder and can only echo the words of the old hymn written by John Newton:

> Amazing grace, how sweet the sound
> That saved a wretch like me
> I once was lost, but now I'm found
> Was blind but now I see.[22]

---

[21] For an extended argument to this effect, see Adam Johnson's *Divine Love Theory* (Grand Rapids: Kregel, 2023).

[22] John Newton, "Amazing Grace," 1772, public domain.

BIBLIOGRAPHY

Adams, Marilyn McCord. *Horrendous Evils and the Goodness of God*. Ithaca, NY: Cornell University Press, 1999.

———. "Redemptive Suffering: A Christian Solution to the Problem of Evil." In *The Problem of Evil: Selected Readings*, edited by Michael L. Peterson, 210–34. Notre Dame, IN: University of Notre Dame Press, 1992.

Adams, Robert Merrihew. *Finite and Infinite Goods: A Framework for Ethics*. New York: Oxford University Press, 1999.

Almeida, Mike. "Review of *God and Moral Law: On the Theistic Explanation of Morality*." Notre Dame Philosophical Reviews, Last modified May 6, 2012. https://ndpr.nd.edu/reviews/god-and-moral-law-on-the-theistic -explanation-of-morality/.

Alston, William P. *Divine Nature and Human Language: Essays in Philosophical Theology*. Eugene, OR: Wipf & Stock, 1989.

Baggett, David. *Did the Resurrection Happen? A Conversation with Gary Habermas and Antony Flew*. Downers Grove: IVP, 2009.

———. "Is Divine Iconoclast as Bad as Cosmic Sadist?" In *C. S. Lewis as Philosopher: Truth, Goodness, and Beauty*, edited by David Baggett, Gary R. Habermas, and Jerry L. Walls, 115–30. Downers Grove: IVP Academic, 2008.

————. Review of "Erasing Hell: What God Said about Eternity and the Things We Made Up." *Wesleyan Theological Journal* 48, no. 2 (Fall 2013): 219–22.

Baggett, David, and Jerry L. Walls. *Good God: The Theistic Foundations of Morality.* New York: Oxford University Press, 2010.

————. *The Moral Argument: A History.* New York: Oxford University Press, 2019.

Baggett, David, and Marybeth Baggett. "Self-Knowledge, Who God Is, and a Cure for Our Deepest Shame: A Few Reflections on *Till We Have Faces.*" *Perichoresis* 20, no. 3 (2022): 3–20.

Baggett, David, and Ronnie Campbell. "Omnibenevolence, Moral Apologetics, and Doubly Ramified Natural Theology." *Philosophia Christi* 15, no. 2 (2013): 337–52.

Baggett, Marybeth, and David Baggett. *Telling Tales: Intimations of the Sacred in Popular Culture.* Houston: Moral Apologetics, 2021.

Barth, Karl. "The Doctrine of God." vol. 2, part 1. In *Church Dogmatics.* Edited by G. W. Bromiley and T. F. Torrance. London: T&T Clark, 2000.

————. "The Doctrine of the Word of God." vol. 1, part 1. In *Church Dogmatics.* Edited by G. W. Bromiley and T. F. Torrance. New York: T&T Clark, 2004.

Becker, Ernest. *The Denial of Death.* New York: Free Press Paperbacks, 1997.

Beilby, James. "Divine Aseity, Divine Freedom: A Conceptual Problem for Edwardsian-Calvinism." *Journal of the Evangelical Theological Society* 47, no. 4 (2004): 647–58.

Campbell, Ronnie. *Worldviews and the Problem of Evil.* Bellingham, WA: Lexham, 2019.

Carson, D. A. *The Difficult Doctrine of the Love of God.* Greenville, SC: Crossway, 1999.

Chisholm, Roderick M. "Human Freedom and the Self." In *Metaphysics: The Big Questions*, edited by Peter Van Inwagen and Dean W. Zimmerman, 356–64. Malden, MA: Blackwell, 1998.

Clayton, Philip. *Adventures in the Spirit: God, World, and Divine Action.* Philadelphia: Fortress, 2008.

Cleveland, Lindsay K. "Divine Aseity and Abstract Objects." In *T&T Clark Handbook of Analytic Theology,* edited by James M. Arcadi and James T. Turner Jr., 165–80. New York: T&T Clark, 2022.

Cobb, John B., Jr., and David Ray Griffin. *Process Theology: An Introductory Exposition.* New York: Westminster, 1976.

Copan, Paul. "Reinforcing the Moral Argument: Appealing to the Historical Impact of the Christian Faith." Paper presented at the Annual Meeting of the Evangelical Theological Society, San Diego, November 20, 2014.

Copan, Paul, and William Lane Craig. *Creation Out of Nothing: A Biblical, Philosophical, and Scientific Exploration.* Grand Rapids: Baker Academic, 2004.

Copan, Paul, and Thom Wolf. "Another Dimension of the Moral Argument: The Voice of Jesus and the Historical Fruits of the Christian Faith." In *A New Theist Response to the New Atheists,* edited by Kevin Vallier and Joshua Rasmussen. Routledge New Critical Thinking in Religion, Theology, and Biblical Studies. London: CLC/Routledge, 2020.

Craig, William Lane. "A Middle Knowledge Response." In *Divine Foreknowledge: Four Views,* edited by James K. Beilby and Paul R. Eddy, 55–60. Downers Grove: IVP, 2001.

———. *Consciousness and the Existence of God: A Theistic Argument.* New York: Routledge, 2008.

———. *God and Abstract Objects: The Coherence of Theism: Aseity.* Cham, Switzerland: Springer, 2017.

———. *God, Time, and Eternity.* Dordrecht, NEL: Kluwer Academic, 2001.

———. *Time and Eternity: Exploring God's Relationship to Time.* Wheaton: Crossway, 2001.

———. "The Middle Knowledge View." In *Divine Foreknowledge: Four Views*, edited by James K. Beilby and Paul R. Eddy, 119–45. Downers Grove: IVP, 2001.

———. "Timelessness and Omnitemporality." *Philosophia Christi* 2, no. 1 (2000): 29–33.

———. *God Over All: Divine Aseity and the Challenge of Platonism*. New York: Oxford University Press, 2018.

———. *The Only Wise God: The Compatibility of Divine Foreknowledge and Human Freedom*. Eugene, OR: Wipf and Stock, 1999.

Craig, William Lane, and James D. Sinclair. "The Kalam Cosmological Argument." In *The Blackwell Companion to Natural Theology*, edited by William Lane Craig and J. P. Moreland, 101–200. Malden, MA: Wiley-Blackwell, 2009.

Creel, Richard E. *Divine Impassibility: An Essay in Philosophical Theology*. Eugene, OR: Wipf & Stock, 2005.

———. *Divine Impassibility: An Essay in Philosophical Theology*. Cambridge: Cambridge University Press, 1986.

Cullmann, Oscar. *Christ and Time: The Primitive Christian Conception of Time and History*. Translated by Floyd V. Filson, 3rd ed. Philadelphia: Westminster, 1962.

Cuneo, Terence. "Duty, Goodness, and God in Reid's Moral Philosophy." In *Reid on Ethics*, edited by Sabine Roeser, 238–57. New York: Palgrave Macmillan, 2010.

Darwin, Charles. *Descent of Man*. Amherst, NY: Prometheus Books, 1997.

Davies, Brian. *An Introduction to the Philosophy of Religion*. New York: Oxford University Press, 2020.

Davis, Stephen T. *Christian Philosophical Theology*. Oxford: Oxford University Press, 2006.

———. *Disputed Issues: Contending for Christian Faith in Today's Academic Setting*. Waco, TX: Baylor University Press, 2009.

———. "God's Action." In *In Defense of Miracles*, edited by R. Douglas Geivett and Gary Habermas, 163–78. Downers Grove: IVP, 1997.

———. *Logic and the Nature of God*. Grand Rapids: Eerdmans, 1983.

DeWeese, Garrett J. *God and the Nature of Time*. Burlington, VT: Ashgate, 2004.

Dolezal, James E. *All That Is in God*. Grand Rapids: Reformed Heritage Books, 2017.

———. *God Without Parts: Divine Simplicity and the Metaphysics of God's Absoluteness*. Eugene, OR: Pickwick, 2011.

Dorner, Isaak August. *Divine Immutablity: A Critical Reconsideration*. Translated by Robert R. Williams and Claude Welch. Minneapolis: Fortress, 1994.

Duby, Steven J. *Divine Simplicity: A Dogmatic Account*. New York: Bloomsbury, 2016.

Elshof, Gregg Ten. *For Shame: Rediscovering the Virtues of a Maligned Emotion*. Grand Rapids: Eerdmans, 2021.

Erickson, Millard J. *Christian Theology*. Grand Rapids: Baker Academic, 2013.

———. *The Word Became Flesh: A Contemporary Incarnational Christology*. Grand Rapids: Baker, 1991.

Feinberg, John S. *The Many Faces of Evil: Theological Systems and the Problems of Evil*. Wheaton: Crossway, 2004.

———. *No One Like Him: The Doctrine of God*. Wheaton: Crossway, 2001.

Finch, Jeffrey. "Athanasius on the Deifying Work of the Redeemer." In *Theosis: Deification in Christian Theology*, edited by Stephen Finlan and Vladimir Kharlamov, 104–21. Eugene, OR: Pickwick, 2006.

———. "Irenaeus on the Christological Basis of Human Divinization." In *Theosis: Deification in Christian Theology*, edited by Stephen Finlan and Vladimir Kharlamov, 86–103. Eugene, OR: Pickwick, 2006.

Fretheim, Terence E. *The Suffering of God: An Old Testament Perspective*. Philadelphia: Fortress, 1984.

Freud, Sigmund. *Civilization and Its Discontents*. Edited and translated by James Strachey. New York: W. W. Norton, 2010.

Gage, Logan Paul. "Newman's Argument from Conscience: Why He Needs Paley and Natural Theology After All." *American Catholic Philosophical Quarterly* 94, no. 1 (2020): 141–57.

Gavrilyuk, Paul. *The Suffering of the Impassible God: The Dialectics of Patristic Thought.* New York: Oxford University Press, 2004.

Geach, Peter. "Omnipotence." In *Contemporary Philosophy of Religion*, edited by Steven M. Cahn and David Shatz, 46–60. New York: Oxford University Press, 1982.

Geisler, Norman. *Chosen but Free: A Balanced View of Divine Election.* Minneapolis: Bethany House, 2001.

Gould, Paul. "Christian Metaphysics and Platonism." In *Four Views on Christian Metaphysics*, edited by Timothy M. Mosteller, 1–34. Eugene, OR: Cascade Books, 2022.

Greene, Graham. *The Power and the Glory.* New York: Penguin, 1940.

Grenz, Stanley J. *Theology for the Community of God.* Grand Rapids: Eerdmans, 1994.

Guinness, Os. *Fool's Talk: Recovering the Art of Christian Persuasion.* Downers Grove: IVP, 2015.

Habermas, Jürgen. *Time of Transitions.* Edited and translated by Ciaran Cronin and Max Pensky. Cambridge: Polity, 2006.

Habets, Myk. "Reformed *Theosis*?: A Response to Gannon Murphy." *Theology Today* 65, no. 4 (2009): 489–98.

Hare, John E. *God's Command.* New York: Oxford University Press, 2015.

———. *The Moral Gap: Kantian Ethics, Human Limits, and God's Assistance.* Oxford: Clarendon, 1997.

Harrison, Verna. "Perichoresis in the Greek Fathers." *St Vladimir's Theological Quarterly* 35, no. 1 (1991): 53–65.

Hart, David Bentley. *The Experience of God: Being, Consciousness, Bliss.* New Haven, CT: Yale University Press, 2013.

Hart, Matthew J. *Calvinism and the Problem of Evil.* Edited by David E. Alexander and Daniel M. Johnson, 248–72. Eugene, OR: Pickwick, 2016.

Hartshorne, Charles. *The Divine Relativity*. New Haven, CT: Yale University Press, 1964.

Hasker, William. "A Philosophical Perspective." In *The Openness of God: A Biblical Challenge to the Traditional Understanding of God*, 126–54. Downers Grove: IVP, 1994.

———. *Metaphysics: Constructing a World View*. Downers Grove: IVP, 1984.

———. *Providence, Evil and the Openness of God*. New York: Routledge, 2004.

———. *The Triumph of God over Evil: Theodicy for a World of Suffering*. Downers Grove: IVP, 2008.

Hazony, Yoram. "An Imperfect God." *New York Times*, November 25, 2012. https://archive.nytimes.com/opinionator.blogs.nytimes.com/2012/11/25/an-imperfect-god/.

———. *The Philosophy of Hebrew Scriptures*. Cambridge: Cambridge University Press, 2012.

Heiser, Michael S. "Monotheism, Polytheism, Monolatry, or Henotheism: Toward an Assessment of Divine Plurality in the Hebrew Bible." *Bulletin for Biblical Research* 18, no. 1 (2008): 1–30.

Helm, Paul. "Divine Timeless Eternity." In *God and Time: Four Views*, edited by Gregory Ganssle, 28–60. Downers Grove: IVP, 2001.

———. *Eternal God: A Study of God without Time*, 2nd ed. New York: Oxford University Press, 2011.

Hoekema, Anthony A. *Created in God's Image*. Grand Rapids: Eerdmans, 1994.

Horrell, J. Scott. "Toward a Biblical Model of the Social Trinity: Avoiding Equivocation of Nature and Order." *Journal of the Evangelical Theological Society* 47, no. 3 (Sept 2004): 399–421.

Howard-Snyder, Frances. "Christian Ethics." In *Reason for the Hope Within*, edited by Michael J. Murray, 375–98. Grand Rapids: Eerdmans, 1999.

Inman, Ross D. "Retrieving Divine Immensity and Omnipresence." In *T&T Clark Handbook of Analytic Theology*, edited by James M. Arcadi and James T. Turner Jr., 127–40. New York: T&T Clark, 2022.

James, William. *The Dilemma of Determinism*. Whitefish, MT: Kessinger, 2010.

Johnson, Adam. *Divine Love Theory: How the Trinity Is the Source and Foundation of Morality*. Grand Rapids: Kregel, 2023.

Kant, Immanuel. *Critique of Practical Reason*. Translated by Mary Gregor. Cambridge Texts in the History of Philosophy. Cambridge: Cambridge University Press, 2015.

———. *Religion Within the Bounds of Bare Reason*. Translated by Werner S. Pluhar. Hackett Classics. Indianapolis: Hackett, 2009.

Kharlamov, Vladimir. "*Theosis* in Patristic Thought." *Theology Today* 65, no. 2 (2008): 158–68.

Leftow, Brian. *Time and Eternity*. Ithaca, NY: Cornell University Press, 1991.

Lewis, C. S. *God in the Dock*. Grand Rapids: Eerdmans, 1970.

———. *A Grief Observed*. New York: Bantam Books, 1976.

———. *Mere Christianity*. New York: Macmillan, 1960.

———. "On Obstinacy of Belief." In *Philosophy of Religion: An Anthology*, edited by Louis P. Pojman. Belmont, CA: Wadsworth, 1987.

———. *The Problem of Pain*. New York: HarperOne, 1996.

———. *Reflections on the Psalms*. New York: Houghton Mifflin Harcourt, 1964.

———. *Till We Have Faces*. New York: HarperOne, 2017.

———. *The Weight of Glory*. New York: HarperOne, 2017.

Linville, Mark. "The Moral Argument." In *The Blackwell Companion to Natural Theology*, edited by William Lane Craig and J. P. Moreland, 391–448. Malden, MA: Blackwell, 2009.

Loke, Andrew Ter Ern. "*Creatio Ex Nihilo*." In *T&T Clark Handbook of Analytic Theology*, edited by James M. Arcadi and James T. Turner Jr., 297–310. New York: T&T Clark, 2022.

Mavrodes, George. "Religion and the Queerness of Morality." In *Ethical Theory: Classical and Contemporary Readings*, edited by Louis P. Pojman, 2nd ed. New York: Wadsworth, 1995.

Mawson, T. J. *The Divine Attributes*. Cambridge: Cambridge University Press, 2019.

McCain, Kevin, and Ted Poston. *Best Explanations: New Essays on Inference to the Best Explanation*. New York: Oxford University Press, 2018.

Migliore, Daniel L. *Faith Seeking Understanding: An Introduction to Christian Theology*. Grand Rapids: Eerdmans, 1991.

Moltmann, Jürgen. *The Crucified God*. Minneapolis: Fortress, 1993.

———. *The Trinity and the Kingdom*. Minneapolis: Fortress, 1993.

Moreland, J. P., and William Lane Craig. *Philosophical Foundations for a Christian Worldview*. Downers Grove: IVP, 2003.

Morris, Thomas V. *Anselmian Explorations: Essays in Philosophical Theology*. Notre Dame, IN: University of Notre Dame Press, 1987.

———. *Our Idea of God*. Vancouver: Regent University Press, 2002.

Morris, Tom, and David Baggett. "A Perfect God." *First Things*, Last modified January 28, 2013. https://www.firstthings.com/web-exclusives /2013/01/a-perfect-god.

Moser, Paul K. *The Divine Goodness of Jesus: Impact and Response*. Cambridge: Cambridge University Press, 2021.

———. *The Elusive God: Reorienting Religious Epistemology*. Cambridge: Cambridge University Press, 2009.

———. *The Evidence for God: Religious Knowledge Reexamined*. Cambridge: Cambridge University Press, 2009.

———. *The God Relationship: The Ethics for Inquiry about the Divine*. Cambridge: Cambridge University Press, 2018.

Mullins, Ryan T. "Classical Theism." In *T&T Clark Handbook of Analytic Theology*, edited by James M. Arcadi and James T. Turner Jr., 85–100. New York: T&T Clark, 2022.

———. "The Divine Timemaker." *Philosophia Christi* 22, no. 2 (2020): 211–37.

———. *The End of the Timeless God*. New York: Oxford University Press, 2016.

———. "Simply Impossible: A Case against Divine Simplicity." *Journal of Reformed Theology* 7, no. 2 (2013): 181–203.

Murphy, Gannon. "Reformed *Theosis?*" *Theology Today* 65, no. 2 (2008): 191–212.

Nash, Ronald H. *The Concept of God: An Exploration of Contemporary Difficulties with the Attributes of God*. Grand Rapids: Zondervan, 1983.

Newman, John Henry. *An Essay in Aid of a Grammar of Assent*. Notre Dame, IN: University of Notre Dame Press, 1979.

Noble, Alan. *Disruptive Witness*. Downers Grove: IVP, 2018.

Oord, Thomas Jay. "God Always Creates out of Creation in Love: *Creatio ex Creatione a Natura Amoris*." In *Theologies of Creation: Creatio ex Nihilo and Its New Rivals*, edited by Thomas Jay Oord, 109–22. New York: Routledge, 2015.

———. *The Uncontrolling Love of God: An Open and Relational Account of Providence*. Downers Grove: IVP, 2015.

Padgett, Alan G. *God, Eternity, and the Nature of Time*. Eugene, OR: Wipf & Stock, 2000.

Pascal, Blaise. *Pensées*. Translated by Honor Levi. New York: Oxford University Press, 1995.

Peckham, John C. *Divine Attributes: Knowing the Covenantal God of Scripture*. Grand Rapids: Baker Academic, 2021.

———. *The Love of God: A Canonical Model*. Downers Grove: IVP, 2015.

———. "Qualified Passibility." In *Divine Impassibility: Four Views of God's Emotions and Suffering*, edited by Robert J. Matz and A. Chadwick Thornhill, 87–128. Downers Grove: IVP, 2019.

Pike, Nelson. *God and Timelessness*. New York: Schocken Books, 1970.

Pinnock, Clark. *Most Moved Mover: A Theology of God's Openness* (The Didsbury Lectures). Grand Rapids: Baker Academic, 2001.

———."Systematic Theology." In *The Openness of God: A Biblical Challenge to the Traditional Understanding of God*, 101–25. Downers Grove: IVP, 1994.

Plantinga, Alvin. "Does God Have a Nature?" In *The Analytic Theist: An Alvin Plantinga Reader*, edited by James F. Sennett. Grand Rapids: Eerdmans, 1998.

———. *Does God Have a Nature? The Aquinas Lecture, 1980*. Milwaukee: Marquette University Press, 1980.

———. *God and Other Minds: A Study of the Rational Justification of Belief in God*. Ithaca, NY: Cornell University Press, 1990.

———. *The Nature of Necessity*. New York: Oxford University Press, 1982.

———. "Self-Profile." In *Alvin Plantinga*, edited by James Tomberlin and Peter van Inwagen, 3–100. Dordrecht: Kluwer Academic, 1985.

Polkinghorne, John C. "Kenotic Creation and Divine Action." In *The Work of Love: Creation as Kenosis*, edited by John C. Polkinghorne, 90–106. Grand Rapids: Eerdmans, 2001.

Rakestraw, Robert V. "Becoming Like God: An Evangelical Doctrine of *Theosis*." *Journal of the Evangelical Theological Society* 40, no. 2 (1997): 257–69.

Reichenbach, Bruce R. *Divine Providence: God's Love and Human Freedom*. Eugene, OR: Cascade, 2016.

Reid, Thomas. *Essays on the Active Powers of the Human Mind*. Cambridge, MA: MIT Press, 1969.

———. *Practical Ethics: Being Lectures and Papers on Natural Religion, Self-Government, Natural Jurisprudence, and the Law of Nations*. Edited by Knud Haakonssen. Princeton, NJ: Princeton University Press, 1990.

Rice, Richard. "Biblical Support for a New Perspective." In *The Openness of God: A Biblical Challenge to the Traditional Understanding of God*. Downers Grove: IVP, 1994.

Richards, Jay Wesley. *The Untamed God: A Philosophical Exploration of Divine Perfection, Simplicity and Immutability*. Downers Grove: IVP, 2003.

Robinson, Marilynne. *Gilead*. New York: Farrar, Straus and Giroux, 2004.

Russell, Norman. *Fellow Workers with God: Orthodox Thinking on* Theosis. Crestwood, NY: St Vladimir's Seminary Press, 2009.

Senor, Thomas. "Incarnation and Timelessness." *Faith and Philosophy* 7, no. 2 (April 1990): 149–64.

Smith, S. M. "Perichoresis." In *Evangelical Dictionary of Theology*, edited by Walter A. Elwell, 2nd ed. Grand Rapids: Baker Academic, 2001.

Spiegel, James S. "Christian Metaphysics and Idealism." In *Four Views on Christian Metaphysics*, edited by Timothy M. Mosteller, 71–102. Eugene, OR: Cascade, 2022.

Stump, Eleonore. *Wandering in Darkness: Narrative and the Problem of Suffering*. New York: Oxford University Press, 2012.

Stump, Eleonore, and Norman Kretzmann. "Eternity." *The Journal of Philosophy* 78, no. 8 (Aug. 1981): 429–57.

Swinburne, Richard. *The Christian God*. New York: Oxford University Press, 1994.

———. *The Coherence of Theism*, 2nd ed. New York: Oxford University Press, 2016.

———. *The Existence of God*. Oxford: Clarendon, 2004.

———. "Natural Theology, Its 'Dwindling Probabilities' and 'Lack of Rapport.'" *Faith and Philosophy* 21, no. 4 (2004): 533–46.

Taylor, A. E. *Faith of a Moralist*. New York: Macmillan, 1930.

Taylor, Charles. *A Secular Age*. Cambridge, MA: Harvard University Press, 2007.

The Westminster Standard. "Chalcedonian Creed (451 A.D)." The Westminster Standard, Last modified 2023. https://thewestminsterstandard .org/the-chalcedonian-creed/.

Thiessen, Henry C. *Lectures in Systematic Theology*, revised by Vernon D. Doerksen. Grand Rapids: Eerdmans, 2000.

Vanhoozer, Kevin J. *First Theology: God, Scripture, and Hermeneutics*. Downers Grove: IVP, 2002.

Wainwright, William. *Reason and the Heart: A Prolegomenon to a Critique of Passional Reason*. Ithaca, NY: Cornell, 2006.

Walls, Jerry L., and Trent Dougherty. *Two Dozen (or So) Arguments for God.* New York: Oxford University Press, 2018.

Walton, John H. *The Lost World of Genesis One: Ancient Cosmology and the Origins Debate.* Downers Grove: IVP, 2009.

Wolterstorff, Nicholas. "God Everlasting." In *Contemporary Philosophy of Religion*, edited by Steven M. Cahn and David Shatz, 77–98. New York: Oxford University Press, 1982.

———. *Justice: Rights and Wrongs.* Princeton, NJ: Princeton University Press, 2008.

———. *Lament for a Son.* Grand Rapids: Eerdmans, 1987.

WPBS-TV. "MRN Clip Jeff Erlanger." WPBS-TV. Streamed live on August 26, 2023. YouTube video, 1:58. youtube.com/watch?v=UNUficgWE3U.

Primary Sources:

Anselm. "Monologion." In *Anselm of Canterbury: The Major Works*, edited by Brian Davies and G. R. Evans. New York: Oxford University Press, 1998. 5–81.

Aquinas, Thomas. *On the Eternality of the World (De Aeternitate Mundi).* Translated by Robert T. Miller. https://sourcebooks.fordham.edu/basis /aquinas-eternity.asp.

———. *Summa Contra Gentiles. Book One.* Translated by Anton C. Pegis. Notre Dame, IN: University of Notre Dame Press, 1975.

———. *Summa Theologica.* Vol. 1. Part 1. Translated by the Fathers of the Dominican Province. New York: Cosimo Classics, 2007.

Athanasius. *Ad Adelphium.* Vol. 4, in *Nicene and Post-Nicene Fathers*, edited by Philip Schaff and Henry Wace, translated by A. Robertson. Peabody, MA: Hendrickson, 2004.

———. *Against the Arians.* Vol. 4, in *Nicene and Post-Nicene Fathers*, edited by Philip Schaff and Henry Wace, translated by A. Robertson. Peabody, MA: Hendrickson, 2004.

————. *On the Incarnation.* Edited by Cliff Lee. Lexington, KY: Paradox Media, 2007.

Augustine. *Homilies On the Gospel of John.* Translated by H. Browne. Nicene and Post-Nicene Fathers: A Select library of the Christian Church. Series One. Vol. 7. Edited by Philip Schaff. Peabody, MA: Hendrickson, 2004.

————. *The Letters of Saint Augustine.* Translated by J. G. Cunningham. Nicene and Post-Nicene Fathers: A Select Library of the Christian Church. Series One. Vol. 1. Edited by Philip Schaff. Peabody, MA: Hendrickson, 2004.

Boethius, *Consolation of Philosophy*, Book V: VI. Translated by V. E. Watts. New York: Penguin, 1969.

Irenaeus. *Against Heresies.* Vol. 1. In *Ante-Nicene Fathers*, edited by Alexander Roberts and James Donaldson. Peabody, MA: Hendrickson, 2004.

NAME INDEX

SUBJECT INDEX

SCRIPTURE INDEX

5:8–9 *179*
6:17–18 *63, 96*
9:25 *51*
11:3 *51, 83*
13:8 *77*

James

1:13 *96, 108*
1:17 *63, 77, 83, 86, 107*

1 Peter

1:3–4 *142*
1:20 *51*

2 Peter

1:3 *140, 142*
1:4 *140*
1:5–7 *140*
1:8 *140*
1:9 *140*
3:4 *51*
3:9 *187*

1 John

1:5 *25, 108*
2:2 *22*
3:2 *161*
3:20 *99*
4:8 *124*
4:20 *128*

Revelation

1:8 *52*
2:17 *153, 198*
3:14 *51*
4:11 *83*
12:9 *96*
13:8 *51, 114*
17:8 *51*
20 *117*
20:7–10 *96*
21:1 *96*